TH

are a series

each of which re-creates the life of a
great man and the era upon which he
left his imprint. Lively source
materials and the comments of
contemporary historians are quoted
in a running text which provides
a unique insight into the
excitement, the controversy, the
hopes and fears of an age.

Thus, a generation ago,
one man, "That Man in the White
House," dominated a constitutional
revolution in American life which
it is the purpose of this
volume to reconstruct.

ALFRED B. ROLLINS, JR., *has been a
fellow of the Fund for Advancement
of Education. He is currently in the
Department of History at Harpur
College, State University of New York.*

Laurel Editions in American History

FRANKLIN D.

ROOSEVELT

and the AGE OF ACTION

Edited and with a text by ALFRED B. ROLLINS, JR.

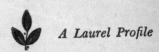

A Laurel Profile

Published by
DELL PUBLISHING CO., INC.
750 Third Avenue
New York 17, N.Y.

Designed and produced by
Western Printing and Lithographing Company

DEDICATION: *For Ernestine, Nancy and John.*

First printing—December, 1960
Second printing—March, 1967

Printed in U.S.A.

ACKNOWLEDGMENTS: *The following selections in this volume are reproduced by permission of the authors, their publishers, or their agents:*

from AFTER SEVEN YEARS by Raymond Moley. Copyright, 1939, by Raymond Moley. Reprinted by permission of Brandt and Brandt.

from GOVERNMENT AND ECONOMIC LIFE by Leverett S. Lyon and Victor Abramson. Reprinted by permission of The Brookings Institution.

from SEEDS OF REVOLT by Mauritz Hallgren, Alfred A. Knopf, Inc., 1933. Reprinted by permission of Curtis Brown, Ltd.

from ROOSEVELT AND THE RUSSIANS: THE YALTA CONFERENCE by Edward R. Stettinius, Jr. Copyright 1949 by The Stettinius Fund, Inc. Reprinted by permission of Doubleday & Company, Inc., Harold Ober Associates, and Jonathan Cape, Ltd.

from THE ART OF POLITICS by Rexford G. Tugwell. Copyright 1958 by Rexford G. Tugwell. Reprinted by permission of Doubleday & Company, Inc., and Russell & Volkening, Inc.

from "Sources of the New Deal: Reflections on the Temper of a Time," COLUMBIA UNIVERSITY FORUM, Vol. II (Fall 1959). Reprinted by permission of the Columbia University Forum.

from F.D.R., HIS PERSONAL LETTERS, Elliott Roosevelt, editor. Vol. I c/r 1947 by Elliott Roosevelt. Vol. II c/r 1948 by Elliott Roosevelt. Vol. III c/r 1950 by Elliott Roosevelt. By permission of Duell, Sloan & Pearce, Inc.

from THE HISTORY OF THE NEW DEAL, 1933-1938, by Basil Rauch, Creative Age Press, 1944. Reprinted by permission of the author and of Farrar, Straus & Cudahy, Inc.

from AMERICA MUST CHOOSE by Henry Wallace, World Affairs Pamphlet No. 3, 1934. Reprinted by permission of the Foreign Policy Association and the World Peace Foundation.

from ARSENAL OF DEMOCRACY, copyright, 1946, by Donald M. Nelson. Reprinted by permission of Harcourt, Brace and Company, Inc.

from BEHIND THE BALLOTS, copyright, 1938, by James A. Farley. Reprinted by permission of Harcourt, Brace and Company, Inc.

CONTENTS

PREFACE

This is a narrative history of the Roosevelt era, but it is also an anthology of source materials and of the best in the secondary literature. Yet the book as a whole reflects a point of view. With all its faults, the Roosevelt leadership was one of the great and germinal phenomena of modern history. This book seeks to plot errors as well as victories, but without losing sight of this essential greatness.

Of my many obligations which ought to be acknowledged, one is pre-eminent. To Herman Kahn and the staff of the Franklin D. Roosevelt Library, this editor, like every Roosevelt scholar, is permanently and deeply indebted.

Alfred B. Rollins, Jr.

State University College of Education
New Paltz, N. Y.

chapter 1 THE SHOCK OF DISASTER

Between October, 1929, and March, 1933, the old America fell apart. Her tired economy wheezed and knocked in the aftermath of the most shocking market crash since stocks had been invented. Her spirit was near breaking, her institutions deeply shaken. No facet of American life escaped the scars of the marvelous mischief which economic collapse had wrought. On a thousand street corners, in a million drab and hopeless homes, human misery marked the pace of the disaster. Four million unemployed in 1930, eight million in 1931. By the ghastly winter of 1932–1933, at least twelve and a half million Americans, one-quarter of the active manpower, drifted haplessly in search of work. The jobless had outrun the machinery of statistics; there may have been twenty million. But there they stood, as the country moved toward a presidential election, an often mute, but monstrous token of a deadly puzzle which few understood and no one seemed able to solve.

Statistics tell the story with stunning drama. Between 1929 and 1932 the Gross National Product fell by more than 28%. The Federal Reserve Board's Index of Manufacturing Production showed a spectacular drop from 110 to 57. Bank deposits were down nearly 22%. Measured in 1947 dollars, average hourly factory wages plummeted from fifty-six to forty-four cents, and corporate profits disappeared.

But no generalized measure could catch the nagging realities of life in a prostrate America. A drop of 24% in per capita real disposable income told little of hunger in a home with no income. Behind the unemployed, veiled in shadows which the statistical "graphsmen" could never penetrate, stood millions of women, grimly watching as beauty, love and laughter were mashed under the leveling steamroller of despair. And children! "Have you ever heard a hungry child cry?" asked a New York social worker. America learned the sound. How could a nation deal with twenty-five famished children who raided the luncheon set out for the heroes in a veterans' parade, with mobs of kids who followed the garbage wagons? Boston and Chicago called the police to drive them away.

The anguish of America was everywhere, too elusive and human for charts and graphs, too common to be denied. It was a tired little man in Connecticut, losing in two years the bungalow he had saved two decades to buy. It was a disillusioned Aroostook County farmer who had carted his seed potatoes to the starch factory for fifty cents a barrel at the height of Coolidge prosperity. Now he left them to rot in fields choked with mustard in September breezes. It was the rough fraternity of hoboes and bums, a fluid proletariat, cadging meals where the chalked code on sidewalk or lamp post marked a sympathetic household. A smart one would check the phone book for names like his own. "Mornin', ma'am. I'm your husband's Uncle John from Vermont."

The misery of America had as many faces as the people themselves. It was the confident predictions made by a stock market executive while he hedged against fate with financial sleight of hand that would lead him to prison. It was the grim expediency of the Illinois farmer who burned his corn because coal was too expensive, and the nagging plight of the Kansan who needed an acre of wheat to put one child in shoes. It was the skittish small town Californian who joined the mob to keep the "Okies" moving on. What little you had, you had to hold. This was no time for sympathy with wild-eyed, ragged men on a safari to nowhere. It was homeless men slapping together a crazy-quilt town in an abandoned Central Park reservoir. There, in "Hoover Valley," they were in sight of Fifth Avenue, a few blocks from the forty-five-thousand-dollar-a-year Park Avenue flats, a little farther from the piers and markets where they scrounged for cast-off food. There were always "Hoover blankets." They rolled off the newspaper presses by the millions every day.

There were sad little jokes. During the wave of financier-suicides: "Do you want this room for sleeping or jumping?" As the bitterness deepened: "Hoover to Secretary Mellon, 'Can you lend me a nickel to call a friend?' Mellon to Hoover, 'Here's a dime. Call both of them.'"

At first, in a trauma of disbelief, the country had taken refuge behind pompous optimism and reckless bravado. Broadway's hit tune was "Happy Days Are Here Again." Signs abounded to help the whistling in the graveyard. "Wasn't the Depression Terrible?" they said in 1930, and President Hoover solemnly announced on March 7, "All the evidences indicate that the worst effects of the crash upon unemployment will have been passed during the next sixty days." [1] Occasional brave bankrupts left notices on the doors of their closed businesses, "Opened by Mistake." While a U. S. Steel official announced in January, 1931, that the worst of the depression had been passed a month before, people began gaily to whistle, "Life Is Just a Bowl of Cherries."

But by 1932 the thin veneer had cracked. All over the country people followed the lead of the Democratic Party's glib press man, Charley Michelson, labeled jack-rabbits "Hoover hogs," mule-drawn shells of dead autos "Hoover chariots," and nastily noted that they need not worry about the President's prediction, "a chicken in every pot," a "car in every garage." Who had the pot to cook it? Who had a garage? Broadway

---

[1] Notes will be found at the end of each chapter.

had long since passed the moment when gay little Mayor Jimmy Walker could ask it to show only the pleasant movies. By October, 1932, it was teaching America:

> Once I built a railroad, made it run—
> Made it race against time.
> Once I built a railroad, now it's done—
> Brother can you spare a dime? [2]

These were not a docile people: these Pittsburgh steelworkers who sent their kids to beg old bread when the bakeries closed—these Connecticut factory girls, working fifty-five hours a week for ten cents a day— these mothers who sent their kids out to gather empty bottles for the local bootleggers at a penny apiece. Even respectable white-collar workers gagged at J. P. Morgan's pious little radio speech for the "Block-Aid" campaign. "We must all do our bit," he told them. All too many remembered the comfortable promise of President Hoover in the campaign of 1928:

> Our country has become the land of oppor- tunity to those born without inheritance, not merely because of the wealth of its resources and industry but because of this freedom of initiative and enterprise. . . . By adherence to the principles of decentralized self- government, ordered liberty, equal opportunity, and freedom to the individual, our American experiment in human welfare has yielded a degree of well-being un- paralleled in all the world. . . . We are nearer today to the ideal of abolition of poverty and fear from the lives of men and women than ever before in any land. [3]

They paused only to sneer at the vacuous confidence they had cheered in 1928.

As humor was swallowed up by hunger, the bastions of law and order began to crumble. People began to understand, as they moved through the second and third sharp winters of depression, the moment of shocking truth that would bring the president of a great railroad to admit publicly, "I would steal before I would starve." The sterile mottoes of the business leaders seemed almost obscene: "Just grin, and keep on working"; "What we must have is faith, hope and charity, and perhaps some day we shall not need charity."

By 1933, it was possible to glean from the press a chronology of violence which covered the nation and increased from month to month:

England, Arkansas, January 3, 1931. The long drought that ruined hundreds of Arkansas farms last summer had a dramatic sequel late today when some 500 farmers, most of them white men and many of them armed, marched on the business section of this town. . . . Shouting that they must have food for themselves and their families, the invaders announced their intention to take it from the stores unless it were provided from some other source without cost. (N. Y. *Herald Tribune.*)

Detroit, July 9, 1931. An incipient riot by 500 unemployed men turned out of the city lodging house for lack of funds was quelled by police reserves in Cadillac Square tonight. (United Press.) . . .

Indiana Harbor, Indiana, August 15, 1931. Fifteen hundred jobless men stormed the plant of the Fruit Growers Express Company here, demanding that they be given jobs to keep from starving. The company's answer was to call the city police, who routed the jobless with menacing clubs. (Federated Press.) . . .

Detroit, November 28, 1931. A mounted patrolman was hit on the head with a stone and unhorsed and one demonstrator was arrested during a disturbance in Grand Circus Park this morning when 2,000 men and women met there in defiance of police orders. (Associated Press.)

Chicago, April 1, 1932. Five hundred school children, most with haggard faces and in tattered clothes, paraded through Chicago's downtown section to the Board of Education offices to demand that the school system provide them with food. (Federated Press.) . . .

Philadelphia, April 30, 1932. More than twenty persons were injured today when police broke up a proposed march on City Hall as it was started from two mobilization points. A dozen marchers were arrested, fifteen were treated or held at hospitals for observation, and five policemen were injured sufficiently to require hospital treatment. (N. Y. Times.) . . .

Cleveland, August 2, 1932. When a local grocery advertised for its opening that it would give away free baskets of food to the first 1,500 persons to enter the store, 6,000 people jammed the surrounding sidewalk. The crowd began to gather at midnight and at 9 A.M. there was a riot. Fifty-two people were injured. (Federated Press.) . . .

Vacaville, California, December 5, 1932. Six reputed leaders of a strike which has disrupted fruit picking in Vaca Valley were kidnaped from Vacaville Jail early today, whisked away in automobiles and reported painted red, beaten, and told never to return to this vicinity. (Associated Press.) . . .

New York, January 21, 1933. Several hundred jobless surrounded a restaurant just off Union Square today demanding they be fed without charge. Their demands were presented by a delegation of five which attacked the restaurant manager when he refused their request. Police riot squads arrived to find the manager stabbed and the several hundred milling outside the restaurant entrance. (N. Y. Evening Post.) . . .

Rochester, New York, February 14, 1933. Menaced by nightsticks and tear gas bombs in the hands of 100 police reserves summoned by radio from every precinct in the city, 400 men and women rioting in a Welfare Bureau station were quickly subdued today after two policemen had been slightly injured. (Associated Press.) . . .[4]

This was only a sample. The quake which had followed the market crash shook the foundations of a values system already deeply undermined. Though Hoover held his faith to the end, the philosophy of individualism he so glowingly idealized had become sadly tarnished by practice in the bold decade of the twenties. Rural America, tormented by chronic agricultural depression since 1921, had seen her ancient distrust of cities, industry and "Wall Street" deeply underscored. By 1930 twelve spokesmen for the agricultural South would sum this up with a complete repudiation of industrialism and all its evils. Taking their "Stand" for the mystical virtues of agrarianism, they announced:

It is an inevitable consequence of industrial progress that production greatly outruns the rate of natural consumption. To overcome the disparity, the producers, disguised as the pure idealists of progress, must coerce and wheedle the public into being loyal and steady consumers, in order to keep the machines running. . . . It is the great effort of a false economy of life to approve itself. But it's task grows more difficult each day. . . . Men are prepared to sacrifice their private dignity and happiness to an abstract social ideal, and without asking whether the social ideal produces the welfare of any individual man whatsoever. But this is absurd. The responsibility of men is for their own welfare and that of their neighbors; not for the hypothetical welfare of some fabulous creature called society.[5]

Middle-class, urban America began to doubt, not industrialism, but individualism itself. While the Southerners yearned for Jefferson, Charles Beard lashed out at "The Myth of Rugged American Individualism." He showed that the advocates of laissez faire had in fact

promoted massive governmental intervention of their
own kind. Flaunting Al Capone as the "supreme in-
dividualist," insisting that no one really had the courage
of the old dogmas, he proclaimed:

> The cold truth is that the individualist creed
> of everybody for himself and the devil take the hind-
> most is principally responsible for the distress in which
> Western civilization finds itself—with investment
> racketeering at one end and labor racketeering at the
> other. . . . Every thoughtful business man who is en-
> gaged in management as distinguished from stock specu-
> lation knows that stabilization, planning, orderly pro-
> cedure, prudence, and the adjustment of production
> to demand are necessary to keep the economic machine
> running steadily and efficiently. . . . The task before us,
> then, is not to furbish up an old slogan, but to get rid
> of it, to discover how much planning is necessary, by
> whom it can best be done. . . .[8]

Walter Lippmann, already the demigod of American
newspaper readers, reminded the nation of its moral
bankruptcy:

> . . . It is not the facts of the crisis which we
> have to fear. They can be endured and dealt with. It
> is demoralization alone that is dangerous.
> A demoralized people is one in which the individual
> has become isolated and is the prey of his own sus-
> picions. He trusts nobody and nothing, not even him-
> self. He believes in nothing, except the worst of
> everybody and everything. He sees only confusion in
> himself and conspiracies in other men. That is panic.
> That is disintegration. That is what comes when in
> some sudden emergency of their lives men find them-
> selves unsupported by clear convictions that transcend
> their immediate and personal desires . . . in this decade
> the change in life brought about by science and ma-

chinery and the modern city, by democracy and by popular education, had struck with full impact and with cumulative force against the traditional morality, the social conventions and the ideals of the mass of men.

That a period of profound spiritual bewilderment had to ensue was inevitable. But this bewilderment has been greatly aggravated in the United States by what I believe may truthfully be called the moral apathy of those in high places. . . .

. . . if you teach a people for ten years that the character of its government is not greatly important, that political success is for those who equivocate and evade, and if you tell them that acquisitiveness is the ideal, that things are what matter, that Mammon is God, then you must not be astonished at the confusion in Washington, or the nonchalance of James J. Walker. . . .⁷

For most Americans the first clear recognition that anything was wrong had come on Black Thursday, October 24, 1929. This second day of the lurid crash dispelled most hopes that the stock market was merely seeking a "more secure technical position." Within a week the whole world knew that "the permanently high plateau," which Yale professor Irving Fisher had pleasantly forecast on October 17, was a miserable fantasy that belonged to the world of the Mad Hatter and the March Hare.

It was not until November 13 that a wildly erratic market finally hit its low for the year, and a preliminary assessment of the shambles could be made. "The Big Bull Market was dead," and with it were shattered the faiths and fancies of a whole generation.

As the public slowly reacted, other figures suggested broader collapse. In the next three years over 5,000 banks failed. While farm production actually increased, average net farm income dropped from $962 to $288, and farm mortgage foreclosures doubled. Marriages fell

off 22%. The birth rate dropped sharply. In 1932 the
suicide rate was 40% higher than it had been in 1929.

As historians and economists looked back beyond the
great financial debauch, they began to see that the
market madness had been merely the symptom of a
deep economic malaise. Infection had been spreading
since the World War. The whole nation had mistaken
the flush of fever for the bloom of health. Arthur
Schlesinger, Jr., has summed up the underlying problems:

1) Management's disposition to maintain
prices and inflate profits while holding down wages and
raw material prices meant that workers and farmers
were denied the benefits of increases in their own productivity. The consequence was the relative decline of
mass purchasing power. As goods flowed out of the
expanding capital plant in ever greater quantities,
there was proportionately less and less cash in the
hands of buyers to carry the goods off the market. The
pattern of income distribution, in short, was incapable
of long maintaining prosperity.

2) Seven years of fixed capital investment at high
rates had "overbuilt" productive capacity (in terms of
existing capacity to consume) and had thus saturated
the economy. The slackening of the automotive and
building industries was symptomatic. The existing rate
of capital formation could not be sustained without
different governmental policies—policies aimed not at
helping those who had money to accumulate more but
at transferring money from those who were letting it
stagnate in savings to those who would spend it.

3) The sucking off into profits and dividends of the
gains of technology meant the tendency to use excess
money for speculation, transforming the Stock Exchange from a securities market into a gaming-house.

4) The stock market crash completed the debacle
. . . business men, in trying to save themselves, could

only wreck their system; in trying to avoid the worst, they rendered the worst inevitable. . . .[8]

But the sickness of the twenties had gone far beyond economics. Inexorably through the decade of "rugged individualism," there had accumulated a backlog of problems crying for solution. And there was a restlessness in the Roaring Twenties that went much deeper than prohibition-hypocrisy or the antics of flaming youth. Schlesinger has noted:

What was wrong with the New Era was not (as yet) evidence of incompetence or stupidity in public policy. Rather, there was a profound discontent with the monopoly of power and prestige by a single class and the resulting indifference of the national government to deeper tensions. Those excluded from the magic circle suffered boredom, resentment, irritation and eventually indignation over what seemed the intolerable pretensions and irrelevancies of their masters. Now it is the gravest error to underrate the power of boredom as a factor in social change. . . . the human capacity for boredom sets limits on conservatism. The dominant official society—the Establishment—of the Twenties was an exceedingly boring one, neither bright nor witty nor picturesque nor even handsome, and this prodded the human impulse to redress the balance by kicking up heels in back streets.

All this encouraged the defection of specific groups from a social order which ignored their needs and snubbed their ambitions. Within the business community itself there were dissident individuals, especially in the underdeveloped areas of the country, who considered that opportunities for local growth were unduly restrained by Wall Street's control of the money market. The farmers felt themselves shut out from the prevailing prosperity. Elements in the labor movement resented their evident second-class citizenship. Members of foreign nationality groups, especially the newer immigration and its children, chafed under the prevalent assumption that the real America was Anglo-Saxon, Protestant, middle-class and white. In time some of the younger people of the nation began to grow restless before the ideals held out to them; while others, in accepting these ideals, acquired a smug mediocrity which even depressed some of their elders.

Gravest among the symptoms was the defection of the intellectuals. . . . The fact of their particular estrangement and discontent guaranteed the articulation, and thus, to a degree, the coordination of the larger unrest. The intellectuals put the ruling class in its place by substituting for its own admiring picture of itself a set of disrespectful images, which an increasing number of people found delightful and persuasive; . . . Together the satirists and the prophets drew a new portrait of America—both of the American present and of the American promise—and the increasingly visible discrepancy between what was and what might be in America armed the spreading discontent.

The well of idealism was rising again; energies were being replenished, batteries recharged. . . .'

NOTES, *chapter 1*

1. *New York Times,* March 8, 1930.
2. E. Y. Harburg and Jay Gorney in J. P. McEvoy's "Americana, 1932," *Stage,* X (November, 1932), (Music Publisher's Holding Corporation).
3. Herbert Hoover, *The New Day, Campaign Speeches of Herbert Hoover, 1928* (Stanford, 1928), 167-168, 175.
4. Mauritz Hallgren, *Seeds of Revolt* (Knopf, 1933), 165-169.
5. Twelve Southerners, *I'll Take My Stand, the South and the Agrarian Tradition* (Harper, 1930), xvii-xviii.
6. Charles Beard, "The Myth of Rugged Individualism," *Harper's Magazine,* CLIV (1931-1932), 22.
7. Walter Lippmann, *Interpretations, 1931–1932* (Macmillan, 1933), 27-28.

8. Arthur M. Schlesinger, Jr., *Crisis of the Old Order, 1919–1933* (Houghton, Mifflin, 1957), 159-160.

9. Arthur M. Schlesinger, Jr., "Sources of the New Deal: Reflections on the Temper of a Time," *Columbia University Forum,* II (Fall, 1959), 6.

chapter 2 "NOTHING TO FEAR"

Saturday, July 2, 1932, the nation looked to Chicago. There in the vast Convention Hall and in the lake front hotels the Democrats had nominated the next President. There, at six in the afternoon, Franklin D. Roosevelt stood to sketch the image of the dawning Age of Action.

This man commanded attention. Not since Jackson had a candidate seemed so certainly fated to victory so early in the game. Not since Lincoln had so much depended upon the quality of one man. And this was no ordinary man. With one magnificent gesture he had broken the pattern of the past. The first candidate ever to start his campaign at the Convention which nominated him, he had flown dramatically from Albany, bucking headwinds and storms. The nation and his party had waited breathlessly until his chartered trimotor had settled through the low-hanging scud, two hours late, at Chicago's airport. But there was more than a talent for dramatic gesture here. This Governor of New York exuded a radiance and a confidence all but forgotten in American politics. The easy smile and the jaunty wave made the cheering crowds forget, if they had ever known, that from the waist down this man was cased in brutal steel braces. The firm grip on the lectern, the square set of the massive shoulders, and the confident cock of the chin dominated the Convention Hall mob and blotted out in moments the memory of the awkward gait with which he had swung on crippled legs to the front of the stage.

And this was a voice, as well as a presence. As he

launched into his acceptance speech, the strange blend
of his delivery—broad Harvard accents, but warm and
friendly tones, deeply resonant on the radio—carried
the magic of his confident mood to a million homes
from coast to coast.

Strangely, it was a long speech, and sometimes dull.
But it was filled with the promise of action, salted with
symbols of faith. Careful of commitment, it was laced
with phrases that aroused old sympathies and new
hopes—phrases that would be remembered:

> We will break foolish traditions and leave it
to the Republican leadership, far more skilled in the
art, to break promises.

Let us now and here highly resolve to resume the
country's uninterrupted march along the path of real
progress, of real justice, of real equality for all of our
citizens, great and small. . . .

To meet by reaction that danger of radicalism is to
invite disaster. Reaction is no barrier to the radical.
It is a challenge, a provocation. The way to meet that
danger is to offer a workable program of reconstruction,
and the party to offer it is the party with clean
hands. . . . I invite those nominal Republicans who
find that their conscience cannot be squared with the
groping and the failure of their party leaders, to join
hands with us; here and now, in equal measure, I warn
those nominal Democrats who squint at the future
with their faces turned toward the past, and who feel
no responsibility to the demands of the new time, that
they are out of step with their Party. . . .[1]

*Roosevelt's analysis of the depression set the tone
for the campaign and for much of his later program:*

> In the years before 1929 we know that this
country had completed a vast cycle of building and
inflation; for ten years we expanded on the theory of

repairing the wastes of War, but actually expanded far beyond that, and also beyond our natural and normal growth. . . . The consumer was forgotten. Very little of it [profits] went into increased wages; the worker was forgotten, and by no means an adequate proportion was even paid out in dividends—the stockholder was forgotten. . . .

What was the result? Enormous corporate surpluses piled up—the most stupendous in history. Where, under the spell of delirious speculation, did those surpluses go? . . . first, into new and unnecessary plants which now stand stark and idle; and second, into the call-money market of Wall Street, either directly by the corporations, or indirectly through the banks. Those are the facts. Why blink at them? . . . Never in history have the interests of all the people been so united in a single economic problem . . . . Danger to one is danger to all. . . .

What do the people of America want more than anything else? To my mind, they want two things: work, with all the moral and spiritual values that go with it; and with work, a reasonable measure of security. . . .

Our Republican leaders tell us economic laws—sacred, inviolable, unchangeable—cause panics which no one could prevent. But while they prate of economic laws, men and women are starving. We must lay hold of the fact that economic laws are not made by nature. They are made by human beings. . . .

I pledge you, I pledge myself to a new deal for the American people. . . .[1]

The mood of confidence had been set. Within days the phrase "new deal" was a national watchword. The drama unfolded in Chicago that muggy July evening was a token of new hope for a distraught nation. But for Roosevelt, for Louis McHenry Howe, his shadowy aide, for James A. Farley, his bluff, dynamic manager, this was the climax of an exhausting struggle to the top. In September, 1921, eleven short years before, F.D.R. had seemed a most unlikely candidate. Lying in a New York hospital, his legs useless, some of the muscles in his upper body affected, he was so massively blighted by polio that the future seemed to hold only the image of a discarded invalid, crabbedly sitting out his life on the broad porch at Hyde Park.

His had been a truly remarkable career, built upon amazing good fortune, but guided by a nearly unique political genius and charm. At twenty-nine he swept into the New York State Senate from a heavily Republican Hudson Valley district. Within three months he was a national figure, the attractive spokesman of an anti-Tammany rebellion among upstate Democrats. At thirty-one, he was tapped as the New York "progressives' " representative in Woodrow Wilson's family. Eight years as Assistant-Secretary of the Navy taught him the limits of political rebellion and the infinite mazes of Washington administration. He learned to live with Tammany; he mastered the art of compromise. In 1920, aged thirty-eight, he was the kind of vice-presidential candidate who ran an unprecedented whistle-stop campaign, even in a hopeless year. Now, not quite forty, he seemed to be finished.

That Roosevelt did not slip back into genteel obscurity was a miracle wrought by his own deep resilience, and by the courage of Eleanor Roosevelt and Louis Howe. The road back was built at first with tiny paving stones—countless letters to Democrats all over the country, on one excuse or another, but always designed to remind them that Franklin Roosevelt was no man to forget. And the fight for publicity: between 1921 and 1928, this political "has-been" was mentioned in the New York Times on nearly 200 ocasions. But the highway was smoothed immensely when Roosevelt and Howe fell in with New York's dramatic Governor,

Alfred E. Smith. As Roosevelt swung himself painfully to the rostrum to nominate "the Happy Warrior" for the Presidency in 1924, he gave notice to the Democracy that he was back in the wars to stay. Though Smith failed to receive the nomination in 1924, he was the standard-bearer four years later. When Roosevelt accepted reluctantly the 1928 gubernatorial nomination, the die was cast. Unhappy at the draft—he and Howe thought the timing was wrong—he nevertheless pitched in to prove that a Roosevelt could outrun a Smith even in New York.

F.D.R.'s two terms in Albany were a conscious apprenticeship for the Presidency. While he played the old game of being "full-time Governor," Roosevelt planned every move with an eye on its national implications. Carefully choosing the State issues which would sell him to Wilson progressives and rural Democrats of the West and South, he evolved specific farm, conservation and public-power programs to which he could point as precedents for national policies. He took refuge in his State office to avoid foreign policy, but he attracted national attention in the fight against crime. Late in discovering the depression, he had the immense advantage of watching from Albany, instead of being on the spot in Washington. Though he muffed badly the State's responsibility for the collapse of New York banks, his timing proved perfect in the end. He could go to Chicago as the author of the dramatic New York State Temporary Emergency Relief Administration. Above all, he proved his political mastery in the toughest school the nation could provide. He managed a striking program of accomplishment with a firmly Republican legislature. He skirted for three and a half years the messy corruption of his party's Manhattan organization. He strengthened the upstate Democracy, without losing Tammany completely. And he lived in the glare of the searchlights for nearly four years without stumbling once.

There were some who found his performance too slick. Walter Lippmann summed up the misgivings in January, 1932:

> It is now plain that sooner or later some of Governor Roosevelt's supporters are going to feel badly let down. For it is impossible that he can continue to be such different things to such different men. . . .
> The art of carrying water on both shoulders is highly developed in American politics, and Mr. Roosevelt has learned it. . . . Thus at one place we learn that the public demands "plans for the reconstruction of a better ordered civilization" and in another place that "the American system of economics and government is everlasting." The first sentence is meant for Senator Wheeler and the second for the New York Times. . . . In the case of Mr. Roosevelt, it is not easy to say with certainty whether his left-wing or his right-wing supporters are the more deceived. The reason is that Franklin D. Roosevelt is a highly impressionable person, without a firm grasp of public affairs and without very strong convictions. . . . Franklin D. Roosevelt is an amiable man with many philanthropic impulses, but he is not the dangerous enemy of anything. He is too eager to please. . . . Franklin D. Roosevelt is no crusader. He is no tribune of the people. He is no enemy of entrenched privilege. He is a pleasant man who, without any important qualifications for the office, would very much like to be President.³

The politicians, perhaps less concerned with principles, were more deeply impressed by his vote-getting. A man who could carry New York in 1930 by 725,001 votes seemed a man who could win in 1932. To this strength Jim Farley and Louis Howe played in their painstaking maneuver for Convention votes in the twenty months before Chicago. Building on their basic strategy to make Roosevelt appealing in the West and South, Howe developed an intricate network of correspondence from his grubby, understaffed office on Madison Avenue. Meanwhile, Farley, now New York State Democratic Chairman, concentrated on the personal contact with the "leaders"—he never called them "bosses." With the help of key Southern and Western Senators, they worked together to block the plans of the increasingly hostile National Chairman, John Raskob—a General Motors executive, a Smith man and an archconservative. By the summer of 1931 they were ready for a sales tour of the West. Farley has told the story:

Shortly after noon on Monday, June 29, I was off on a journey from coast to coast that was to enable me to cover eighteen states in nineteen days, a journey that was to consist mostly of "sleeper jumps" from state to state, while sandwiched in between were all kinds of meetings, conferences, confabs, and luncheon engagements with Democratic chieftains. I was a kind of roving "listening post," ...

Perhaps the role of "political drummer" had never before been attempted on such a wide scale, or in such a plain manner. . . . If I got to a city and found as many as five hundred people waiting there to look me over, I shook hands with each one personally. I was extremely careful to get first and last names correctly and of course never disputed the views of others if it was at all possible to agree. It always creates a bad impression to start off with an argument. By carefully observing those simple and essential rules, I managed to strike up the kind of informal, easy-going friendships that make future understandings a great deal easier to arrive at. . . .

I never talked to individuals about the presidential nomination unless I was certain of the other fellow's position. Usually, I sparred around a bit by suggesting

that we had three outstanding potential candidates for
the Presidency in New York State—Alfred E. Smith,
Owen D. Young, and Franklin D. Roosevelt—and that
it was my purpose to discover what the public thought
of them as possible standard-bearers. This was the line
I was using on William W. (Bill) Howes, the national
committeeman of South Dakota, as we sat in a lunch-
room at Aberdeen on a roasting hot day. . . . Just before
it was time to go, Bill decided to let me know what he
really thought. He plumped his fist on the table and
growled in a deep voice:

"Farley, I'm damned tired of backing losers. In my
opinion, Roosevelt can sweep the country, and I'm going to support him. . . .

". . . the consensus of opinion among the leaders
[Farley went on to report to Roosevelt] is that you are
the one man who can win. . . . If I continue to find the
same sentiment in the other states that I have found
already, my statement upon reaching New York will
be so enthusiastic that those who read it will think I
am a fit candidate for an insane asylum. . . ." [8]

*The campaign in the West and South went almost as
well as Farley had predicted. Late in the autumn of
1931 he began to forecast a first-ballot victory. Nevertheless, the Roosevelt boom was seriously threatened as
the winter wore on. His artful dodging of the Tammany
issue brought him the contempt of many reformers and
liberals. Almost simultaneously he was pilloried by the
Hearst press as a dangerous internationalist. Hearst was
supporting John Garner of Texas, the Speaker of the
House. Early in February, personally bitter, uneasy
about what he thought to be Roosevelt demagoguery,
Al Smith himself entered the race. Governor Albert
Ritchie of Maryland and Harry Byrd of Virginia,
Newton D. Baker of Ohio and a handful of others had
scattered blocks of votes.*

Smith and Tammany took Roosevelt's own delega-

tion out of his camp. Ill-advised and poorly managed fights in Massachusetts, Connecticut and Rhode Island were lost to Smith. The crucial Pennsylvania block was split. Illinois, Indiana and Ohio were waiting to jump on the winner's wagon. Texas and California stood for Garner.

Thrown off-balance by Hearst's attack, Roosevelt repudiated sharply the Wilsonian position on foreign policy which he had steadily promoted since 1920. On February 2, 1932, he told the New York State Grange:

> . . . the League of Nations is not the League conceived by Woodrow Wilson. It might have been, had the United States joined. Too often through these years its major function has been not the broad overwhelming purpose of world peace, but rather a mere meeting place for the political discussion of strictly European political national difficulties. In these the United States should have no part. . . . American participation in the League would not serve the highest purpose of the prevention of war and a settlement of international difficulties in accordance with fundamental American ideals. Because of these facts, therefore, I do not favor American participation.
>
> What the world needs most today is a national policy which will make us an example of national honor to other nations. . . .
>
> Europe owes us. We do not owe her. Therefore, we should call a meeting of our debtors here and not in Europe and demand an understanding. . . . Europe has indulged herself in an orgy of spending and finds herself at the moment in a crippled financial position. . . . The world ship of state cannot regain its safe course to port by reckless spending and by reckless vituperation, but it can steer safely home by unity of action and a determination eventually to meet its just obligations. . . .'

By early spring Roosevelt had come to see that he had far too many vague notions, and far too few specific plans. His legal counsel and speech-writer, Samuel Rosenman, began to collect for him an informal staff of Columbia University professors who were soon labeled the "Brain Trust." Their ideas were often disparate, sometimes conflicting—but they had ideas. While Farley, Howe and their aides dug for the votes, Rosenman and Raymond Moley rode herd on the professors who were sketching the first tentative outlines of the New Deal. As it happened, however, the most effective statement of Roosevelt's public posture during the preconvention months was written for him by a friendly newsman, Ernest K. Lindley. From Lindley's draft, Roosevelt told an Oglethorpe University Commencement:

> . . . it seems to me probable that our physical economic plant will not expand in the future at the same rate at which it has expanded in the past. We may build more factories, but the fact remains that we have enough now to supply all of our domestic needs, and more, if they are used. . . . Our basic trouble was not an insufficiency of capital. It was an insufficient distribution of buying power coupled with an oversufficient speculation in production. . . .
>
> The country needs and, unless I mistake its temper, the country demands bold, persistent experimentation. It is common sense to take a method and try it: if it fails, admit it frankly and try another. But, above all, try something. The millions who are in want will not stand by silently forever while the things to satisfy their needs are within easy reach. . . .[5]

When Farley and Howe reached Chicago they faced, not the easy first-ballot sweep on which they had gambled, but the outlines of a dogged stop-Roosevelt movement. James MacGregor Burns has described their struggle:

At Roosevelt headquarters in Chicago Farley posted a gaudy map—"Field Marshal Farley's map," it was soon dubbed—showing his chief's strength across the nation. The map also showed Roosevelt's weakness. For it was clear when the Democratic Convention opened on June 27, 1932, that Roosevelt could not win the often predicted first-ballot victory unless a stampede was touched off at the end of the roll. Who would touch it off? Farley still did not know. He had met disappointment after disappointment in trying to win the extra one hundred votes that would mean victory. . . .

Under mounting pressure, the Roosevelt forces at the eleventh hour embarked on a risky maneuver that almost lost them the fight. This was the repeal of the two-thirds rule. The idea was simple: Each national convention at the outset adopted its own rules by straight majority vote; sure of commanding such a majority the Roosevelt men needed only to change the rule and then nominate their candidate by a straight majority.

The tactic might have worked if it had been properly timed. But it was not. The issue came up at an organization meeting of Roosevelt delegates. . . . Suddenly Senator Huey P. Long of Louisiana took the floor to offer a resolution setting forth that the governor's friends would fight for a straight majority rule. Coat open, arms pumping, the Kingfish raised his pudgy, pock-marked face in a bellowing call to action. Farley dared not restrain the man who held Louisiana's delegates' votes in his pocket, and who had told Flynn that he backed Roosevelt only because he had met the other contenders. The resolution went through.

The opposition blazed up in wrathful indignation. A nomination won in such a way, said Senator Carter

Glass, would be "damaged goods obtained by a gambler's trick." Roosevelt's opponents, hitherto divided, now had a moral issue around which to unite. Even worse, pro-Roosevelt delegations in the South showed signs of deserting on the majority rule issue, for the two-thirds rule had become a venerable mechanism for protecting the power of the South in the party.

After conferring over the telephone with Roosevelt in Albany and with Howe in Chicago, Farley decided to surrender. . . .

At last came the roll call on nomination. Farley was everywhere, pumping hands, claiming victory, exhorting delegations to get on the bandwagon while there was still room. In a hotel room Howe was conducting last-minute espionage operations and putting out feelers to key men in favorite-son delegations. In Albany, Roosevelt waited by the radio, frequently counseling with his lieutenants over a private telephone wire. Biting on a cigar, Smith sat amid Tammany delegates so hostile to Roosevelt that Farley had difficulty finding a seat in order to vote during roll calls. It was past four o'clock on the morning of July 1 when the nominating and seconding speeches finally came to an end. Exhausted by ten hours of turgid oratory, demonstrations, and blaring band music, the delegates slumped in their chairs.

The first roll call went according to expectations. Roosevelt moved far ahead near the outset and kept a long lead. His final tally on the first roll call of 666¼ dwarfed Smith's 204¾, Garner's 90¼, and White's 52, but it was about one hundred short of two-thirds. While tellers were making their check, Farley sat back on the platform, waiting for the bandwagon rush to start.

Nothing happened.

Farley sprinted down to the floor and pleaded with delegations to shift. He had the vice-presidential

nomination to offer, but the delegations were stalling
while they waited to see if the current went in another
direction. Weary delegates were eager to adjourn but
the Roosevelt forces wanted another roll call before their
own delegations weakened. On the second roll call
Roosevelt picked up 11½ votes, an increase so small
that it dramatized the extent to which Farley had staked
his hopes on the first ballot.

Still no delegation came over. Now it was the opposition forces that wanted another roll call. Roosevelt,
they proclaimed, was stopped. On the third ballot
Roosevelt crept up five more votes. His ranks at least
were holding firm—but so were the enemy's. At 9 A.M.,
after the third roll call, the convention adjourned and
the delegates tottered out into the sunshine.

The next few hours would be decisive. Farley had to
win a sizeable bloc of votes before his own ranks
buckled. The breaking away of one delegation might
start an avalanche toward Garner, who had picked
up eleven votes on the third ballot. Already Mississippi's
twenty votes were in jeopardy. . . . Alabama, Arkansas,
and Minnesota also had soft spots.

The only card Farley had left was a big one. For some
time he had been in touch with a group of men close
to Garner, including Representative Sam Rayburn of
Texas. Garner was a serious candidate, but he did not
want a deadlocked convention, and he personally
opposed the two-thirds rule. Farley had also been in
direct touch with Hearst, warning him that in a deadlock the prize might go to Baker, whose internationalist
views the publisher hated. Hearst hated Smith even
more. Farley had been putting every possible form of
pressure on Garner's men at the convention. Now—while
Roosevelt leaders were proffering the vice-presidency
in a dozen different directions—Farley was able to make
a definitive offer. The deal was quickly made. All during
the day Smith was trying to reach Garner in Washing-

ton, but the Speaker would talk to no one but Rayburn. Late in the afternoon Rayburn got an official release from Garner. It was none too soon. Mississippi had cracked and gone over to the coalition. . . .

Now the Roosevelt avalanche began. The shift of Texas brought around California too. On the fourth roll call McAdoo, a victim of the two-thirds rule eight years before, came to the rostrum. The pro-Smith galleries drowned him out with groans and boos, but finally his voice came through. "California came here to nominate a President of the United States," he shouted. "She did not come to deadlock the Convention or to engage in another devastating contest like that of 1924. California casts 44 votes for Franklin D. Roosevelt."

The frenzied cheering echoed over the radio in Roosevelt's study. He leaned back and grinned broadly. "Good old McAdoo." The delegations swiftly fell in line—all but Smith's diehard supporters, who refused to make the nomination unanimous.

On a roof garden in Washington a little man [Garner] sat smoking a cigar. A reporter recognized him. "You've gone to Roosevelt?" "That's right, son." The reporter expressed surprise. The cigar glowed. "I'm a little older than you are, son. And politics is funny." [*]

As the summer of 1932 wore on, Roosevelt's chief embarrassment was the need, finally, to hold hearings which looked toward the removal of Tammany's Jimmy Walker as Mayor of New York. Walker happily obliged by resigning as the fateful moment approached. President Hoover's embarrassments were more fundamental. One was the Bonus Marchers, a loosely organized mob of veterans who descended on Washington in June and camped at Anacostia Flats, in dreary desperation. A jittery administration finally authorized troop action against them; bayonets, tear gas and fire rooted the pitiful, disintegrating group of men, women and chil-

dren from their makeshift town onto the road to nowhere again. The commanding general, Douglas Mac-
Arthur, thought he saw a "mob" about to seize the
government. The *Washington News* saw "the great
American Government, mightiest in the world, chasing
unarmed men, women and children with Army
tanks. . . ." The Bonus Marchers' own shabby newspaper suggested an inscription for the tombstone of the
only child born at the Flats: "Here lies Bernard Myers,
aged three months, gassed to death by order of President Hoover." '

But this was no campaign to be taken for granted.
Roosevelt and his friends knew that their worst enemy
was overconfidence. They fought against it with a
compulsion to organization and activity scarcely
matched in the country's political history. And Roosevelt insisted on a busy personal campaign. With his
peculiar handicap, he must demonstrate his physical
vigor. He must arouse enthusiasm, maximize the sense
of urgency which was turning tired Democrats into
vigorous workers again. He must capitalize on his personal dynamism. Just as important, he loved the con-
catenation of confusion and excitement. He would
not be kept on the front porch. Nevertheless there
were dangers. To many it seemed stupidly reckless
for the candidate who had only to avoid stumbling to
insist on such an expansive and public obstacle course.

Worse yet, Roosevelt was caught dead center in
what Arthur Schlesinger, Jr., has called "a triangle of
advice." Behind him the Garners and Byrds, the Al
Smiths and Carter Glasses of the party urged a trun-
cated budget, regressive taxes, a return to States' Rights,
all matters to which Roosevelt had paid his tokens of
respect on occasion. At one side the descendants of the
farmer radicals, such men as Burton K. Wheeler, Huey
Long and Bob La Follette, Jr., pressed for vigorous
attack on the vested interests, for trust-busting, infla-

tion and economic regulation. They were aided by Felix Frankfurter, the supercharged, imaginative, and scholarly Harvard law professor who distrusted both architectural social planning and the status quo. Frankfurter had Roosevelt's deep respect. On the other hand stood some of the most influential of F.D.R.'s brain trusters, among them Rexford Tugwell and Adolph Berle. For them integrated social planning was the essential; Garner and Frankfurter, and Wheeler, were all anathema.

While all of his advisers stewed intermittently, Roosevelt proved himself a gambler capable of the large rewards which came with large risks. His own end-of-campaign summary suggests the pace and scope of his nationwide swing, with each major speech a national performance as he played to the strengths of his radio personality:

At Topeka I outlined a complete national plan for the restoration of agriculture to its proper relationship to the Nation.

At Salt Lake City I outlined a definite program to give us a national transportation policy, including the rehabilitation of the railroads of the Nation.

At Portland I set forth in definite terms a national policy for the conduct of utilities and especially those engaged in manufacturing and distributing electric power.

At Sioux City I proposed a tariff policy aimed to restore international trade and commerce not only with this Nation but between all nations.

At Boston I championed the principle that the national government has a positive duty to see that no citizen shall starve.

At Columbus I proposed the protection of the investing public against evils and the fraud perpetrated against them during the past 10 years.

At Pittsburgh I proposed an honest, national budget system.[8]

This was the bare outline. As the speeches emerged after relentless hammering by disparate craftsmen, Roosevelt seemed to be choosing among the sides of his triangle experimentally. Often he appeared to follow some near-mystical sense of fluctuations in the public mood. Sometimes he seemed merely an insouciant opportunist. Faced with two sharply conflicting drafts of his tariff speech, he told Raymond Moley to "weave the two together." He could reflect in San Francisco the sober views of Berle: that American society had passed beyond the age of progress, that only integrated social planning could meet the crisis. In Pittsburgh, a few weeks later, he could mouth the economic conservatism of Bernard Baruch in his advocacy of governmental retrenchment, the "honest" policy of economy.

Above all he sought to arouse the hopes of the masses of voters, but without freezing the direction of the experiment before the laboratory was his. To some the total effect betrayed a deep uncertainty about even the major patterns. Richard Hofstadter suggests:

Roosevelt's 1932 campaign utterances indicate that the New Deal had not yet taken form in his mind. He was clear on two premises: he rejected Hoover's thesis that the depression began abroad, insisting that it was a home-made product, and he denounced Hoover for spending too much money. . . .

And yet he was "unwilling that economy should be practiced at the expense of starving people." Still, he did not indicate how he proposed to relieve starving people. Public works? They could be no more than a "stopgap," even if billions of dollars were spent on them. He was firm in ascribing the depression to low domestic purchasing power, and declared that the government must "use wise measures of regulation which will bring the purchasing power back to normal." On the other hand, he surrendered to Hoover's idea that America's productive capacity demanded a large outlet in the export market. . . .

Roosevelt delivered one speech at the Commonwealth Club in San Francisco, however, which did generally foreshadow the new tack that was about to be taken under the New Deal. . . .

A glance at the situation today only too clearly indicates that equality of opportunity as we have known it no longer exists. . . . Put plainly, we are steering a steady course toward economic oligarchy, if we are not there already. . . .

Clearly, all this calls for a re-appraisal of values. Our task now is not discovery or exploitation of natural resources, or necessarily producing more goods. It is the soberer, less dramatic business of administering resources and plants already in hand, of seeking to re-establish foreign markets for our surplus production, of meeting the problem of underconsumption, of adjusting production to consumption, of distributing wealth and products more equitably, of adapting existing economic organizations to the service of the people. The day of enlightened administration has come. . . .

As I see it, the task of government in its relation to business is to assist the development of an economic declaration of rights, an economic constitutional order. . . .

Happily, the times indicate that to create such an order not only is the proper policy of Government, but it is the only line of safety for our economic structures as well. We know, now, that these economic units cannot exist unless prosperity is uniform, that is, unless purchasing power is well distributed throughout every group in the nation.

In cold terms, American capitalism had come of age, the great era of individualism, expansion, and opportunity was dead. Further, the drying up of "natural" economic forces required that the government step in and guide the creation of a new economic order. . . . But in the Commonwealth Club speech two different and potentially inconsistent lines of government action are implied. One is suggested by the observation that the industrial plant is "overbuilt," that more plants will be "a danger," that production must be "adjusted" to consumption; the other by phrases like "meeting the problem of underconsumption," making prosperity "uniform," distributing purchasing power, and "an economic declaration of rights." The first involves a retrogressive economy of trade restriction and state-guided monopoly; the second emphasizes social justice and the conquest of poverty. . . .[9]

Roosevelt was more interested in the effects than in the logic of his campaign. And the people appeared more caught by the man than by what he said. "People began to look for the Roosevelt characteristics: the upthrust head; the confidential look with eyebrows arched when he let fly a gibe at the opposition, followed by the slow grin as the audience caught on; the sly mockery; the biting scorn; the righteous wrath."[10] President Hoover, who could not manage and could never respect these mobile acrobatics, dubbed him "a chameleon on plaid." Intellectuals broadly suspected him. He was too slippery, too superficial.

But the voters ratified the Roosevelt technique and the Roosevelt pragmatism. 22,815,539 to Hoover's 15,759,930! Forty-two States! 472 electoral votes! A twenty-two seat majority in the Senate, a one hundred and eighty-nine margin in the House of Representatives!

While Roosevelt rested at Warm Springs—on Vincent Astor's yacht, Nourmahal—and at Hyde Park, the "triangle of advice" closed in on him. Bernard Baruch, Rex Tugwell, Huey Long, and a score more, each hinted broad confidence that his program would win. The uneasy party regular, Sam Rayburn, worried that the administration might fall prey to "some god-damn Rasputin," and Ray Moley skittered about trying to yoke this balky team of off-oxen who pulled in all directions at once. But, as James Burns later saw it:

> Roosevelt knew how to use these men for his own purposes; he resembled Hawthorne's picture of Andrew Jackson as one who compelled every man who came within his reach to be his tool, and the more cunning the man, the sharper the tool. But the process worked the other way too. Through these men Roosevelt. . . . was sinking taproots into the whole American experience. . . .
> Many of . . . [their] ideas were mutually contradictory, and some would be squeezed out in the press of crisis. In any event, Roosevelt did not swallow them all equally. He had an order of priority which amounted to something of a political creed. He believed—most of the time—that government could be used as a means to human betterment. He preached the need to make government efficient and honest. He wanted to help the underdog, although not necessarily at the expense of the top dog. He believed that private, special interests must be subordinated to the general interest. He sought to conserve both the natural resources and the moral values of America.
> These made up a collection of general concepts rather than an operating program, and some of Roosevelt's associates were amazed and even frightened by his receptivity to any notion that might fit under the broad umbrella of his mind. . . . He had, observed Tugwell, a flypaper mind.[11]

While the battle raged for Roosevelt's mind—and

power—the stage on which the act would be played out darkened month by month. December 15 would see the next installment due on the war debts. President Hoover's one-year moratorium had run out. The lame-duck Congress met on December 5, anxious to act, but hamstrung by public repudiation not only of many of its members, but of the President himself. Outside, over a thousand "hunger marchers," crowded beyond the lines of armed Washington police to chant in unison: "Feed the hungry, tax the rich." Early in February, the imminent collapse of the entire banking structure of Michigan forced the Governor to declare a "holiday." Meanwhile, before a congressional investigating committee, the giants of the money markets were sadly describing the shabby practices which had helped create a pathetic paper structure behind the ornate façades and massive bronze doors. By the end of the month the entire money structure of the nation was on the verge of collapse.

On February 15, 1933, in Miami, a pain-ridden psychotic peppered Roosevelt's car with bullets. F.D.R. escaped; but Chicago's Mayor Tony Cermak died a few days later of his wounds.

President Hoover sought to enlist the prestige of his successor in the deepening crisis, and at the same time to commit him to the policies of the old administration. Personal conferences between Hoover and Ogden Mills, his Secretary of the Treasury, Roosevelt and Ray Moley, collapsed in November 1932, over the international debt issue, and again just before inauguration, on the banking problem. Hoover wanted F.D.R.'s stamp on a program of balanced budget, sales tax, the renegotiation of international debts, and a federal order controlling bank withdrawals. But the two presidents did not trust each other. Their commitments were inconsistent. To Hoover the crisis was still an international and a psychological problem. To Roosevelt it had become increasingly a domestic problem. F.D.R. could muster only those minimal gestures of co-operation expected by the public. He would not tie his hands in advance of his new responsibilities. He would not fritter away on a discredited administration his immense popular support. Hoover, frozen by personal resentment, by grief and responsibility, and by his immense self-righteousness, would not negotiate and could not bend.

By March 4 when Hoover and Roosevelt rode side by side through the crowded Capital streets, their rapport was as somber as the chill and cloudy weather that overhung the city. F.D.R., who could never stand a silence, was reduced to the level of idiocy in his desperate bid for conversation.

Roosevelt's aides carried in their luggage the texts of the proclamations necessary for a bank holiday, but Treasury officials had spent the night in hectic telephone surveys of the nation's banks, uncertain whether the crisis would wait for the moment of inauguration. While Democrats whooped it up for victory and the city massed to watch the colorful military parade, the nation turned aside to listen to the voice of the new era.

The voice was sober, resolute. The younger figure of the new President stood as dignified and firm as the familiar, bearded Chief Justice who faced him while the oath was taken. The words themselves seemed to warm the cutting wind which whipped across the park and through the thousands of silent spectators below the stand:

This is pre-eminently the time to speak the truth, the whole truth, frankly and boldly. Nor need we shrink from honestly facing conditions in our country today. This great nation will endure as it has endured, will revive and will prosper.

So first of all let me assert my firm belief that the only thing we have to fear is fear itself—nameless, unreasoning, unjustified terror which paralyzes needed efforts to convert retreat into advance.

In every dark hour of our national life a leadership of frankness and vigor has met with that understanding and support of the people themselves which is essential to victory. I am convinced that you will again give that support to leadership in these critical days.

In such a spirit on my part and on yours we face our common difficulties. They concern, thank God, only material things. . . .

Plenty is at our doorstep, but a generous use of it languishes in the very sight of the supply.

Primarily, this is because the rulers of the exchange of mankind's goods have failed through their own stubbornness and their own incompetence, have admitted their failure and abdicated. . . .

They have no vision, and when there is no vision the people perish.

The money changers have fled from their high seats in the temple of our civilization. We may now restore that temple to the ancient truths.

The measure of the restoration lies in the extent to which we apply social values more noble than mere monetary profit. . . .

Restoration calls, however, not for changes in ethics alone. This nation asks for action, and action now.

Our greatest primary task is to put people to work. This is no unsolvable problem if we face it wisely and courageously.

It can be accomplished in part by direct recruiting by the government itself, treating the task as we would treat the emergency of a war, but at the same time, through this employment, accomplishing greatly needed projects to stimulate and reorganize the use of our natural resources.

Hand in hand with this, we must frankly recognize the overbalance of population in our industrial centers and, by engaging on a national scale in the redistribution, endeavor to provide a better use of the land for those best fitted for the land.

The task can be helped by definite efforts to raise the values of agricultural products and with this the power to purchase the output of our cities.

It can be helped by preventing realistically the tragedy of the growing loss, through foreclosure, of our small homes and our farms.

It can be helped by insistence that the Federal, State and local governments act forthwith on the demand that their cost be drastically reduced.

It can be helped by the unifying of relief activities which today are often scattered, uneconomical and unequal. It can be helped by national planning for and supervision of all forms of transportation and of communications and other utilities which have a definitely public character.

There are many ways in which it can be helped, but it can never be helped merely by talking about it. We must act, and act quickly.

Finally, in our progress toward a resumption of work we require two safeguards against a return of the evils of the old order; there must be a strict supervision of all banking and credits and investments, so that there will be an end to speculation with other people's money; and there must be provision for an adequate but sound currency. . . .

Our international trade relations, though vastly important, are, in point of time and necessity, secondary to the establishment of a sound national economy.

I favor as a practical policy the putting of first things first. I shall spare no effort to restore world trade by international economic readjustment, but the emergency at home cannot wait on that accomplishment. . . .

In the field of world policy I would dedicate this nation to the policy of the good neighbor—the neighbor who resolutely respects himself and, because he does so, respects the rights of others—the neighbor who respects his obligations and respects the sanctity of his agreements in and with a world of neighbors.

If I read the temper of our people correctly, we now realize as we have never before, our interdependence on each other; that we cannot merely take, but we must give as well; that if we are to go forward we must move as a trained and loyal army willing to sacrifice for the good of a common discipline, because, without such discipline, no progress is made, no leadership becomes effective. . . .

Action in this image and to this end is feasible under the form of government which we have inherited from our ancestors.

Our Constitution is so simple and practical that it is possible always to meet extraordinary needs by changes in emphasis and arrangement without loss of essential form. . . .

It is to be hoped that the normal balance of Executive and legislative authority may be wholly adequate to meet the unprecedented task before us. But it may be that an unprecedented demand and need for undelayed action may call for temporary departure from that normal balance of public procedure.

I am prepared under my constitutional duty to recommend the measures that a stricken nation in the midst of a stricken world may require.

These measures, or such other measures as the Congress may build out of its experience and wisdom, I shall seek, within my constitutional authority, to bring to speedy adoption.

But in the event that the Congress shall fail to take one of these two courses, and in the event that the national emergency is still critical, I shall not evade the clear course of duty that will then confront me.

I shall ask the Congress for the one remaining in-strument to meet the crisis—broad Executive power to wage a war against the emergency, as great as the power that would be given to me if we were in fact invaded by a foreign foe. . . .

We do not distrust the future of essential democracy. The people of the United States have not failed. In their need they have registered a mandate that they want direct, vigorous action.

They have asked for discipline and direction under leadership. They have made me the present instrument of their wishes. In the spirit of the gift, I take it.

In this dedication of a Nation we humbly ask the blessing of God. May He protect each and every one of us! May He guide me in the days to come.[12]

There was politics here, and there was promise of action. But mostly, the country sensed, there was resolution, strength and hope.

If Roosevelt and his writers had caught the drama of the moment, every gesture of the new administration maintained the pitch. On all sides there were tokens of dynamic change. The dramatic bank holiday: the ready-drawn bills rushed through an eager Congress—one was passed by the House before it had been printed. Children and dogs and gaiety in the White House. The new presidential press conference—oral questions now, and direct, off-the-cuff answers. Help of all kinds for the second battalion of Bonus Marchers camped in the flats, and a clever maneuver to guide them into CCC camps. "Hoover sent the Army," someone said, "Roosevelt sent his wife." For Eleanor Roosevelt was an integral part of the mood. Tramping through the mud with the veterans and poking into Washington slums, visiting from house to house in the grimy coal-mining hamlets of Logan County, West Virginia, she

brought the White House to the people in a way her
husband could not manage.

And the Fireside Chats! The first week was scarcely
over before Roosevelt went to the people to explain the
banking crisis so simply, as Will Rogers said, that even
the bankers understood it. Hoover had never seemed so
much a part of one's family, had never managed the
subtle friendliness which this man aroused in seven
days.

But this was more than a blend of natural warmth
and clever public relations. The action came, and it was
effective if not always consistent.

This was the Hundred Days; and in this
period Franklin Roosevelt sent fifteen messages to
Congress, guided fifteen major laws to enactment, delivered ten speeches, held press conferences and cabinet
meetings twice a week, conducted talks with foreign
heads of state, sponsored an international conference
[in Montevideo], made all the major decisions in
domestic and foreign policy, and never displayed fright
or panic and rarely even bad temper. . . . Washington,
Arthur Krock reported, was experiencing the sensation
of a man traveling on a life-and-death errand thousands
of miles away who suddenly found himself switched
from an ox cart to an airplane. . . . And there could be
no question, Krock added, who was responsible: "The
President is the boss, the dynamo, the works."

For a deceptive moment in 1933, clouds of inertia
and selfishness seemed to lift. A despairing land had
a vision of America as it might someday be. "For the
first time since we can remember," said Frances
Perkins, "we are trying to be a unified people." Anne
O'Hare McCormick described the response as "the
rising of a nation." "It's more than a New Deal," said
Harold Ickes. "It's a new world. People feel free again.
They can breathe naturally. It's like quitting a morgue

for the open woods." "We have had our revolution," said Collier's, "and we like it." [18]

Eight years later, as the American people approached their day of reckoning with the world, they could look back on not one, but two, disparate New Deals. There had been a revolution made by the collapse of an old way of life and guided by an inspired opportunist with a conscience. There was a new Constitution, with hardly a word of textual change, a new politics, a new economy. But the Roosevelt revolution had been a far cry from the march of hysteria Unter den Linden, the paralysis of decay on the Champs Elysées, the dance of death along the Ginza.

NOTES, *chapter 2*

1. Samuel Rosenman, ed., *The Public Papers and Addresses of Franklin D. Roosevelt, 1928–1936,* 5 vols. (Random House, 1938), I, 647-652, 657, 659.

2. Walter Lippmann, *Interpretations, 1931–1932,* 259-262.

3. James A. Farley, *Behind the Ballots: the Personal History of a Politician* (Harcourt, Brace, 1938), 81-86.

4. Franklin D. Roosevelt, *Public Papers of the Governor, 1932* (Lyons, 1933), 551-552.

5. *Papers, Governor,* 589, 591.

6. James MacGregor Burns, *Roosevelt, the Lion and the Fox* (Harcourt, Brace, 1956), 134-138.

7. Arthur M. Schlesinger, Jr., *Crisis of the Old Order, 1919–1933,* 263, 265.

8. *Papers, Governor,* 664.

9. Richard Hofstadter, *The American Political Tradition and the Men Who Made It.* (Vintage ed., 1954), 328-331.

10. Schlesinger, *Crisis,* 429.

11. Burns, *Roosevelt,* 154-155.

12. *Public Papers,* II, 11-16.

13. Arthur M. Schlesinger, Jr., *The Coming of the New Deal* (Houghton, Mifflin, 1959), 21-23.

chapter **3** F.D.R. AND THE WORLD WHICH
MADE HIM

"You'll find me just the same, and I'll wear the same size hat," Roosevelt once wrote. More perceptively, John Gunther later said of him, "Roosevelt was like a cornucopia; one can draw out of him inexhaustibly."[1]

The fact is, of course, that no personality is recorded except through interaction with another, and through action in context. There can no longer be the real Roosevelt; there never was. There were as many Roosevelts as the situations he met, as many as the personalities with whom he talked.

Eleanor Roosevelt has long since gently warned, ". . . no human being ever completely knows another human being. . . ." And she has touched deftly the peculiar problem of really knowing this particular man:

. . . . a man like my husband, who was particularly susceptible to people, took color from whomever he was with, giving to each one something different of himself. Because he disliked being disagreeable, he made an effort to give each person who came in contact with him the feeling that he understood what his particular interest was. . . .

Often people have told me that they were misled by Franklin. . . . This misunderstanding not only arose from his dislike of being disagreeable, but from the interest that he always had in somebody else's point of view and his willingness to listen to it. If he thought it was well expressed and clear, he nodded his head and frequently said, "I see," or something of the sort. . . .[2]

The same incident could lead one person to see him as a master of decision, another as a weak will-o'-the-wisp. Huey Long would complain, "I wonder if he says 'Fine!' to everybody." *Henry Morgenthau, Jr., would record an unusually direct example of Roosevelt's indirection. Thinking he had his boss's firm agreement to oppose a soldiers' bonus, he was appalled to hear F.D.R. say at lunch:*

"You know we may have to compromise. . . ."
I had a sort of sinking feeling and found myself sort of gradually crumpling up and I said, "If you want me to go on please do not talk that way to me because I am building a bonfire of support for you in your veto message." He said rather quickly with a smile, "Let's agree that I will not talk to you about any compromise if you will not talk to me about any bonfire." He said, "In other words, never let your left hand know what your right is doing." I said, "Which hand am I, Mr. President?" And he said, "My right hand." He said, "But I keep my left hand under the table."
This is the most frank expression of the real F.D.R. that I ever listened to and that is the real way that he works. . . .[3]

Yet there were patterns in this personality on which most observers would agree. One was the immense joie de vivre, the resilience of the man, and this was closely allied with the indiscriminate warmth to all comers which Mrs. Roosevelt recognized confused so many. He loved a fight, but not a face-to-face, personal one. He could chat warmly with Tammany bosses he had pilloried publicly. He could joke at the height of the banking crisis with his sworn political enemy, Ogden Mills, who brought him a lengthy and serious memo: "You must have stayed up all night working on that, Ogden." Harold Ickes could gloat at chopping off a careless subordinate while Roosevelt could not; it was only rarely that F.D.R. could ruin his own day this way. He could relax at the most awful times and at pursuits that struck his stuffier aides as sheer childishness: stamps, and cartoon movies, fishing and "who-dun-its." He could laugh uproariously at anti-Roosevelt cartoons.

His sense of humor was spontaneous, although sometimes a little stilted and awkward in expression, and often rough on his close associates. When reporters badgered him about whether he would fly to the 1932 National Convention, he cracked:

> Now I'll tell you what I'm going to do. . . . I'm going to bicycle out to Chicago.
> I'm going to get one of those quintets—you know, five bicycles in a row.
> Father will ride in the first seat and manage the handlebars, Jim will ride second, then Elliott, then Franklin, Jr., and then John.
> Sam [Rosenman] . . . will follow—on a tricycle.[4]

Later he jokingly protested to Jim Farley:

> Thank you for the N.R.A. postage stamp and cover. The honest farmer, who looks like me; the honest business man, who looks like Grover T. Whalen; and the honest blacksmith, who looks like Lionel Barrymore, are magnificent. But Oh Heavens what a girl! She is wearing a No. 11 shoe, also a bustle, and if recovery is dependent on women like that, I am agin recovery.[5]

When Tommy Corcoran suggested that F.D.R. never "faked" as his cousin, Theodore, had done, the President himself chuckled and said, "But I do, Tommy! I do!" Only when his patriotism or his personal morality were impugned, or his sense of decency violated, did he explode in wrath.

Above all, he was a gentleman, and this confused many who put politics or causes above manners. He could be incensed at raucous arguments about personalities across the Cabinet table. He could enjoy off-color jokes with close friends; but all women must be treated as ladies, and he insisted upon it. He liked people, and he respected them as individuals, and he wanted to be liked by them. But he seldom allowed gentility and friendship to dictate decision.

Urbane, genteel and warm though he might be, the thing which characterized the man most was his immense confidence: in himself, in his country, in the future. This was a confidence so great that it could shuck off major mistakes as if they were nothing, forgetting or rationalizing them until they no longer existed for him. There were few moments of deep, nagging doubt such as Lincoln suffered.

This lack of fear was not something at which he had to work. It was founded deeply on faith. One frequently repeated story goes that, when asked what he believed, he replied that he was a Christian and a Democrat. Cynics, weaned on Freud, Marx and Mencken, thought him vacuous, or a fake. But this was a man who could refuse to go to church in Washington because he couldn't say his prayers in a "goldfish bowl," who could be shocked at the attempts of a Washington clergyman to sign him up for a grave in the Cathedral—"The old body snatcher, the old body snatcher," he grumbled. This was also the man who could read Kierkegaard, and who could, on his way to Yalta, say quietly to Miss Perkins, who would understand, "You'd better pray for me, Frances."

The roots of his character are so simply traced that they are often missed. Much of Roosevelt's immense confidence and buoyancy grew from the fact that he bounced from the genteel progressivism of the 1910s to the challenge of the 1930s without transition. He missed the whole jarring cataclysm of the 1920s be-

cause he was an invalid, and because he was not an
intellectual. While his peers were learning to distrust
tradition, to discredit the old mores and question the
old ethics, Roosevelt was insulated and dominated by
his personal fight with polio and despair. He emerged
with the indomitable confidence that comes only to a
man who has won gloriously the worst battle he could
ever fight. His personal orientation remained the sense
of obligation he had learned from Sara Roosevelt, and
the human kindness he had learned from Eleanor. His
ethics and his spiritual anchor remained the ones he
had taken easily in childhood from the ritual and
practice of his Episcopalian parents. His faith in the
common people carried to the end an almost mystical
note of Jefferson's idealism.

Above all, this man was an idealist, not in any rigid
devotion to this or that cause, but in his outlook on
life. He could be cynical about individuals and doubt
their motives. He could not doubt the inevitability of
progress, the goodness of God, the goodness of the
universe, the dignity of the human being, in the large.
The most important single fact about Roosevelt was the
inordinately simple faith which he brought to domestic
crisis, to war and to planning for peace. To others,
whose faith had been corroded by the acid of frustration
and much thought, he often seemed dangerously naïve.
But his essential confidence in his country and its
people cut through the haze of words and problems to
touch men and women in crisis, to shore up their
faltering hopes.

But this remarkable continuity could have been
maintained only by a man who enjoyed unusual security.
This Roosevelt certainly did. He faced psychological
and physical challenges. He struggled clear of his
mother's domination. He fought to make himself a
man again after the blight of polio. But never did he
face a moment of real financial insecurity, a moment
without friends or devoted family, a moment without

a clear and certain place in his society. Someone suggested of him, "He must have been psychoanalyzed by God." He could drop off to sleep with the ease of a growing boy.

Nevertheless, security created its own challenges. Most important was his ambition for power in a realm he had not inherited. Money did not interest him greatly; he could take it for granted. There was no incentive to social achievement. His name and training had given him an unimpeachable passport to Wall Street and Tuxedo Park. Often those who admired the attainments his family had given him were enraged at the flip insouciance with which he took them for granted, or even cast them aside. This restless man seemed almost to resent the gifts he had not won for himself.

Richard Hofstadter has put the early life from which these qualities emerged into brief but precise vignette:

James and Sara Delano Roosevelt, Franklin's parents, are reminiscent of secondary characters in Edith Wharton's novels who provide the climate of respectable and unfriendly opinion in which her unfortunate heroines live. James Roosevelt, vice-president of several corporations, was a handsome country gentleman who dabbled in Democratic politics, enjoyed a stable of trotting-horses, and lived in leisure on his Hyde Park estate. Sara Delano, James's second wife, was also from an upper-class family with deep roots in American history; her father had owned copper lands, iron and coal mines, acreage on New York harbor, and a fleet of clipper ships. When they were married Sara was twenty-six and James was fifty-two. Two years later, on January 30, 1882, an entry in James Roosevelt's diary noted the birth of "a splendid large baby boy."

The only child of a fond mother, treated like a grandson by his father, Franklin was brought up with unusual indulgence. He had governesses and tutors; his playmates were from his own class; he owned a pony and a twenty-one-foot sailboat. Eight times before his adolescence he was taken on jaunts to Europe. At fourteen he entered the Reverend Endicott Peabody's Groton School, a little Greek democracy of the elite, which, as its headmaster said, stood for "everything that is true, beautiful, and of good report." The Groton boys, about ninety per cent from social-register families, lived in an atmosphere of paternal kindness and solicitude and swallowed huge gulps of inspiration at Peabody's weekly chapel performances.

From Groton Roosevelt followed a well-beaten path to Harvard. Although he was privileged to hear James, Royce, Norton, Shaler, and other illuminati, his life flowered chiefly outside the classroom. He became a prodigious doer and joiner, with memberships in more than a half-dozen campus clubs and a position on the *Crimson* that won him a good deal of college renown. A large part of his work on the *Crimson* was devoted to petty crusades for campus reforms. At an age when many boys are kicking over the traces, flirting with heresies, defying authority, and incidentally deepening their intellectual perspectives, young Roosevelt was writing exhortations about "school spirit" and football morale. On one occasion he urged in patriarchal fashion that "the memories and traditions of our ancestors and of our University be maintained during our lives and be faithfully handed down to our children in the years to come." His most serious public interest and possibly his first manifestation of sympathy for an underdog was in a college relief drive for the Boers. He left Harvard in 1904; his youth is summed up in his mother's words: "After all he had many advantages that other boys did not have."

Since it had been decided that Franklin should become a lawyer, he entered Columbia Law School. The following year he married his distant cousin Eleanor, to whom he had secretly been engaged, and moved into a home in New York City under the managerial eye of his mother. He was not happy in law school. "I am . . . trying to understand a little of the work," he wrote plaintively to Rector Peabody. Bored by the tenuous subtleties of the law, he failed some of his courses and left school without taking a degree, although he had absorbed enough to pass bar examinations.°

The young Roosevelt who was tapped for the hapless role of State Senatorial candidate in 1910, was a far cry from the polished practitioner who stormed the country in 1932. His speeches then were stilted and unconvincing. He betrayed the most transparent flattery and the most shallow thought. His humor was strained.

In the State Senate Roosevelt proved himself aggressive, generally progressive, not at all humbled by his lack of experience. He put himself at the head of a coterie of maverick Democrats who challenged the regulars' choice for the United States Senate, William F. Sheehan. "Blue-Eyed Billy" was beaten down; Tammany chose a "compromise" candidate. Within three months the publicity surrounding the incident made Roosevelt nationally known. His cartooned stereotype was already beginning to form (see the following page).

He learned fast. Within five months he had already grasped two matters of fundamental technique. You couldn't fight all the time, and you must claim even the worst defeat as a moderate victory. The rough edges of his personality obtruded bluntly at points. Reactions to him were mixed and uncertain. Someone in Albany suggested that the thing to do with any Roosevelt was to drop him off the dock before he caused the kind of trouble the dynamic Teddy had. The New York Times Albany reporter wrote:

*First published sketch
of Roosevelt, Jan. 19, 1911,
J. Norman Lynd, New
York Herald, © New York
Sun, Inc.*

. . . Nature has left much unfinished in the
modeling of the face of the Roosevelt of greater fame.
On the face of this Roosevelt, younger in years and in
public service, she has lavished all her refining processes
until much of the elemental strength has been lost in
the sculpturing.

Senator Roosevelt is less than thirty. He is tall and lithe. With his handsome face and his form of supple strength he could make a fortune on the stage and set the matinee girl's heart throbbing with subtle and happy emotion. But no one would suspect behind that highly polished exterior the quiet force and determination that now are sending cold shivers down the spine of Tammany's striped mascot.

. . . Unlike his Uncle-in-law, Senator Roosevelt would never indulge in pell-mell pedestrianism where angels would tread with soft foot falls.[7]

Even Frances Perkins, years later when she had come to respect this man as she did few others, would remember her first impression:

I have a vivid picture of him operating on the floor of the Senate: tall and slender, very active and alert, moving around the floor, going in and out of committee rooms, rarely talking with the members, who more or less avoided him, not particularly charming (that came later), artificially serious of face, rarely smiling, with an unfortunate habit—so natural that he was unaware of it—of throwing his head up. This, combined with his pince-nez and great height, gave him the appearance of looking down his nose at most people . . . this habit of throwing his head up, which when he was young and unchastened gave him a slightly supercilious appearance, later had a completely different effect. By 1933, and for the rest of his life, it was a gesture of courage and hope, and people were responsive to it as such.

Many staunch old Tammany Democrats in those days felt that he did look down his nose at them. I remember old Tim Sullivan . . . saying after a bout with Roosevelt, "Awful arrogant fellow, that Roosevelt."

I can see "that Roosevelt" now, standing back of the

brass rail with two or three Democratic senators arguing
with him to be "reasonable," as they called it, about
something; his small mouth pursed up and slightly
open, his nostrils distended, his head in the air, and his
cool, remote voice saying, "No, no, I won't hear of it."
. . . He never wholly ignored these youthful traits
himself. He once said to me when he was President,
"You know, I was an awfully mean cuss when I first
went into politics." [8]

"Packy" McCabe, the redoubtable boss of the Albany
Democratic machine, would have agreed with this bit
of Roosevelt self-analysis. Stung by one of the young
maverick's frequent attacks, he poured out all the
venomous resentment which most regulars felt about
F.D.R. in the early years:

In the book of Proverbs we find, "The pro-
motion of fools is a disgrace," and in this wise pre-
monition is embodied the primary cause of the disease
from which the Democratic party in this State is at
present suffering.
I am glad that Senator Roosevelt took occasion to
mention me in . . . a speech bristling with the silly con-
ceits of a political prig. . . .
Mr. Roosevelt admits that he is the best-informed
man in the party . . . on obsolete and remote questions
of government. I have heard him time and time again
quote, or misquote, in the most friendly and neighborly
way, Solon who spent so many years among the Egyp-
tians studying their laws. He also gave several years of
his life on the Continent conning the Governments of
Europe . . . my leadership here in Albany depends absolutely upon human sympathy, human interest, and
human ties among those with whom I was born and
bred. . . . Some leaders may stand for the impudence
and arrogance of these political prudes but I won't.[9]

The personality which emerged in 1920 after seven years of Wilsonian Washington was still dynamic and confident. But it was more sensitive to the pounding of reality, more conspiratorial and devious, more smoothly buffed. A three-year crusade to build a progressive, anti-Tammany—and incidentally pro-Roosevelt—machine in New York had failed monumentally. He had been whipped in 1914 in a primary election challenge to Tammany's senatorial candidate.

Assistant-Secretary of the Navy Roosevelt constructed an uneasy alliance with his old enemies of the Fourteenth Street Wigwam. He learned much as he maneuvered among such experienced in-fighters as Tammany's Charles Francis Murphy and the unobtrusive Presidential shadow, Colonel Edward M. House. And his ambition was beginning to check his impulsive instinct to rebellion. Thus, he could confide to a friend early in 1920:

> Do not believe everything you hear about my running for Senator or Governor or dog catcher. . . . I can tell you confidentially, but perfectly frankly, that I do not propose to make an early Christian martyr of myself this year if the Democratic Party does make some fool mistake at San Francisco.[10]

Yet he could not comply completely with the political forces he despised. Before the 1920 convention he did fight to break the unit rule in the New York delegation to free some votes for a Wilsonian candidate. When he had himself been nominated for the Vice-Presidency, he did conduct a rigorous crusade for the League of Nations, although he must have known it was hopeless.

He had learned to improvise. But sometimes his glib facility betrayed him, as it did when he boasted inanely:

Well, I will say that the United States has at least twelve votes in the Assembly to England's six. . . . I have something to do with the running of a couple of little Republics. Until last week, I had two of these votes in my pocket. . . . One of them was Haiti. I know, for I wrote Haiti's Constitution myself, and, if I do say it, I think it was a pretty good little Constitution.[11]

There were not many foul blows. For the most part he was a hard, clean puncher, as well as an artist at fancy footwork. Most reporters agreed with the New York Post's man who noted:

. . . Without being in the least florid, Mr. Roosevelt knows his trade as a public speaker. He gets, that is, the last ounce of appeal-power out of each sentence. . . . The physical impression leaves nothing to be asked—the figure of an idealized college football player, almost the poster type in public life; over six feet in height, weight perhaps 180-200 pounds, standing straight on both feet, making clean, direct, and few gestures; always with a smile ready to share, sincerely, one is sure, in the audience's humor.[12]

No matter how vigorous and competent, a mere vice-presidential candidate could not hold back the tidal reaction of 1920. But it was the crippling illness, not the premature fame, that marked the watershed of Roosevelt's career. There were important shifts in the shadings of the man's personality. Frances Perkins thought:

Franklin Roosevelt underwent a spiritual transformation during the years of his illness. I noticed when he came back that the years of pain and suffering had purged the slightly arrogant attitude. . . . The man emerged completely warmhearted, with humility of spirit and with a deeper philosophy. Having been to the depths of trouble he understood the problems of people in trouble.[18]

Certainly the dimensions of his life were sharply curbed by physical facts. A man who could not walk alone might save immense amounts of time that other men lose in pointless moving about. But such a man must also rely incessantly on the effectiveness with which his staff and family understood his needs. Every change of scene presented major logistical problems. John Gunther has catalogued some of the barriers against which Roosevelt constantly brushed:

> Nobody with legs can easily appreciate what it is like to be without them. I do not mean in such obvious realms as that FDR could never take a hike, kick a football, dance, climb a fence, skate or play with his toes in the sand. So long as he lived, he was never able to climb a stair more than two or three inches high, lean deeply to kiss a child, crouch to catch an object, scuff with his feet, squat on the grass, tap a foot, do a deep bend, or kneel in prayer. . . .
> I do not even mention such items as . . . that the simple business of getting in and out of an automobile was an almost intolerable strain; that he could not completely dress or undress himself; that he wore a cape instead of an overcoat, and a sweater instead of a bathrobe, because they were easier to get into; that he could never fulfill one tenth or one twentieth of all manner of ideas that came to him. . . .
> If he were making a speech in a hall, he had to brace himself accurately on the lectern. This was always tested beforehand, to see if it would bear his weight. . . . During his first presidential campaign, while making a speech in Georgia, he toppled over when the table against which he was leaning slipped. Members of his entourage quickly helped him to his feet; he kept on

with his speech at the exact point where it had been broken off, and made no reference to the mishap; the audience cheered wildly. In Philadelphia four years later, a bolt in one of the braces became unlocked just before he was to address the Democratic convention, and he lost balance. The pages of his speech splashed to the floor, but Gus Gennerich, his bodyguard, and Mike Reilly caught him before he actually fell. They reached down and relocked the brace while Jim Farley and his son James closed in around him to keep the mishap from the eyes of the crowd. But there was a good deal of confusion and the President was badly shaken; his words to Reilly were a curt snap, "Clean me up!"

But the worst agony lay in subtler fields. For instance the President could never, except when he slept, be left alone; once he told Ambassador Winant that his utter lack of privacy was the hardest single thing he had to bear. Occasionally, by error, he was left alone. Once Frances Perkins was with him in the Oval Room just before he was going to bed; he rang, but unaccountably no one answered; finally he turned to Miss Perkins and said, "Please find Prettyman [the valet]; I am helpless without him." [14]

He was really afraid of only one thing—fire.

His own attitude toward his handicap was carefully contrived. He seemed always to ignore it; others were always set at ease by the nonchalance with which he accepted the humiliating business of being helped. This was the brave mask of a proud man. He made it easy for others to forget the seven long years of crawling, crablike, about his New York home, of inching endlessly back and forth along exercise rails, of crashing again and again as he tried to balance on steel legs and wooden crutches, of the interminable exercises in the buoyant waters of Warm Springs, of the dogged insistence that he would play golf again, that he would *walk with only a cane. Sympathy he did not want and could not afford.*

Those around him were dominated by his charm. Frances Perkins, in one of the most sensitive pictures of an American president at home, was struck by the common unpretentiousness of this pleasant and contented man:

> Wherever the Roosevelts lived, whether at Hyde Park, the Executive Mansion in Albany, or the White House, there was always the sense of a big family. Their own children were a considerable company, and there were others who seemed like members of the family. . . . Roosevelt moved in this family commotion with joyous relish. Having so many people around did not seem to get on his nerves. He was responsive, courteous, very much the paterfamilias, giving advice freely to members of the family with an amiability that was not diminished if the suggestions were ignored or even openly derided. . . .

Roosevelt's personal habits and way of life were simple to the point of bareness. He had practically no personal luxurious needs or tastes. . . . Books, stamps, boats, ship models—these things he spent money on gladly and without thought, but for his personal use he preferred the old to the new—the old sweater, the old coat, the old hat. No fancy desk sets—just a common pen and an ordinary blotter sufficed.

The simplicity of his taste in food is proverbial. Mrs. Roosevelt has often said that if anyone asked him what he wanted to eat, he would think a minute and look up, always with the same innocent look, and say, "Scrambled eggs." It was the only food he could remember. As a matter of fact, he liked all kinds of food, he merely wasn't particular.

Later, in the White House, he continued to live with complete personal simplicity. . . .

The President chose the Oval Room on the second

floor as a study. Here he could have people come in the evening, Sundays, and other unusual times for conferences. Here he could work at a desk near the door to his bedroom, which was the room directly off the study. He often received his secretaries and some close associates in his bedroom in the early morning. Occasionally when he had a cold and I had a matter of important business to transact, I saw him there.

I have a photographic impression of that room. A little too large to be cozy, it was not large enough to be impressive. A heavy dark wardrobe stood against a wall. . . . A marble mantelpiece of the Victorian type carved with grapes held a collection of miniature pigs— Mexican pigs, Irish pigs, pigs of all kinds, sizes, and colors. Snapshots of children, friends, and expeditions were propped up in back of the pigs. There was an old bureau between the windows, with a plain white towel on top and the things men need for their dressing arrangements. There was an old-fashioned rocking chair, often with a piece of clothing thrown over it. Then there was the bed—not the kind you would expect a President of the United States to have. Roosevelt used a small, narrow white iron bedstead, the kind one sees in the boy's room of many an American house. It had a thin, hard-looking mattress, a couple of pillows, and an ordinary white seersucker spread. A folded old gray shawl lay at the foot. "Just the right weight," the President once said. "Don't like these great heavy things." An old gray sweater, much the worse for wear, lay close at hand. He wore it over night clothes to keep his shoulders warm when he had a cold. A white, painted table, the kind one often sees in bathrooms, stood beside the bed, with a towel over it, and with aspirin, nose drops, a glass of water, stubs of pencils, bits of paper with telephone numbers, addresses, and memoranda to himself, a couple of books, a worn old prayer book, a watch, a package of cigarettes, an ash tray, a couple of telephones, all cluttered together. Hanging on the walls were a few pictures of the children and favorite familiar scenes. And over the door at the opposite end of the room hung a horse's tail. When one asked what that was, he would say, "Why, that's Gloucester's tail." Gloucester, a horse raised by the President's father, had been regarded by the family as one of the finest examples of horseflesh in the world.[15]

One of the most important portraits of Roosevelt's personality appears in a private letter from Raymond Moley to a close relative:

You ask what he is like. . . . One thing is sure—that the idea people get from his charming manner —that he is soft or flabby in disposition and character— is far from true. When he wants something a lot he can be formidable—when crossed he is hard, stubborn, resourceful, relentless. I used to think on the basis of casual observation that his amiability was "lord-of-the-manor"—"good-to-the-peasants"—stuff. It isn't that at all. He seems quite naturally warm and friendly—less because he genuinely likes many of the people to whom he is pleasant (although he does like a lot of people of all sorts and varieties) than because he just enjoys the pleasant and engaging role, as a charming woman does. And being a born politician he measures such qualities in himself by the effect they produce on others. He is wholly conscious of his ability to send callers away happy and glowing and in agreement with him and his ideas. And he particularly enjoys sending people away who have completely forgotten (under his spell) the thing they came to say or ask. On the whole, his cordiality and his interest in people is, to all appearances, unfeigned.

The stories about his illness and its effect upon him are the bunk. Nobody in public life since T.R. has been so robust, so buoyantly and blatantly healthy as this fellow. He is full of animal spirits and keeps himself and the people around him in rare good humor with a lot of horseplay . . . a good many cabbages will be thrown by this man at respectable doors—not because he feels it is an act of justice but because it is so much fun. He likes to do it on a parlor scale; broad, never really witty . . . and seldom even funny, but bold and cheerful and exuberant. Sam Rosenman is "Sammy the Rose" and Morgenthau, Jr. "Henry the Morgue." There is teasing and loud laughing at teatime. . . .

The man's energy and vitality are astonishing. I've been amazed with his interest in things. It skips and bounces through seemingly intricate subjects and maybe it is my academic training that makes me feel that no one could possibly learn much in such a hit or miss fashion. . . . There is a lot of autointoxication of the intelligence that we shall have to watch. But he gets a lot from talking with people who come in. A typical approach to a big problem is "so and so was telling me yesterday." Another is "now we found in dealing with the state so-and-so that we had to deal with such-and-such." . . .

The frightening aspect of his methods is F.D.R.'s great receptivity. So far as I know he makes no effort to check up on anything that I or anyone else has told him. I wonder what would happen if we should selfishly try to put things over on him. . . .

As I look back at what I have scribbled here I see I haven't conveyed any sense of his gallantry, his political sophistication, his lack of the offensive traits of men who have a bloated sense of personal destiny.[16]

If Moley knew his man's personality, he failed completely to grasp the deep convictions which lay behind it. Roosevelt did have commitments, though his nonchalance often confused his associates for the moment. Brain Truster Rex Tugwell has written:

The governor's mind may have been a *tabula rasa*, but the *tabula* had clearly labelled pages to be written on. He did not very much care what kind of farm relief, or how the principle of cheap and universally available power was arrived at. Banking regulations might be of any practicable sort, and the methods used for relieving the unemployed were open to argument. But he was committed to some action in all these matters.[17]

Roosevelt also understood the long cycles of American politics. In 1924 he wrote an old acquaintance, "Every war brings after it a period of materialism and conservatism; people tire quickly of ideals and are now repeating history."[18] The fact that he did not believe in stubbornly advocating the unpopular has obscured how much of his New Deal had its origins in his own youthful orientation.

Most important in the long continuity of his ideas was his belief in positive government, in social experiment and planning. As a young State Senator, he was pushed to recognize the new directions most starkly in the matter of conservation. Loving trees almost passionately, and finding himself Chairman of the Senate Committee on Forest, Fish and Game, he flung himself into a fight for compulsory reforestation of private lands. He even launched an impassioned attack on economic individualism in a speech at Troy early in 1912:

... competition has been shown to be useful up to a certain point and no further. Co-operation must begin where competition leaves off and co-operation is as good a word for the new theory as any other. ...

One hundred and fifty years ago in Germany the individual was not restricted from denuding his lands of the growing trees. To-day he must cut only in a

manner scientifically worked out, which is calculated to
serve the ends of the community and not his ends.

They passed beyond the liberty of the individual to
do as he pleased with his own property and found it
was necessary to check this liberty for the benefit of the
freedom of the whole people. . . .

There are many persons left to-day that can see no
reason why if a man owns land he should not be permitted to do as he likes with it. . . .

With them the motto is "After us the deluge." . . .

It is the same way with all of our natural resources in
addition to forests. Why, let me ask, are so many of the
farms in the State of New York abandoned? The answer
is easy. Their owners 50 or 100 years ago took from the
soil without returning any equivalent to the soil. In
other words they got something for nothing. . . . Today the people in the cities and the people on the farms
are suffering because these early farmers gave no thought
to the liberty of the Community.[19]

In the twenties he made his own farms into a model
tree plantation. As Governor he fought for a scientific
land-use survey, a regular plan for fostering reforestation
and expansion of the state's forest reserves.

His commitment to positive, experimental government was more often acted than articulated. The most
eloquent evidence of what it meant lay in his youthful
struggles for regulation of agricultural markets and
public utilities, and for cheap, public electric power. As
early as 1927 he advised Al Smith:

It is a long distance job, but eventually we as a nation
will undertake the storing of waters on the higher
reaches of the tributary rivers and, in conjunction with
those, will develop hydroelectric power for the benefit
of the people of the United States. This is sound doctrine and it is time it was said by somebody in authority.[20]

The same year he wrote, "The phrase 'the best government is the least government' is a sound phrase, but it applies only to the simplification of governmental machinery and to the prevention of improper interference with the legitimate activities of the citizens. But the nation or state which is unwilling by governmental action to tackle new problems caused by immense increase of population and the astounding strides of modern science is headed for a decline and ultimate death from inaction." [21]

A second concern was cleaning up politics. He had led an advance patrol in the fight to break Tammany, to bring the direct primary to New York State, and he gave his name and support easily to the movement for urban "home rule," city managerships and the short ballot. But here he lost faith. In 1914 he had run against an organization candidate for the U.S. Senate. A stunning defeat taught him how sharply the direct-primary cards were stacked in favor of the organization. From 1916 on he worked with the regulars. He had learned to rationalize that it was more important to use the machinery at hand for constructive purposes than to lose influence, and usefulness, by hopeless assaults upon it.

He had an early compulsion to administrative efficiency. In 1911 he had been outraged by a Tammany move to give the state's highway program three bosses, and had written:

It seeks to set up a hitherto absolutely untried method of department administration. . . . You might just as well make the train dispatcher of a railroad responsible for the running of all trains and at the same time insist that he obtain the approval of every member of the board of directors of the railroad before allowing a single wheel to turn . . . no human being can possibly tell where the responsibility begins and where it ends. [22]

He set one of the major themes of the 1920 campaign with his persistent demands for a budget system and reorganization of the executive departments in Washington. Throughout three years of his governorship he preached the reorganization and simplification of his state's antique local government. Yet this was merely concern with blueprint efficiency, and in the White House he would rely on personal improvising, at the cost of monumental overlapping and confusion.

There were aspects of reform to which the progressivism of the younger Roosevelt did not extend. Only well after he had entered the White House did he begin to grasp the real dimensions of the labor problem. His views on government's relations with business were often conservative. As a businessman in the twenties, he complained of the Secretary of Commerce:

> Mr. Hoover has always shown a most disquieting desire to investigate everything and to appoint commissions and send out statistical inquiries on every conceivable subject under Heaven. He has also shown in his own Department a most alarming desire to issue regulations and to tell businessmen generally how to conduct their affairs.[38]

As head of a trade association, the American Construction Council, he came to believe firmly in industrial self-regulation to solve problems of overproduction and cyclical unemployment. As Governor, he was slow to move in the banking crisis, immensely respectful and trustful of the big men of finance.

For agriculture, however, Roosevelt always had a special love. Romanticist that he was, he liked to think of himself as a tree farmer. In 1912 he warmed to an issue which political friends had created for him during a campaign illness—the regulation of the commission merchants. In the twenties, he groped uneasily for a solution of agricultural overproduction: this was, he *thought*, the nation's number-one problem. His first gesture as Governor was a crash program for farm relief in upstate New York.

There was amazing continuity in F.D.R.'s thought. In foreign affairs only did he undergo a significant revolution in attitudes before 1932. The turning point was 1919; the major force, Wilson's League.

As a young man Roosevelt had absorbed Teddy's imperialism and jingo nationalism as easily as his domestic progressivism. As Assistant-Secretary he could wax almost lyrical over the sheer power of his Navy: "Soon the nine battleships bound for the Mediterranean came along. . . . The big gray fellows were magnificent as they went past, with all hands at the rail, and I only wish a hundred thousand people could have seen them." [22]

He was restless under the restraints of Wilson's neutralism. At one point he wrote his wife:

> To my astonishment on reaching the Dept. nobody seemed the least bit excited about the European Crisis—Mr. Daniels feeling chiefly sad that his faith in human nature and civilization and similar idealistic nonsense was receiving such a rude shock. So I started in alone to get things ready and prepare plans for what ought to be done by the Navy end of things. . . . These dear good people like W.J.B. [William Jennings Bryan] and J.D. have as much conception of what a general European war means as Elliot has of higher mathematics.[23]

Early in 1915 he confessed, "I just know I shall do some awful unneutral thing before I get through!" [24] There were no doubts for him about the Navy's intervention in Haiti or Mexico. In fact, he gloated in his role as one of Haiti's bosses, and acted like an adolescent romantic on a holiday when he went there for an inspection tour. Unlike the President, he found the

front in France more glamorous than horrible. But
observation of the Versailles Conference from its fringes
and long talks aboard ship with the homebound Wilson
tamed this thoughtless jingo. In the 1920 campaign
he committed himself to the League of Nations.

In 1928, he sent to one of Al Smith's close advisers
the outlines of his future Good Neighbor policy for the
western hemisphere:

I am one of many Americans disturbed by
the war in the Republic of Nicaragua, in which the
United States Navy and Marine Corps are now engaged. . . . Only in rare cases, when internal dissensions
or chaos in an individual nation over a long continued
period of time begin harmfully to affect sister nations,
can there be any possible justifications for intervention,
even of a peaceful kind. When such a rare case happens,
it seems to me that the civilized world now demands
that action should not be taken by one outside nation
alone without consultation with its neighbors.

Surely, in this great continent there is enough of
civilization for us to get together with our sister republics for the preservation of the peace and to lend
a helping hand to those in need in the Americas, north
and south.[25]

By campaign time he had to swallow his regret at the
party's retreat from international co-operation. None-
theless, his essentially Wilsonian approach would
lie in the recesses of his mind to guide the subtle
evolution of foreign policy in the mid-thirties. His
critics were often blinded to his consistency in objectives by his adaptability in methods. "This is a step
in the right direction," he would say over and over
again when he had to accept less than he wished. For
Roosevelt, principles and political tactics could never
be divorced. An impractical principle was a dead one.
But the most effective politicking was bankrupt unless

*it moved in a meaningful direction. He always sought
to stake out the comfortable position just left of center,
where the votes lay. In 1924 he explained:*

> ... The Democratic Party is the Progressive
> party of the country, but it is not and I hope never will
> be the radical party of the country which is a very
> different thing. We cannot surely progress unless each
> advancing footstep is placed on firm and tried ground.
> To rush blindly along the paths proclaimed as highways
> to Utopia by some of our radical friends would be to
> find ourselves hopelessly mired in the quicksand of un-
> sound political theories and unworkable doctrines of
> Government. . . . I believe there is a place for the
> most optimistic dreamers in our party, because our party
> in its very foundation principles is committed to the
> doctrine of adopting every new thing that makes for the
> comfort and happiness and well being of all the people
> of our country just as soon as it is certain that such new
> ideas are sound and will have that effect. . . . In the race
> of modern civilization I believe the victory will not go
> to the swift, and I believe that it will certainly not go to
> those who hold to the Republican theory of standing still.
> The greatest real progress will be made by that country
> which is always looking for something better but never
> risking something which is untried and unproven. . . . [26]

NOTES, *chapter 3*

1. John Gunther, *Roosevelt in Retrospect, A Profile in
History* (Harper, 1950), 110.

2. Eleanor Roosevelt, *This I Remember* (Harper, 1949),
1-2.

3. John Blum, *From the Morgenthau Diaries, Years of
Crisis 1928–1938* (Houghton, Mifflin, 1959), 254.

4. Samuel Rosenman, *Working with Roosevelt* (Harper,
1952), 74.

5. Elliott Roosevelt, ed., *F.D.R., His Personal Letters,
1928–1945* (Duell, Sloan and Pearce, 1950), 358.

6. Richard Hofstadter, *The American Political Tradition and the Men Who Made It,* 318-319.

7. *New York Times,* Jan. 22, 1911.

8. Frances Perkins, *The Roosevelt I Knew* (Viking, 1946), 11-12.

9. *New York Times,* Dec. 25, 1911.

10. Roosevelt to Nelson Drummond, Feb. 14, 1920, Franklin D. Roosevelt Library [FDRL], Hyde Park, N. Y.

11. *New York Times,* Aug. 19, 1920.

12. *New York Evening Post,* Aug. 10, 1920.

13. Frances Perkins, *Roosevelt,* 29.

14. Gunther, *Roosevelt,* 235-237.

15. Frances Perkins, *Roosevelt,* 61-62, 64-66.

16. Raymond Moley, *After Seven Years* (Harper, 1939), 10-11.

17. Rexford G. Tugwell, *The Democratic Roosevelt, A Biography of Franklin D. Roosevelt* (Doubleday, 1957), 150.

18. Roosevelt to Willard Saulsbury, Dec. 9, 1924, FDRL.

19. Edgar B. Nixon, ed., *Franklin D. Roosevelt and Conservation, 1911–1945* (Franklin D. Roosevelt Library, 1957), I, 17-18.

20. Roosevelt to Alfred E. Smith, May 20, 1927, FDRL.

21. Ernest K. Lindley, *Franklin D. Roosevelt, A Career in Progressive Democracy* (Bobbs, Merrill, 1931), 324.

22. Roosevelt to James Forrestal, June 6, 1911, FDRL.

23. Roosevelt to Ward Melville, Sept. 21, 1928, FDRL.

24. Elliott Roosevelt, ed., *F.D.R., His Personal Letters, 1905–1928* (Duell, Sloan and Pearce, 1948), 211, 238, 267.

25. Memorandum for Frederick Greene, Jan. 13, 1928, FDRL.

26. Roosevelt to James Edgerton, Dec. 12, 1924, FDRL.

chapter 4 THE ROOSEVELT TEAM AND
THE ROOSEVELT PARTY

After 1932 Roosevelt seemed often to lack direction. This was largely because the team behind which he had driven to Washington was an ill-matched collection of spirited broncos. And all kinds of mavericks were finding their way back to the stables in search of the feed troughs. Notable among them were the big city bosses and the conservatives who had rallied behind Smith or Garner at Chicago.

In fact there were several teams. One was his close personal staff, dominated by the sardonic Louis McHenry Howe. A second was the fluid group of Brain Trusters, held in check rein for the moment by Raymond Moley. A third was the Cabinet, a cross section of reformers, professional politicians and financial angels. The most potentially balky, and yet the strongest for the long haul, were the Congressmen, led by the regulars who had kept the party alive in the dry years of the twenties. None of these groups was homogeneous. They had been united during the campaign by Depression, Disillusionment and the Democratic party. All that held them together now was the emergency and Franklin Roosevelt.

At first attention centered on the Brain Trust. This informal and unofficial group had drafted the issues and the speeches during preconvention days. It consisted mainly of Raymond Moley, Rexford Tugwell and Adolph Berle, all Columbia University professors, Samuel Rosenman and General Hugh Johnson.

Moley became for the moment Assistant-Secretary

of State, a position from which he actually continued to
function as the President's chief policy aide. The flamboyant Johnson—"Old Iron Pants"—became the dynamic dictator of the NRA. Tugwell carried on his
advisory role from the Department of Agriculture. Berle
operated from a variety of posts. Rosenman remained in
New York for a time, but from 1936 to 1945 he would
flit easily in and out of Washington as the President's
manager of the speech-writing projects. But these were
merely the first in a tidal wave of New Dealers whom
Arthur Schlesinger, Jr., has described:

. . . The old capital did not know what to
make of the invasion. "A plague of young lawyers
settled on Washington," wrote George Peek, the
veteran farm leader, sourly. "They all claimed to be
friends of somebody or other and mostly of Felix Frankfurter and Jerome Frank. They floated airily into offices,
took desks, asked for papers and found no end of things
to be busy about. I never found out why they came,
what they did or why they left."

This was one view, and certainly the change was
startling. Depression, by cutting off normal outlets in
law practice or in the universities, had made men of
intellectual ability available as never before; and government had never been so eager to hire them. Like circles
beyond circles, both the legal network and the academic
network were limitless. With each prominent New
Dealer acting as his own employment agency, Washington was deluged with an endless stream of bright young
men. . . . They brought with them an alertness, an
excitement, an appetite for power, an instinct for crisis
and dedication to public service which became during
the thirties the essence of Washington. "No group in
government," said Arthur Krock, "has ever been more
interesting, dull, brilliant, stupid, headstrong, pliable,
competent, inefficient; more honorable in money mat-

ters, more ruthless in material methods." Their élan, their bravado, their sense of adventure, their cocky assurance, their inexhaustible activism were infectious. They often were irritating, but they always were alive. "The Filii Aurorae make me actively sick at my stomach," Judge Learned Hand said early in 1934; "they are so conceited, so insensitive, so arrogant. But on the whole the Old Tories are intellectually so moribund . . . so stupid and emit such dreary, hollow sounds."

The sounds of the New Dealers were rarely dreary or hollow. They altered the whole tempo and tone of Washington as a community. . . . "In times of relaxation," said Krock, "they are a merry group, the New Dealers. They like singing and dancing and a fair amount of drinking. They are hearty eaters and colossal workers." Above all, they talked. . . . Chat after dinner no longer consisted of tedious anecdotes about quail shooting and golf. Instead, it dealt in issues and ideas and went on till early in the morning. . . .

Who were the New Dealers? They represented all classes—from the wellborn, like Franklin Roosevelt, Averell Harriman, Francis Biddle, to the sons of poverty, like Harry Hopkins—but they were predominantly middle class. They represented a variety of occupations; but they were mostly lawyers, college professors, economists, or social workers. They came from all parts of the land and from both city and country, though most of them had been educated in state universities or Ivy League colleges, and many had their first political experience in the fight for decent city government. They were all ages, though most of them were born between 1895 and 1905. But the common bond which held them together, as Herman Kahn has acutely noted, was that they were all at home in the world of ideas. They were accustomed to analysis and dialectic; and they were prepared to use intelligence as an instrument of government. They were more than

specialists. As Kahn has further pointed out, they were
—or considered themselves—generalists, capable of
bringing logic to bear on any social problem. They de-
lighted in the play of the free mind.

They were by no means of a single school. Indeed,
they represented divergent and often clashing philoso-
phies. The laissez faire liberalism of the Democratic
Party, dedicated, in the tradition of Grover Cleveland,
to sound money, fiscal orthodoxy, and tariff reduction,
found its voices in Lewis Douglas and Cordell Hull. . . .
The agrarian tradition, [was] stronger in Congress than
in the administration, harking back to William Jennings
Bryan and demanding monetary inflation as a means of
turning the terms of trade more favorably to the farmer.
. . . The trust-busting liberalism of the Brandeis-
Wilson school, seeking to liberate the economy from
business bigness, spoke especially through Professor
Felix Frankfurter of Harvard. . . . And to these traditional Democratic strains there was now added an in-
fusion of the Theodore Roosevelt–Herbert Croly
Progressivism of 1912, finding advocates from Raymond Moley on the right to Rexford Tugwell on the
left, and seeking to counter the anarchy of competition
by government-business collaboration.

What Roosevelt gave the New Dealers was an opportunity to put ideas to work. Motives, of course, were
mixed. For some it was a job, or a passing enthusiasm,
or a road to personal power. But for the best of them,
the satisfaction lay, as Francis Biddle once put it, "in
some deep sense of giving and sharing. . . . The satisfaction derived from sinking individual effort into the
community itself, the common goal and the common
end. . . ." They often suffered frustration and disillusion.
They worked to the edge of collapse. They had moments when they hated Washington and government
and Roosevelt. Yet for most of them this was the hap-
piest time and the deepest fulfillment they would ever

know. . . . The memories would not soon fade—the interminable meetings, the litter of cigarette stubs, the hasty sandwich at the desk or (if there was time) the lazy lunch along sun-drenched wharves by the Potomac, the ominous rumor passed on with relish, the call from the White House, the postponed dinner, the neglected wife, the office lights burning into the night, the lilacs hanging in fragrance above Georgetown gardens while men rebuilt the nation over long drinks, the selflessness, the vanity, the mistakes, the achievement. At his worst, the New Dealer became an arrant sentimentalist or a cynical operator. At his best, he was the ablest, most intelligent, and most disinterested public servant the United States ever had.[1]

They were often resented. Postmaster-General Farley complained politely:

I think a fault common to many of the "Brain-Trusters" and other inexperienced men who have been trusted with high responsibilities and given ready access to the White House is a tendency to forget that Franklin D. Roosevelt is President of the United States. It is well-nigh impossible for a young man to get close to the seat of power without imagining that he himself occupies the place at the head of the table.[2]

They often resented each other. There was bitterness between the Frankfurter individualists and the Tugwell collectivists. But between the dynamic newcomers and the old-timers there was sheer hatred. Over twenty years later Tugwell could still refer to Vice-President Garner as "the malicious little man from Uvalde."[3] Some of this lingering bitterness undoubtedly grew from the fact that most of the Brain Trusters eventually found themselves displaced as Roosevelt moved beyond them. They shared a common expendability which did not apply to the regulars in Cabinet or Congress who had deep roots in the party or in Roosevelt's personal friendship.

Despite his much advertised "inability" to fire anyone, Roosevelt did manage, by one method or other, to change his advisers like his clothes, as policy and politics dictated. In fact after 1932 the Brain Trust was never a formal body. It was merely a loose group of advisers consulting individually with Roosevelt. Rosenman has written of this change:

> Acting together in a consultative and advisory capacity, they could have been of great help. Acting individually, without the natural restraint and check which came from group discussion, some of the members of the Brain Trust who did take administrative positions in Washington in 1933 eventually caused the President embarrassment in one way or another. Ultimately their paths and the President's separated.'

By the end of 1934 Moley and Tugwell were receding from influence. The gaudy and explosive Hugh Johnson was forced out long before his fond creation, the NRA, had collapsed. Lewis Douglas departed with the "economy" mood. During the winter of 1934–1935 their places of intimacy in the White House were gradually pre-empted by a tough-minded, able pair of Frankfurter protégés: the ebullient, resilient and ambitious Thomas Corcoran, and the scholarly, quiet, but effective Benjamin Cohen. The much-publicized team of Corcoran and Cohen were themselves relentlessly pushed aside between 1938 and 1940 by the predominating presence of Harry Hopkins.

Perhaps no one was more influential with Roosevelt on the whole than two men who at different times lived as members of the President's personal family. The first was Louis Howe, who had been F.D.R.'s constant aide since 1912. Howe's influence waned sadly after 1934. Desperately ill, he died early in 1936. The second was Hopkins who moved into the White House in 1940. He had worked for Roosevelt as director of relief programs since 1930 and his power grew rapidly after the 1938 recession. John Gunther has written of Howe and Hopkins:

Both were frail men physically who had long periods of ill-health; both were sharp, honest as the day, and tenaciously loyal; both, a minor point, loved race tracks and the lighter things of life; both were jealous of others close to the throne; both gave up their whole lives to Roosevelt without thought of reward except the not inconsiderable reward which came from membership in the inner circle of power; both died exhausted by their labors in his service. But there were striking differences too. Howe was, one might say, interested only in FDR and making him President; he had little concern with the merits of issues, policy in the abstract, or affairs outside his own orbit; if FDR had come out for the Devil, it wouldn't have mattered to him much. But Hopkins had a deep, vital, unshakeable *belief* in principles and issues. In the early days it was Howe who taught Roosevelt, and told him like a Dutch uncle how to do things; conversely it was Roosevelt who was the teacher, the mentor, so far as Hopkins was concerned. Roosevelt may have loved Hopkins more, but he paid more attention to Howe. I have heard one of FDR's sons say, "The most fascinating man in father's entire life was Howe." His only ambition was to be "manager" of the man whom he genuinely thought to be the greatest human being history had ever produced. . . .

Hopkins was a broader human being, he had a more decisive grip and intellectual capacity, and he moved, after the war began at least, on a much more imposing stage. He had more power than Howe ever had, and he loved power. Probably Howe said No to FDR more often. Hopkins could say No but he seldom persisted in opposition or resistance to the President over a prolonged interval. Howe would stick his No out—even his neck. Hopkins would delay and conciliate and finally come along. . . .

One of Howe's great usefulnesses was his unerring instinct for detecting men with axes to grind, chiselers; he had second sight about politicians who were promoting nothing but themselves. . . .

He was a gadfly, a hair shirt, implacable in his demand for blind unquestioning loyalty to FDR. Once he gave these instructions to a group of recruits helping in the 1932 campaign: "Remember this; you're nothing. Your face means nothing. Your name means nothing. . . . I don't want to catch you or anybody else trying to crowd into a photograph. . . . All you have to worry about, night and day, day and night, is this man Roosevelt, and get him to the White House, no matter what."

Hopkins entered the scene much later. . . . He was an extremely charming person and Roosevelt, a charmer himself, liked charming people. He was an admirable, patient listener. FDR could talk to him as if nobody was in the room. He had great sensitiveness to the President's own moods, and FDR liked him for his habit of irony, his irreverence, and the way he could laugh and banter and give a humorous touch no matter how serious the situation. This is not to say that he was frivolous. Far from it. Churchill called him "Lord Root of the Matter"; his mind was stubborn and penetrating to an advanced degree. Also he knew everything; he was a bottomless well of news and gossip. He brought Roosevelt gaiety and scuttlebutt. Then too FDR liked him because he *did* things, and for the way he would say, "To hell with the cost, let's go ahead." . . . Once a distinguished editor asked the President what Hopkins' function was. FDR replied, "I can answer that with a single illustration. We've just had a cable from the British asking for 375,000 75mm. shells. The army said, 'Sorry, but we haven't got any.' I turned the thing over to Harry. He found 100,000 shells at Fort Bragg left there since 1919, and another 150,000 in Manila. Then he got five manufacturers to produce 10,000 more apiece." [8]

Roosevelt tended to use the Brain Trust and the Cabinet as foils against each other. Sometimes an informal adviser would short-circuit the most distinguished Cabinet officer. Moley, for example, was much more powerful than Hull, though the Secretary of State was technically his boss. But often when a member of the kitchen cabinet was riding high, he would find himself cut loose by the President's sudden resort to one of the official departments.

The importance of the Cabinet members varied. And the roles of individual secretaries changed from year to year. Senator Claude Swanson and Governor George Dern, for example, made little impact as Secretaries of Navy and of War. But Henry Wallace, as Secretary of Agriculture and later as Vice-President, grew constantly in importance. Secretary of State Cordell Hull seemed all but repudiated during the first year. He became a major part of the team the next year with the success of his Reciprocal Trade Agreements program. But much of his authority was firmly delegated by the President to Undersecretary Sumner Welles, and Hull was barred from many of the great decisions after 1939 by the President's personal diplomacy.

Cabinets must often be constructed to satisfy the sharply antagonistic wings of the party; they sometimes reflect personal political indebtedness, rather than competence for the task at hand. Roosevelt's was no exception. Wallace represented the penchant to experi-

ment and the liberal point of view. Secretary of the
Treasury William H. Woodin, Postmaster-General
James A. Farley, Vice-President Garner, and Jesse Jones
at the Reconstruction Finance Corporation claimed a
brand of economic conservatism Wallace despised. Hull
stood for the free-trade traditions of the party; Secretary
of the Interior Harold Ickes, for the fighting spirit of
Bull Moose Progressivism. Secretary of Labor Frances
Perkins was a practical, but devoted, reformer; Henry
Morgenthau, Jr., Governor of the Farm Credit Administration (and later, Secretary of the Treasury),
was a conservative with a strong social conscience.
Morgenthau, Perkins and Farley were tied to Roosevelt
by long association as well as common cause. Perkins,
Ickes and Wallace appealed in one way or another to
the nation's New Deal mood. Farley was the spokesman
for the organization leaders. Jones, Hull and the first
Secretary of Commerce, Daniel C. Roper, had support
among Southern congressional leaders. Some, like
Woodin, Dern and Attorney-General Homer Cummings
would never find their permanent place in the team, and
would be displaced by death or illness or recognition of
their inappropriateness.

But Hull, Ickes, Wallace and Miss Perkins would
remain to the end. And so would the stolid and loyal
Morgenthau, and the relentlessly driving Hopkins, first
as relief administrator, then as Secretary of Commerce,
and finally in a position even above the Cabinet. Farley
and Garner would remain until the third-term issue and
the permanency of the New Deal pushed them aside.
Roosevelt might experiment with his Brain Trust, but
he preferred stability in the Cabinet. This required
strong leadership on the President's part. One of his
chief tasks was the smoothing of ruffled feathers in the
Cabinet. Wallace, Jones and Ickes hated each other.
Some members were chronically impatient with Morgenthau and Miss Perkins. Roosevelt had regularly to

refuse resignations from Morgenthau, Ickes and Perkins. But much of this was politically essential. He could shuck a Moley or a Corcoran, and the country cared little. He could not displace an Ickes without seeming to give in to the conservatives; he could not fire a Hull or a Jesse Jones without raising the hackles of conservative congressmen.

In the management of his administration generally, Roosevelt liked to think of himself as a quarterback, making decisions from play to play within the limits of his team and the terms of the situation. It has become almost conventional, however, to assume that he was careless and inconsistent in management, that he was less than honest in playing his subordinates off against each other, that he did not have the courage to fire incompetents, but preferred the creation of new and overlapping agencies.

Miss Perkins, who worked closely with him for sixteen years and knew him for almost thirty-five, has insisted, "It is my final testimony that he never let me down." She has pointed out:

> . . . I learned to prepare material so that it would photograph itself upon his memory. I habitually prepared a complete memorandum which any subordinate might read; but I also prepared not over two pages, preferably one page, of strictly structural outline material. It was the kind of academic outline that is so tiresome to the average reader but so helpful to one who must recall the principal steps in an argument. . . . With that in his hand and under his eye, I discussed the matter with him. I answered all his questions. I undertook to tell him the opposition to the argument. I persuaded him to read some of the larger memoranda, but to hold the outline in his hand as he read or discussed them with me.

When he had been over the outline, asked his questions, heard explanations, jotted a pencil note on the margin of the outline, I would put the question to him: "Do you authorize me to go ahead with this? Are you sure?" Then we might have a brief discussion of the propriety or timing of the program or the political technique to be used. . . .

After a few more moments of conversation, I would always make occasion to go over the outline with him a second time. "Are you sure you want item number one? Do you want items number two and three? You understand that this is what we do and this is who is opposed?"

With that clearly photographed on his mind, he would say, "Yes, go ahead."

Then I knew I could safely proceed. . . .

There are others who say that Roosevelt sometimes let them down after he had told them he was in favor of a particular project. My own belief is that they did not sufficiently prepare it for him. They did not tell him what the opposition was.[6]

And John Gunther has noted:

FDR is often criticized for being a bad administrator, but this is largely because the circumference he tried to embrace was so limitless; so far as running his own office was concerned he was somewhat eccentric and his executive methods were catch-as-catch-can; of course he had the unendingly faithful cooperation of a first-rate staff. That he was able, year after year, to retain such devotion from a widely variegated and numerous group was, of course, a substantial tribute to his personal power. The White House executive staff numbered 687 men and women in 1944. . . .

One peculiarity in FDR as an executive was that, in certain fields, he disliked and distrusted so-called experts. . . .

He gave assignments like a benevolent city editor to the men he liked and trusted, let them have free rein, and saw them seldom. His men had to guess a good deal as to what he wanted in detail. . . .

Sometimes Roosevelt made terrible appointments. He shopped for ambassadors, it seemed, like a housewife choosing among apples over the telephone. But let us remember (a) that he had to think in terms not merely of hundreds of appointments but of thousands; (b) he had to work with what talent was available; (c) there were always political difficulties. . . . Roosevelt had to have, let us say, the vote of Senator Blank in order to be sure of a majority in the Senate for the Dumbarton Oaks proposals. Therefore it was imperative that he let Senator Blank have his way on the postmastership of Senator Blank's home town. . . . He had to buy his legislation through. Jesse Jones, it was said, had "ten votes in the Senate and forty in the House." So it was difficult to refuse Jones favors. One reason he found Bernard M. Baruch so useful was that Baruch had such prestige among the Southern senators.⁷

But the direction of the administrative team was almost an incidental part of the job. Much more challenging was the management of Congress and of the far-flung resources of the Democratic party. James M. Burns has summarized Roosevelt's problem of congressional leadership:

Supposedly sharing co-ordinate power with the President, even during crises, were 96 Senators and 435 representatives on Capitol Hill. . . .

Within the two Houses . . . powerful forces were working toward both the left and the right. Southerners, generally conservative in outlook, except for their hostility to Wall Street, were chairmen or ranking members of most of the committees as a result of storing up seniority during the long years of Democratic defeats in the North. Along with the time-honored blocs—public works, reclamation, farmers, labor, and the like—were factional groups propelled by depression-sharpened discontent; silverites, inflationists, veterans. A wholly unpredictable factor lay in the scores of freshman representatives, some of them stridently offering panaceas, others silent and bewildered by the capital kaleidoscope. The Senate had responded more slowly to political trends, but it too embraced a multitude of ideological splits, bipartisan blocs, and party factions.

Left without direction the Democratic ranks in Congress would break up into guerrilla armies. . . . Who would direct the steering committee, the whips, the caucus? What program would be followed? The question was not long left in doubt. Casually identifying the Democratic party's program with the administration, [Speaker Henry T.] Rainey said, "We will put over Mr. Roosevelt's program."

The Chief Executive was Chief Legislator. . . . The price of congressional support was that Roosevelt often yielded unduly to congressional pressures. . . .

During the first half of his first term Roosevelt tried a Grand Experiment in government. He took the role of national father, of bipartisan leader, of President of all the people. . . .

As President of all the people Roosevelt tried to stay above the political and ideological battles that raged all around him. Insisting that he did not want to be drawn into controversy, he asked his supporters to take over the burden of answering attacks on the New Deal from the extreme right or left. He was forever acting as umpire between warring administrators or congressmen. . . .

Some Democrats could not understand Roosevelt's nonpartisan line. . . . Republican party leaders were perplexed too. . . . By early 1934 they were trying hard to act as a real opposition party.

But what were they to oppose? . . . the Grand Old Party itself tended to split into factions to the right and to the left of the President's erratic middle-of-the-road course. . . .

The classic test of greatness in the White House has been the chief executive's capacity to lead Congress. . . . By this classic test Roosevelt—during his first years in the White House—was a strong President who dominated Congress with a masterly show of leadership.

If Roosevelt had ever stopped during these turbulent days to list his methods of dealing with Congress, the result might have looked something like this:

1. Full use of constitutional powers, such as the veto.
2. Good timing.
3. Drafting of measures in the executive branch.
4. Almost constant pressure, adroitly applied.
5. Careful handling of patronage.
6. Face-to-face persuasiveness with legislative leaders.
7. Appeal to the people.

But it would have been out of character for the President to catalogue his methods in such systematic fashion. He cheerfully played the legislative game by ear, now trying this device and now that, as the situation dictated.

He experimented even with a policy of hands off for a short period. Late in March 1934 the President ostentatiously left Washington for two weeks of deep-sea fishing off the Bahamas. White House pressure was relaxed. Soon Congress was looking like a schoolroom of disorderly boys with the master gone. . . . Over one hundred representatives, breaking away from their leaders, lined up in favor of a mortgage refinancing bill so inflationary that Roosevelt sent word to Garner and Rayburn from his yacht to tell Congress "if this type of wild legislation passed the responsibility for wrecking recovery will be squarely on Congress, and I will not hesitate to say so to the nation in plain language." . . .

The hands-off experiment was a dismal failure.

Welcomed by a group of congressmen on his return Roosevelt remarked pointedly that he had learned some lessons from the barracuda and sharks. He added with a smile, "I am a tough guy."

The presidential reins were tightened, but the President never got really tough. He depended mainly on conferences with congressional leaders. . . .

"The word 'must' is a terrible word," he told reporters. "I would not use 'must' to Congress. I never have, have I?" he finished amid laughter.

. . . he delivered his reports on the state of the union to Congress in person. He outlined general proposals in well-timed messages, and he followed these up by detailed legislative proposals drafted in the executive departments and introduced by friendly congressmen. . . . In practice he fashioned a kind of "master-ministry" of bureaucrats and congressmen with Roosevelt at the top.

The President could say no, too. . . . More important than the veto was the President's threat to use it. Again and again he sent word through congressional leaders that he would turn down a pending bill unless it was changed. . . .

Roosevelt played the patronage game tirelessly and adroitly. Major appointments were allotted on the basis of lists the President drew up of "our friends" in various states; an opponent he carefully designated simply as "not with me." . . .

Roosevelt was not above back-alley horse trades. In the spring of 1934 Senator "Cotton Ed" Smith of South Carolina pigeonholed the Chief Executive's nomination of Tugwell as Under Secretary of Agriculture. But Smith also badly wanted a United States marshalship for a henchman who had a good reputation except for a slight case of homicide. So Roosevelt made the deal, and greeted an astonished Tugwell with the cheery remark: "You will never know any more about it, I hope; but today I traded you for a couple of murderers!"

Roosevelt often fell back on his own charm and resourcefulness in dealing with congressmen. . . .

The Roosevelt technique with Congress dazzled the country; but there were misgivings. One of those who was not enchanted was a keen student of national politics at Harvard named E. Pendleton Herring. Analyzing the first two sessions of Roosevelt's Congress, Herring noted the extent to which presidential control had rested on unsteady bases such as patronage, government funds and favors, the co-operation of congressional leaders, and the crisis psychology of the people. Even so, Herring noted, the administration could do little more than "keep order in the bread-line that reached into the Treasury." The more powerfully organized groups got much of what they wanted; the weaker groups such as labor and consumers, did not do so well. The President had shown himself as an astute politician rather than a crusader. Responsible executive leadership seemed weak in the face of organized minorities.[8]

This was the first—the crisis Congress. And Herring had seen accurately the limits of Roosevelt's magic with the legislators. The tactics changed little, but the curve of Presidential leadership moved like a barometer with the broad sweep of the weather fronts. In general he was successful when Congress needed him, when the font of executive patronage was full, when a crisis loomed, when an election threatened. The election of 1934, with its significant swing of the congressional balance to the left, helped the President to place more reliance on labor and reform sentiment. In the summer of 1935 Roosevelt leadership was superb in paving the road for a remarkable "second hundred days" of intense White House–Capitol co-operation. But with 1936 safely over, the Congress began to tire of both reform and Roosevelt. A special session in the fall of 1937 obdurately refused every Presidential suggestion. The party crisis of the "Roosevelt Recession" in the spring of 1938 brought a brief resurgence of the old pattern. The war brought others. But there were long gaps in which Congress squabbled with the President and within itself as freely as at any time in the nation's history. In fact after 1936 Congress drew away from F.D.R. The rebuff on his plan to remake the Supreme Court was only the most dramatic instance. Except on the war issues, he would never again be able to play the masterly policy-maker that he had in his first administration.

Throughout all the erratic sparring between Congress and the President, Roosevelt's most significant weapon had remained his remarkable ability to arouse popular support against the legislature. Speech-writing was at the core of his administrative strategy. In this matter he remained the "old master," the master of tone and manner, of emphasis and timing. Yet speech-writing, like everything else in the Roosevelt Administration, was a matter of team-work. For the millions of words Roosevelt wrote and spoke in twelve years were neither entirely his own nor entirely anyone else's. John Gunther has graphically described the process:

> The way Roosevelt wrote speeches was a riot. . . . A speech by the President was, to put it mildly, almost always a composite phenomenon. The list of his literary helpers, from first to last, includes a great number of people—Charles Michelson, Ernest Lindley, Sumner Welles, Moley and the whole Brain Trust, Stanley High ("to take care of the spiritual side," as FDR once expressed it), Archibald MacLeish, Tom Corcoran, Basil O'Connor, Bob Jackson, and above all Rosenman and Sherwood. . . .

In the early days each of two or three advisers would

prepare a long speech, after getting FDR's ideas. Then, facing a manuscript that would have taken four or five hours to deliver, the President would intermix the best points together and get it to manageable length. Next the advisers would consult again, and cut further. Once more FDR would go over it brutally, and it would finally be trimmed to fit into the proper time. Later this procedure became much more elaborate. Sometime in December, say, Missy LeHand or Miss Tully would gently prod the President into recalling that his annual message on the state of the Union was due early in January. FDR would groan, "What—already? Very well, let's start tomorrow night at nine." Then relevant material would be assembled from the State Department, the Treasury, the Navy, the War Production Board, and whatever other government agencies were involved. The President, dictating to Miss Tully, would then outline his own conception of what the speech should eventually contain. Sherwood and Rosenman would go to work furiously on this draft, often with sub-ghosts assisting them. The President's manuscript was by no means sacrosanct. The boys would, in fact, tear it to pieces, muttering phrases like, "He'll forget that he ever said this—it's terrible—let's cut it out." But they were extremely careful to maintain his mood, his pace, his major trajectory, his essential theme. Soon . . . a provisional script would be submitted to the President. He would often as not blow up, exclaiming, "I never said that!" or "What are you trying to make me say?" Then it would be pointed out, "But Economic Warfare wants that in," or, "The Pentagon asks specially that you make that point." Work would go on till midnight, and then after FDR went to bed, until two in the morning, three, four or even six. After three drafts, which would take three or four days to prepare, the advisers had what they called a "ground floor." Then the President himself added walls and rooms. After six or seven drafts FDR would be apt to say, "We're getting along fine now. Let's go back to the beginning and start all over."

The remarkable thing was that, in spite of the mazes and confusions, the speech when finally delivered did have the indisputable imprint of the President himself. Always he blew his own vitality into every passage.[9]

Whether it was in managing the speech-writers, the Brain Trusters, Cabinet officers or congressmen, the one constant in Roosevelt's technique was the fact that he seemed to feel it in his bones. Miss Perkins has noted perceptively:

In the use of his faculties Roosevelt had almost the quality of a creative artist. One would say that it is the quality of the modern artist as distinct from the classical artist. The name for it in the graphic arts is automatism. It describes an artist who begins his picture without a clear idea of what he intends to paint or how it shall be laid out upon the canvas, but begins anyhow, and then, as he paints, his plan evolves out of the material he is painting. So Roosevelt worked with the materials and problems at hand. As he worked one phase, the next evolved.[10]

NOTES, *chapter 4*

1. Arthur M. Schlesinger, Jr., *The Coming of the New Deal*, 16-20.

2. James A. Farley, *Behind the Ballots: the Personal History of a Politician*, 218.

3. Rexford G. Tugwell, *The Democratic Roosevelt, A Biography of Franklin D. Roosevelt*, 378.

4. Samuel Rosenman, *Working with Roosevelt*, 88.

5. John Gunther, *Roosevelt in Retrospect, A Profile in History*, 84-86.

6. Frances Perkins, *The Roosevelt I Knew*, 161-162.

7. Gunther, *Roosevelt*, 126-128.

8. James M. Burns, *Roosevelt, the Lion and the Fox*, 174-175, 183-188, 191.

9. Gunther, *Roosevelt,* 121-124.

10. Frances Perkins, *Roosevelt,* 163.

chapter **5** RELIEF AND RECOVERY FOR A
DESPERATE PEOPLE

The initial New Deal was based upon a strategy that Roosevelt had called during the campaign "a true concert of interests," and that meant in practice something for everybody. Farmers got the A.A.A. Business got the NRA codes. Labor got wage-and-hour provisions and the collective bargaining promise of section 7 (a). The unemployed got a variety of federal relief measures. The middle classes got the Home Owners' Loan Corporation, securities regulation, and other reforms. Some debtors were aided by inflation. As new discontents developed they were met with new expedients.[1]

Roosevelt could himself admit by 1938:

To us, strong vital government action was . . . a prerequisite in any program for material recovery. . . .
. . . those who seek inconsistencies will find them. There were inconsistencies of methods, inconsistencies caused by ceaseless efforts to find ways to solve problems for the future as well as for the present. There were inconsistencies born of insufficient knowledge. There were inconsistencies springing from the need of experimentation. But through them all, I trust, that there also will be found a consistency and continuity of broad purpose.
Consistently I have sought to maintain a comprehensive and efficient functioning of the representative

form of democratic government in its modern sense. Consistently I have sought through that form of government to help our people to gain a larger social justice.[2]

The inconsistencies were, in fact, inevitable, and born of more considerable elements than ignorance and experimentation. Roosevelt had no plan, as such, but almost everyone else did. As Tugwell has pointed out:

> There were at that time several theories about recovery. They are roughly recognizable as: (1) the business solution—deflation, easing up on business regulation, restoration of confidence; (2) monetary—infusing currency into the system to restore price levels and start things going and, because gold was the standard of value, to affect prices by manipulating the value of gold; (3) consumers' purchasing power—by making purchasing power available to consumers, to start factories going, thus reducing unemployment; (4) fiscal—manipulating interest rates (making money "easy") and increasing or decreasing federal spending; (5) balance—the equalizing of income among mutually supporting groups. . . .[3]

Berle and Tugwell insisted upon the path to collectivism. Moley attempted the role of manager and mediator but leaned for the moment toward his Brain Trust friends. Frankfurter yearned for the road back to competition, the re-atomization of economic life. Wallace demanded broad farm relief; Lewis Douglas insisted upon rigid economy. Hull crusaded for international economic co-operation; a dozen others wanted recovery first at home. Congress demanded inflation and public works. Others demanded sound money and a balanced budget. Baruch wanted restoration of business confidence. Senators Robert F. Wagner and Hugo Black, and Frances Perkins persistently pleaded the cause of organized labor and labor reform. And so it went. Roosevelt could play no other role than that of quarterback, though sometimes his team seemed a strange one indeed in which the line and the backfield were playing by different rules. The quarterback's own strategy would remain the pattern of conservatism through change which he had outlined to the New York Legislature in January, 1932: "We should not seek in any way to destroy or tear down, except in order to re-place unsound materials with new. . . . Let us seek not merely to restore. Let us restore and at the same time remodel." [4]

But there were consistencies also, created by the pattern of Roosevelt's own signal-calling. There must be action; confidence must be restored. Neither must be impeded by the irrelevant rigidities of theory. And the action must be human. As Frances Perkins noted, "The intellectual and spiritual climate was Roosevelt's general attitude that the people mattered." [5]

The first move when Congress met in emergency session on March 9, 1933, was legislation to reopen the banks. The Proclamation of March 6, which had closed them, had been based on presidential authority drawn from the half-forgotten wartime Trading with the Enemy Act. It would be useful to get congressional ap-proval; it was essential to set the terms for the liquida-tion of the "holiday."

The Proclamation had also embargoed all foreign-exchange transactions and the export of gold and silver. In the thirty days before inauguration about three hundred million dollars in gold had been withdrawn for export. But perhaps the most striking problem was the restoration of an adequate currency with large blocs of the existing supply in hiding. Between Monday, when the Proclamation was issued, and Thursday, when Congress met, Woodin and Moley conferred constantly with the President, by phone with bankers all over the country, with Hoover's top Treasury men who loyally stayed on to help. There was general agreement that public confidence must be restored by "Swift and Staccato Action," by using traditional methods wherever possible, by a sharp "gesture of governmental economy," by quietly blanketing for the moment the "reputedly left-wing presidential advisers," and by a presidential appeal for co-operation. But on details there was confusion. There was some talk of nationalizing the banks; there was more of issuing scrip. As Moley has explained:

It was Will [Woodin] who tossed the scheme out the window and decided in favor of those in the Treasury . . . who believed the issue of scrip was unnecessary.

Early Tuesday morning, as I came to breakfast with him, he yelled at me with wild enthusiasm, "I've got it! I've got it! . . . after you left, I played my guitar a little while and then read a little while and then slept a little while and then awakened and then thought about this scrip thing and then played some more and read some more and slept some more and thought some more. And, by gum, if I didn't hit on the answer that way! Why didn't I see it before? We don't have to issue scrip! . . . We don't need it. . . . We can issue currency against the sound assets of the banks. The Reserve Act lets us print all we'll need. And it won't frighten people. It won't look like stage money. It'll be money that looks like money." [6]

Woodin and Moley rushed off to the White House and had Roosevelt's enthusiastic approval in twenty minutes. Drafted in forty-eight hours, passed by an hysterical Congress before anyone except the leaders had read it, the bill gave the President broad powers to

control the use of gold by private individuals, authorized
the issuance of Federal Reserve notes against the assets of the member banks, and empowered the Secretary
of the Treasury to reopen the banks under regulations
which he was free to devise. Further, the Reconstruction
Finance Corporation was authorized to help by purchasing the preferred stock of banks.

The next day, March 10, the President's Executive
Order on the reopening of the banks extended the gold
embargo indefinitely, and he rushed to strengthen the
mood with his drastic economy proposal. This "Act to
Maintain the Credit of the United States Government,"
would give the President broad powers to decrease
veterans' pensions and the salaries of government employees. Roosevelt solemnly warned the Congress:

> For three long years the Federal Govern-
> ment has been on the road to bankruptcy. . . . It has
> contributed to the recent collapse of our banking struc-
> ture. It has accentuated the stagnation of the economic
> life of our people. It has added to the ranks of the un-
> employed. Our Government's house is not in order and
> for many reasons no effective action has been taken to
> restore it to order. . . . Too often in recent history
> liberal governments have been wrecked on the rocks of
> loose fiscal policy. We must avoid this danger. . . . We
> must move with a direct and resolute purpose now.
> The members of this Congress and I are pledged to
> immediate economy.[7]

The bill was jammed through a Congress distraught
with the outraged cries of the veterans' lobby. Victory
seemed assured for the prophets of "sound" recovery:
for Lewis Douglas in the Budget Bureau, for Baruch
and Woodin and Moley. And on Sunday night the
President completed his bid for national confidence
with the first of his Fireside Chats:

It has been wonderful to me to catch the note of confidence from all over the country. . . . After all, there is an element in the readjustment of our financial system more important than currency, more important than gold, and that is the confidence of the people. Confidence and courage are the essentials of success in carrying out our plan. You people must have faith; you must not be stampeded by rumors or guesses. Let us unite in banishing fear. We have provided the machinery to restore our financial system; it is up to you to support and make it work.

It is your problem no less than it is mine. Together we cannot fail.[5]

The same night, with the threat of trouble in the Senate over the Economy Bill, he told Louis Howe, "I think it's time for beer." Together they drafted a quick message drawn from the National Platform. The next morning Congress had his welcome suggestion that the Volstead Act be amended to legalize light wine and beer while the nation awaited the repeal of the Eighteenth Amendment. On Thursday and Friday the Senate voted for economy and beer.

Anne O'Hare McCormick reported in the New York Times:

After two weeks of the New Deal it is hardly an exaggeration to say that it is about the biggest surprise Washington ever had. The capital is in a state of exclamation . . . the popular response to the first acts of the new administration is like the rising of a nation. . . .

Perhaps it is more than coincidence that the advent of Roosevelt is marked by two tremendous if temporary abdications, that of Wall Street and that of Congress. During the emergency, at least, both the financial and political capitals have moved into the White House. . . .

The more precedents he breaks, the more authority

he assumes, the more applause the new Executive
receives from his admiring audience. The yearning of
America is for action, almost any kind of action. Roosevelt makes a flying start by satisfying that long-balked
appetite. One suspects that he expresses the kind of
revolution that fires the American mind, a 100 per cent
American revolution, whose manifesto is the Con-
stitution.⁹

There were many who felt the program should go
no further. But such "sound" recovery would have been
possible only if the President had followed his first
impulse and allowed Congress to adjourn as soon as the
banking legislation had passed. He couldn't do this. He
didn't want to do it. The enthusiasm was too great to
waste. In any case the crises of unemployment and farm
disaster could hardly be ignored. As soon as Roosevelt
turned to these more fundamental quandaries, he found
himself committed to spending—not economy, to broad
and disciplined organization, and to inflation. He might
tell the Governors that the Federal Government would
"step in" on relief only when the localities and States
had proven that they could not do the job, and he might
put off the demands of the Senators for a public works
program. But as early as March 15, he was thinking of
both a bill to put 200,000 men to work in the national
forests and an agricultural relief measure. He piously
forecast a minimum of expense. "Obviously a farm bill
is in the nature of an experiment," he said. "We all
recognize that. My position toward farm legislation is
that we ought to try to do something to increase the
value of farm products and if the darn thing doesn't
work, we can say so quite frankly, but at least try it." ¹⁰
    The next day Roosevelt sent to Congress the Ag-
ricultural Adjustment Bill which had been cleared by
Henry Wallace with a conference of farm leaders on
March 10. On March 21 he submitted legislation for a

Civilian Conservation Corps and for a Federal Relief Administrator. And he warned of impending new requests for state relief aid and for a federal public works program. Nothing illustrated better the extent to which the President was playing the tune by ear. At first intending to go ahead with CCC "the way I did on beer," Roosevelt finally agreed to consult his aides and friends in Congress. The result was a package: CCC for the President; half a billion dollars in emergency relief appropriations and a general promise of public works for Frances Perkins and Senators Wagner and La Follette who had been working on an elaborate bill for grants-in-aid to the States. But Roosevelt was also encouraged by the quickening concern of conservatives within his own family. Vice-President Garner spoke up early in the administration:

> Mr. President . . . I think that when we were campaigning we sort of made promises that we would do something for the poorer kind of people, and I think we have to do something for them. We have to remember them. We have to take account of that.[11]

His genial elasticity showed through again in his handling of CCC's practical administrative problems. The Army, the Department of Labor, the Forestry Service were all given a role in its management; and a labor leader, Robert Fechner, was made its director to salve the unions' fears of labor regimentation and wage-scale busting. As Miss Perkins reported with some dismay:

> . . . the Roosevelt theory proved correct. Labor was satisfied that there was no disguised regimentation, and it was uncritically in favor of CCC from that time on.

The fact that this set-up might not make for efficient

administration did not trouble Roosevelt. When it was pointed out to him, he said, "Oh, that doesn't matter. The Army and the Forestry Service will really run the show. The Secretary of Labor will select the men and make the rules and Fechner will 'go along' and give everybody satisfaction and confidence."

It is a technique of administration which drives professors of political science almost mad—but government in a representative democracy has to be adapted to human feelings.[12]

This arrangement proved rough on Fechner. But CCC emerged as one of the most successful Roosevelt innovations. For Roosevelt himself, CCC was less a matter of relief than of human and physiographic conservation. As he told the Congress: "It will conserve our precious natural resources. It will pay dividends to the present and future generations. . . . More important, however, than the material gains will be the moral and spiritual value of such work. . . . We can eliminate to some extent at least the threat that enforced idleness brings to spiritual and moral stability."[13]

Roosevelt might be primarily interested in CCC, but the demand for agricultural relief was the most urgent. Arthur Schlesinger, Jr., has summarized the mood as the planting season wore on:

Already discontent was flaring in the farm belt. In mid-March the Farmers' Holiday Association, speaking through its chief, Milo Reno, had threatened a farm strike if Congress did not accept its demands by May 3. . . . They wanted a guaranteed cost of production for farm products, mortgage relief, and, above all, inflation. . . . With the farm bill bogged down in the Senate, farmers began to take things into their own hands, as they had the previous autumn. They stopped eviction sales, denounced foreclosures, intimidated the agents of banks and insurance companies. On April 27 over five hundred farmers crowded the courtroom in Le Mars, Iowa, to demand that Judge Charles C. Bradley suspend foreclosure proceedings until the state courts had passed on recently enacted state legislation. When Bradley turned the farmers down and rebuked them for wearing hats and smoking in the presence of the court, a sullen murmur rose from the crowd. A Farmers' Holiday leader later described the reaction: "That's not his courtroom. We farmers paid for it with our tax money and it was as much ours as his. The crowd had a perfect right there." As the judge continued to scold the throng, men stepped forward, their faces masked in blue bandanas, and dragged him from the bench. In a fury they slapped him and mauled him, placed a blindfold around his eyes and threw him on a truck. Some shouted, "Get a rope! Let's hang him!" A mile from the city, they stopped, tossed a rope over a telegraph pole, fastened one end about his neck and tightened the knot till he nearly lost consciousness. Someone removed a hub cap from the truck and put it on his head, while others pushed him to his knees and told him to pray. Crowned with the cap, grease running down his face, thrust to the ground, he looked at the angry men around him and prayed: "Oh Lord, I pray thee, do justice to all men." And still he refused to pledge himself not to foreclose mortgages on their farms. They threw dirt on him, then tore off his trousers and smeared them with grease and dirt, till, weary and perhaps abashed, they went away. . . .

The farmers had been through too much—their crops crushed by hailstorm and withered by drought and consumed by plagues of grasshoppers, their hard labor brought to naught by falling farm prices, their homes and livelihood menaced by the banks and insurance companies, their recourse to legislation now threatened by nullification in the courts and apathy in the Congress.[14]

Because it had to be, the conflict among inflationists, advocates of crop reduction, of farm price supports and foreign dumping was resolved. The solution for the moment was a linkage of crop reductions and price supports.

In return for a restriction of output by the individual farmer (the heart of the scheme), benefit payments were offered to growers of a variety of staple commodities, cotton, wheat, corn, hogs, tobacco, and rice. To meet the expense of such a program, a processing tax was levied on the staples affected. But it was necessary to do more. The crops for 1933 were already in the ground. As a purely emergency measure the government ordered the plowing under of a fourth of the cotton crop and the slaughter of more than 6,000,-000 pigs. . . . The scale of payments to farmers was based on a complicated formula known as "parity." The principle of this formula was that the farmer would receive for his product a price that "would give agricultural commodities a purchasing power equivalent to the purchasing power of agricultural commodities in the base period, August, 1909–July, 1914."

The act of 1933 was a profound attempt to alter the free system of agriculture that had historically prevailed in the United States. . . .[15]

Although the Agricultural Adjustment Act was stated in emergency terms, it suggested gradualism and the balanced consideration of consumers as well as producers. In fact, however, it became a catch-all for the varied remedies which had boiled up from the farm states during the previous two years. In addition to parity payments, it provided for acreage reductions and marketing agreements; it authorized the President to issue up to three billion dollars in United States notes in payment of government bonds, and to set the relative prices of gold and silver; it provided extensive powers for emergency farm mortgage refinancing.

The Agricultural Adjustment Administration rolled into action under the uneasy guidance of a staff which bickered constantly over policy. In the fall Roosevelt came under relentless pressure from the great cotton growers of the South and turned to Jesse Jones's Reconstruction Finance Corporation to provide additional aid. As Jones remembered the incident loosely and many years later:

One day, when pickers were just entering the fields of the Southland in full force, Oscar Johnston, a big Mississippi planter, regarded as one of the nation's leading authorities on cotton, went to the White House to tell the President that ruin faced him and all the growers.

"We'll see what Jones can do about it," Roosevelt said. He called Jones and asked him to come to the White House.

Jones had not taken his chair in the President's office before Roosevelt said, "Jess, Oscar says cotton is selling at nine cents a pound, and may go lower if we don't do something to support the market. Cotton ought to be worth ten cents."

"All right," Jones said, "we'll make it worth ten cents."

"How can you do it, and how soon?" Roosevelt asked.

"We will offer to lend ten cents a pound anywhere in the cotton-growing section," Jones replied.

"Yes, but the law says you can lend only on 'full and adequate' security."

"Certainly; I know that. I also know that cotton is worth ten cents a pound; and, if all our loans are as well secured as loans on cotton will be at ten cents, we'll be mighty lucky."

... Thus the Commodity Credit Corporation was set up, and in the six years of its life under RFC it made loans to farmers that topped the government's help to railroads, and was second only to the amount dispensed to banks and other financial institutions. . . .[16]

Prices inched upward throughout the fall and winter. By November, Roosevelt could write jubilantly from Warm Springs: "This Southland has a smile on its face. Ten Cent cotton has stopped foreclosures, saved banks and started people definitely on the upgrade. That means all the way from Virginia to Texas. Sears-Roebuck sales in Georgia are 110 per cent above 1932."[17]

But nature, the Supreme Court and the complexity of the farm population all intervened. In the spring of 1934 the Great Plains faced a nearly unprecedented drought.

        . . . only sun, and no rain; sun, at first, and then the winds. In May the dust storms began to blow. . . . The winds swept topsoil from millions of acres of farm land. They seared the crops of two-dozen states. They left behind wheat and corn withered in the fields, ground baked hard as rock, dead trees lonely against the horizon. Cattle, without water to drink or grass to eat, their lungs strangling with dust, grew thin and lay down in fence corners to die. Some ate so much dirt as they scratched at the grass roots that they died from mudballs in their stomachs. . . . Some [men] saw in the drought and dust the judgment of God on men who had dared to plow under cotton and slaughter baby pigs. A demand arose that AAA be abolished. Washington, confronted with the worst drought in the history of the republic, went into swift action, rushing seed and feed to the distressed areas, buying and removing livestock, and acting in other ways to see the farmers through the emergency. At the same time, the government began to develop plans for the protection of land and water over the longer run. . . .

The black blizzards of 1934 had their major long-run impact in speeding the development of federal conservation policies. But they also had a direct effect on the workings of AAA. For they cut down production, particularly of wheat, with a deadly and harsh efficiency far surpassing the man-made efforts of the AAA administrators. The wheat crop, which had averaged 864 million bushels over the years 1928-32, sank to an average of about 567 million bushels for 1933-35; of this reduction, perhaps 20 million resulted from AAA and the rest from the weather. As a conequence, the wheat carryover was absorbed, wheat prices rose, and by 1935-36 the United States was actually importing wheat in material quantities. . . . In cotton, AAA could claim exclusive credit for price increases. In corn, both AAA and weather helped; but no one could question the results. . . . Between 1932 and 1936, gross farm income increased 50 per cent, and cash receipts from marketing, including government payments, nearly doubled. Even more important was the striking improvement in the farmers' terms of trade. The ratio between prices the farmers received and the prices they paid, including interest and taxes, rose steadily from 55 in 1932 to 70 in 1934 and 90 in 1936. Farmers' prices increased by two-thirds in this period. All this was accompanied by a decrease of a billion dollars in the size of the farm debt, and a wholesome shift of creditors from private banks and insurance companies to federal agencies.[18]

But AAA ignored or exacerbated the desperate straits of the tenants, the small marginal farmers, the agricultural laborer. As late as 1938 there were over a million and a half farm families with incomes of less than $600 a year. There were three million tenant families and hundreds of thousands of migrants. Fated to remain at the bottom of the economic ladder, to scratch at eroded soil or exist in rural slums, the bulk of these remained untouched by AAA.

Chester Davis, the AAA Administrator, was insistent upon working for agriculture within the structure set by the owner-dominated Farm Bureau Federation. A showdown with the reformers on his staff who wanted a direct attack on the problems of the "disadvantaged" resulted in a purge of the department's "liberals" in 1935. But there were other problems. The increasing difficulty of working within a framework of voluntary co-operation, brought Cotton and Tobacco Acts in 1934 which used the tax power to force co-operation. Then in 1936 the Supreme Court threw out the whole program. The processing tax, it said, was discriminatory. More important, the whole matter was beyond the scope of Federal power: agriculture was not in interstate commerce.

As he began to sense the need for long-range revision, Henry Wallace had found himself caught, also, between the approach of the first AAA, which presumed national isolation, and the implications of Cordell Hull's reciprocal trade agreements. In 1934, his best-selling pamphlet, America Must Choose, suggested a policy of splitting the difference which might avoid the hard choice:

> If we continue toward nationalism we must be prepared to make permanent the withdrawal from cultivation of over 50 million acres of fairly good farmland, and face the consequences of all the social and economic dislocations which are bound to ensue. If, on the other hand, we choose not to put our agriculture under so high a degree of interior tension and discipline, we must drastically lower tariffs and reorganize industry,

so that we can receive from abroad another billion dollars' worth of goods each year.

The planned middle course I propose as a basis for present discussion is one precisely halfway between these two extremes: a line of march along which we would lower tariffs enough to bring in another half-billion dollars' worth of goods annually, and permanently retract of our good agricultural land some 25 million acres. . . .

The foreign demand will vary with the facilities we afford other nations to send us goods in exchange—that is to say, how much we dare lower tariffs. Plainly, the farm retreat ties up with our tariff policy, which in turn hangs upon the success of the New Deal.[19]

But the reactions of the New Deal to the challenges of 1934–1936 were shaped by the practical limits of politics and by the Supreme Court. 1936 brought the Soil Conservation and Domestic Allotment Act, designed to rescue the program from the Court's decision by making it more permissive, by gearing it to conservation rather than relief, and by emphasizing the role of the States. Meanwhile the Resettlement Act of 1935, and then the Bankhead-Jones Farm Tenancy Act of 1937, provided funds and administration for a vast program of relief and rehabilitation for tenant farmers and migratory workers. The sharp drop in the wheat surplus inspired Henry Wallace to think of the whole crop-control program in terms of a permanent balance to the natural crop cycles. As early as May, 1934, Roosevelt described to his press conference the concept of an "ever-normal granary":

Over a year ago we began discussing the principle of establishing what might be called a reserve granary which would contain a large carryover, a larger carryover than we have been carrying in normal years.

That reserve emergency granary could be used to store surpluses in the bounteous years; and then we could draw on that granary in years of drought in order to prevent any starvation or anything like abnormally high prices. In that way, it would work both ways. In other words, in years of plenty it would help prevent abnormally low prices, and in years of drought it would help prevent abnormally high prices.[20]

By 1938, the administration was ready to assume that the problem was permanent. The second Agricultural Adjustment Act provided a broad program of acreage allotments and marketing quotas, combined with crop insurance and crop loans to support prices. And there was a marriage of democracy and regimentation. Referenda would be held to allow farmers as a group to decide whether to accept the program. Once adopted, however, strict penalties would enforce its operation.

By 1939 the picture was impressive in terms of farm income. From $2.8 billion in 1932, it had risen to $6.2 billion in 1937. In the recession of 1938, the drop was only to $5.5 billion. But there were fundamental questions still open on the eve of the war. John T. Flynn wrote from South Carolina:

Very obviously the farmer's condition is improved. After all, the South Carolina farmer has collected in cash from the government in outright payments something over $72,000,000 in that time. He has received in addition another $36,000,000 in cash loans on his undisposable crops. But over all this a great tide of federal funds has flowed into the state from a variety of government bureaus for both farming and industrial and social objectives. This sum of money, including the direct cash payments, has touched the great total of $344,936,572. . . .

But the farmer is after all an economic unit who must

get his living out of his farm. The aim of any program must be to make him and his farm self-supporting. He cannot go on enjoying forever this bountiful extra crop of cash from the government. . . . The farmer here was told that the condition which wrecked his cotton crop was the creation of unsalable surpluses each year. . . . Today, at the end of the trail, the cotton surplus is greater than ever. . . . As a means of reducing cotton production it has been a complete failure."[21]

Norman Thomas, Socialist spokesman of the era, reiterated the inherent moral complaint: "It remained for us to invent 'bread lines knee-deep in wheat.' "[22]

NOTES, *chapter 5*

1. Richard Hofstadter, *The American Political Tradition and the Men Who Made It*, 334.

2. Samuel Rosenman, ed., *The Public Papers and Addresses of Franklin D. Roosevelt*, I, xii, xiii.

3. Rexford G. Tugwell, *The Art of Politics: As Practiced by Three Great Americans, Franklin Delano Roosevelt, Luis Muñoz Marín and Fiorello H. La Guardia* (Doubleday, 1958), 184-186.

4. *Public Papers*, I, 124.

5. Frances Perkins, *The Roosevelt I Knew*, 173.

6. Raymond Moley, *After Seven Years*, 151-152.

7. *Public Papers*, II, 49-50.

8. *Public Papers*, II, 64-65.

9. Anne O'Hare McCormick, *The World at Home: Selections from the Writings of Anne O'Hare McCormick* (Marion Turner Sheehan, ed., Knopf, 1956), 173-175.

10. *Public Papers*, II, 72.

11. Frances Perkins, *Roosevelt*, 167.

12. Frances Perkins, *Roosevelt*, 180-181.

13. *Public Papers*, II, 81.

14. Arthur M. Schlesinger, Jr., *The Coming of the New Deal*, 42-44.

15. Dexter Perkins, *The New Age of Franklin Roosevelt, 1932–1945* (University of Chicago, 1957), 19.

16. Bascom N. Timmons, *Jesse H. Jones: the Man and the Statesman* (Holt, 1956), 222-223.

17. Elliott Roosevelt, ed., *F.D.R., His Personal Letters, 1928–1945,* 372.

18. Schlesinger, *New Deal,* 69-71.

19. Henry Wallace, *America Must Choose* (Foreign Policy Association and World Peace Foundation, 1934), 27, 32.

20. *Public Papers,* III, 229.

21. John T. Flynn, "The Farmer—Seven Years After," *New Republic,* CII (1940) , 535.

22. Norman Thomas, *The Choice Before Us* (Macmillan, 1934), 6.

chapter **6** RELIEF AND RECOVERY:
BUSINESS AND THE
WORKING MAN

While the farm program was evolving, the Roosevelt
team was blasting out a similarly nationalistic formula
for planned recovery in industry. The National Industrial Recovery Act would prove the most dramatic, but
most sadly abortive, experiment of the era. It appealed
to Roosevelt particularly because it offered a chance
to marry the disparate demands of capital, labor, and
the unemployed. When the Senate passed Hugo
Black's thirty-hour-week bill a month after inauguration
in 1933, the direction was set. As Dexter Perkins has
noted:

> By meeting the demands of businessmen for
codes of fair competition and by combining this with
protection for the worker in the form of minimum
wages and reasonable restrictions on the hours of
labor, it might be possible to produce a statute that
would satisfy both sides and lay a broad foundation for
business recovery. . . . This far-reaching measure ex-
empted from the operation of antitrust laws those
business groups to be formed under the new law. It
permitted these groups to draw up codes for their own
industries subject to governmental approval. It provided
punishment for violators of these codes. At the same
time, it stipulated for the establishment of minimum
wages and maximum hours under the new agreements.
Most important of all from the point of view of labor, it
guaranteed the right of collective bargaining with employers through representatives freely chosen by the
employees.

This last provision was a masterpiece of equivocation. It by no means signified full recognition of the organized trade union. It was drafted in such terms as to leave the way open for the company, or industry-controlled, union as well. It was to cause much trouble in the future, but it is a fair sample of the process of compromise that lay behind much of the legislation of the New Deal.[1]

Raymond Moley, who was assigned the job of bringing together the sharply conflicting plans of Roosevelt's advisers, has explained the basic assumptions of the NRA:

The beliefs that economic bigness was here to stay; that the problem of government was to enable the whole people to enjoy the benefits of mass production and distribution (economy and security); and that it was the duty of government to devise, with business, the means of social and individual adjustment to the facts of the industrial age—these were the heart and soul of the New Deal. Its fundamental purpose was an effort to modify the characteristics of a chaotic competitive system that could and did produce sweatshops, child labor, rackets, ruinous price cutting, a devastated agriculture, and a score of other blights even in the peak year of 1928. It's chief objective was the initiation of preliminary steps toward a balanced and dynamic economic system.[2]

As he signed the National Recovery Act, Roosevelt indicated clearly the extent to which business and labor relief and recovery from depression were interwoven, the degree to which he looked to business for co-operation:

The law I have just signed was passed to put people back to work, to let them buy more of the products of farms and factories and start our business at a living rate again. This task is in two stages; first, to get many hundreds of thousands of the unemployed back on the payroll by snowfall and, second, to plan for a better future for the longer pull. While we shall not neglect the second, the first stage is an emergency job. It has the right of way.

The second part of the Act gives employment through a vast program of public works. . . .

In my Inaugural I laid down the simple proposition that nobody is going to starve in this country. It seems to me to be equally plain that no business which depends for existence on paying less than living wages to its workers has any right to continue in this country . . . and by living wages I mean more than a bare subsistence level—I mean the wages of decent living . . . decent living, widely spread among our 125,000,000 people, eventually means the opening up to industry of the richest market which the world has known. It is the only way to utilize the so-called excess capacity of our industrial plants. . . .

On this idea, the first part of the Act proposes to our industry a great spontaneous cooperation to put millions of men back in their regular jobs this summer. The idea is simply for employers to hire more men to do the existing work by reducing the work-hours of each man's week and at the same time paying a living wage for the shorter week.

No employer and no group of less than all employers in a single trade could do this alone and continue to live in business competition. . . . The challenge of this law is whether we can sink selfish interest and present a solid front against a common peril. . . .[3]

NRA committed the administration to an unparalleled delegation of legislative power, first to the President then to industry itself. This would finally destroy it in the courts. But the Blue Eagle was fettered from the start by the idiosyncrasies of its flamboyant director, Hugh Johnson, by the stark conflict between capital and labor, by the interminable struggles between the collectivists and the conservatives in the administration. James MacGregor Burns has described the erratic flight of Johnson's Blue Eagle:

. . . Within weeks the NRA burst on the American people like a national call to arms. The NRA eagle was suddenly in every shop window, on magazine covers, in the movies, on girls in chorus lines. Rushing from city to city in an army plane, issuing pronunciamentos at every stop, Johnson orated, politicked, wisecracked, coaxed businessmen into signing codes drawn up by industry representatives hurriedly collected in Washington. The general became the symbol of recovery; for hours he reviewed a climactic parade up Fifth Avenue, trying desperately to greet the endless river of humanity without appearing to give the despised Mussolini salute. Not since 1917 had the whole nation savored such a throbbing sense of unity, of marching together.

But marching where? Almost at the start the President had virtually lost control of the NRA. He told the cabinet one day how Johnson, coattails standing out behind, had rushed into his office, and handed the President three codes to sign. As Roosevelt was signing the last one, Johnson looked at his watch, said he had five minutes to catch his plane, and dashed out, the codes in his pocket. "He hasn't been seen since," Roosevelt added brightly. The President was hardly more than a front man in whose name an elaborate re-employment agreement was arranged and a thousand other actions taken. Johnson himself had to delegate huge policy-making powers to hastily summoned businessmen who might or might not be representative of the myriad interests in their industries. And in the first flush of enthusiasm the NRA coverage was extended so far that the machinery was nearly swamped. An extreme case was the St. Louis bootblack who signed the reemployment agreement, cut his hours to forty a week, and promptly asked the NRA to make up his pay.

The NRA was essentially an expression of the broker state—that is, of the government acting for, and mediating among, the major interest groups. The NRA was the institutional expression of Roosevelt's plan for a partnership of all groups, achieved through friendly cooperation between the government and group leaders. But who were the leaders? It is not surprising that in the haste and confusion Johnson dealt with the business and labor leaders closest at hand, those who were most vocal, best organized, most experienced in dealing with politicians and bureaucrats. Who could speak for that amorphous group, the consumers? . . .

By the end of 1933 the NRA eagle was fluttering through heavy weather "N.R.A. is the worst law ever passed," some disillusioned Cleveland grocers wired the President. . . . the President could not ignore the protests. In March 1934 he appointed a review board under the old reformer and defense attorney Clarence Darrow, which soon was reporting that the codes had allowed the more powerful interests to seize control or extend their control of industries. Roosevelt trimmed NRA's powers, limited its jurisdiction, eased Johnson out, and put a more domesticated chief, Donald Richberg, in his place. But by the time the Supreme Court administered the *coup de grâce* shortly before NRA's second birthday, it was near administrative and political collapse.[4]

Roosevelt himself was resolute. In February, 1935, when he requested a two-year extension of NRA, he claimed:

It is now clear that in the spring and summer of 1933, many estimates of unemployment in the United States were far too low and we are therefore apt to forget today that the National Industrial Recovery Act was the biggest factor in giving reemployment to approximately 4,000,000 people.

In our progress under the Act the age-long curse of child labor has been lifted, the sweatshop outlawed, and millions of wage earners released from starvation wages and excessive hours of labor. Under it a great advance has been made in the opportunities and assurances of collective bargaining between employers and employees. Under it the pattern of a new order of industrial relations is definitely taking shape.

Industry as a whole has also made gains. It has been freed, in part at least, from dishonorable competition brought about not only by overworking and underpaying labor, but by destructive business practices. We have begun to develop new safeguards for small enterprises; and most important of all, business itself recognizes more clearly than at any previous time in our history the advantages and the obligations of cooperation and self-discipline, and the patriotic need of ending unsound financing and unfair practices of all kinds.[5]

And there were pitiful evidences that many had found hope. The most touching were the piles of letters from working people which found their way into NRA files:

A woman in . . . [the southwest wrote];
"Before the New Deal came into effect we was compelled to work 15 hours of each day during the rush and no overtime and fired if you get a [union] card. Now we got our union and we got our decent workweek and we got more girls working here and we got better wages. Where I used to never get more than $8 a week now I don't never get under $13.50. Our life

is no bed of roses because that ain't the way it is for the workers yet but it's better for us than ever I seen it and I been in a factory 9 years since I was 15." . . .

This is from a mid-western town:

"I am a salesman in a chain store. Before NRA I worked 7 A.M. to 10 or 11 P.M. Now two of us work 8 hours a day each. If they don't extend NRA one of us gets fired and the other works 14 or 15 hours." [6]

The permanent result was difficult to fix. Two economists, studying the question in 1940, concluded:

> On the primary question of whether the N. R. A. was in general promotive of recovery, the record is not clear. . . .
> Nor is it possible with assurance to isolate the effects of the N. R. A. from those of the many other forces present during its existence. There is general agreement that in the beginning it "made a definite contribution toward changing the prevailing mood of the country from apprehension to hopeful effort." However, in the later months of its existence it is probable that the uncertainty and conflict of its policies, together with its efforts to raise wages, fix prices, and restrict production, had a retarding effect on recovery. It has been estimated that its policy of spreading work brought about the reemployment of from 1,750,000 to 2,000,000 men. This, however, is no measure of its contribution to recovery.
> Although the Schechter decision ended the legal life of the N. R. A., the forces which gave rise to it were by no means spent. . . .
> In several states "little N. R. A.'s" continued in existence for some time, and the recent movement to secure so-called fair-trade and unfair-trade laws may be traced in part to N. R. A. influences. In the federal sphere, the current regulation of the bituminous coal industry is patterned after the controls attempted in that industry under the N. R. A., and proposals for the

revival of similar N. R. A. controls have been made for
several other industries, notably the cotton textile industry. The present National Labor Relations Act had
its origin in part in the forces stimulated by the
N. R. A. . . .

More significant than these specific results, however,
have been the lessons the N. R. A. has taught organized
groups—both industry and labor—concerning the advantages of united action in pressing for the fulfillment
of their partisan interests; and the precise crystalliza-
tion of sentiment within those groups which it brought
about. The desire thus stimulated to achieve group
advantages has been tempered somewhat, however, by
the realization that conflicting groups may pursue a
similar strategy, and by the fear that there may be pro-
voked more extensive controls by government.[7]

*A later student would point to NRA's monumental
role as a pioneer in social reform and would go on to
remark:*

. . . the experience of solidarity prepared the
nation for a greater and more arduous crisis, which,
when it came, almost seemed an NRA reunion. The
child of the War Industries Board, NRA was the father
of the War Production Board. Leon Henderson, Donald
Nelson, Sidney Hillman, Averell Harriman, William H.
Davis, Isador Lubin, Edward R. Stettinius, Jr.—all had
their training in national mobilization in the breathless
days of 1933 and 1934. For all its defects, NRA represented an essential continuity which in face of crisis
helped preserve American unity.[8]

*AAA, CCC and NRA together fell far short of solving
the most immediate problem—relief to the unemployed.
The proportions of the challenge were ghastly. Dixon
Wecter tells the story of the administration's reaction:*

. . . FERA [Federal Emergency Relief Administration], admittedly a makeshift because of the urgency of the crisis, was set up by Congress on May 12, 1933, to help the needy chiefly with money for direct relief administered through established channels of state and municipal welfare. Beginning with funds of half a billion dollars, it spent eventually about three billion. . . .

Hopkins's thinking drifted steadily away from direct help—the quickest, cheapest and most inclusive type—toward "made work" paid for according to need and, finally, toward a systematic work program at minimum wage rates, which would utilize idle skills. Once he had the immediate crisis under control, he looked about for employment that might foster morale, for the usefulness of the task raised the doer's self-respect and kept his hand in. Hopkins's ideas, however, did not meet with universal agreement. While organized labor feared the effect of low pay for relief work on wages in private industry, many conservatives objected to such relief on quite other grounds. They favored the dole as cheaper, and argued that a public-works program would divert funds from the money market, sometimes undermining existing values (as in the low-cost housing field), and would saddle the nation with huge debts, which in themselves would further retard recovery.

That the mass of people, however, indorsed Hopkins's choice admitted little doubt. After four years of the New Deal, a Gallup poll in May, 1937, reported that four persons out of five approved relief through public works. . . .

The shift from the dole to work relief proceeded so far in later phases of the FERA that in 1935, during the last months of its existence, the agency counted nearly half of its beneficiaries as workers, a total of two and a half million during the peak month of January in that year. The previous winter, however, that of 1933–34, had witnessed the widest expansion of the FERA and of relief rolls in the Great Depression, with nearly eight million households, representing almost twenty-eight million persons, on the lists in February, 1934.

That enormous dilation was due to the fleeting development of a special work-relief branch called the Civil Works Administration, which operated straight from Washington through regional subdivisions, thus avoiding local red tape. . . .

If the usefulness of certain CWA projects was dubious, their general effect was to demonstrate the psychological value of job relief. A Michigan county administrator, observing that "the joy of the men at having even this brief opportunity to earn a decent living wage knew no bounds," saw some leave her office "weeping for sheer happiness." With their initial pay checks many went straight to the barber for their first professional haircut in months, and during the weeks that followed their appearance mirrored further stages in the recovery of self-respect. Naturally the barber himself, along with the grocer, druggist and clothier, also benefited. True, not every relief worker took so blithe an attitude. For the man who had come down in the scale from a professional or technical career to the ranks of crude labor, a certain bitterness was apt to rankle against the whole system. A mechanical engineer, the forty-one-year-old father of seven children, after toiling a few weeks for the CWA wrote ironically about "the idea that ditch-digging is a noble occupation." This agency reached the end of its allotted span in the spring of 1934, its uncompleted projects being taken over by the general FERA program.

On the whole, the FERA raised the tone of state and municipal relief and supported only a small minority of spongers, probably never exceeding ten per cent. Against the stubborn pride of many of the newly poor it sought to lend a certain dignity to the acceptance of aid. . . .

When, within the limits of seasonal fluctuation, it grew clear that New Deal policies were not reducing but apparently augmenting the number on relief, the administration decided to scrap the FERA, returning direct relief wholly to local governments and devoting the federal outlay to able-bodied clients and projects of more durable value. December, 1935, saw the demise of the FERA. . . .

The defects of the FERA and its short-lived offshoot, the CWA, appeared striking beside the record of another venture, the Public Works Administration, organized on June 16, 1933, with an appropriation of $3,300,000,000. The PWA was designed to stimulate heavy industry by fostering public works that required huge quantities of material. President Roosevelt placed it in the hands of cautious, hard-headed Harold L. Ickes, secretary of the interior and self-styled "curmudgeon," whose aversion to using federal funds "to hire grown men to chase tumbleweeds on windy days" colored the whole doctrine of the PWA. . . .

The PWA was conceived by New Dealers as the pump-priming agency best calculated to stimulate private employment, upon the Keynesian theory of compensatory spending. This figure of speech was suggested by the old-fashioned pump, into which water sometimes had to be poured to swell the leather valve before it drew properly. Whether Uncle Sam by priming could coax the pump of industry into efficient operation, or whether he got out of the pump merely the water he had poured into it, occasioned much dispute. Although the PWA was mistrusted by those fearful of a planned economy, it seems early to have had a stimulating effect upon private business. Not adapted primarily to succor the unemployed, the PWA nevertheless kept an average of half a million men steadily at work through the year 1934 under a thirty-hour week. By the time it began liquidation in the early forties, it had spent over four billion dollars upon more than thirty-four thousand projects.

Their social usefulness admitted no question. . . .

Of special significance for the future, the PWA between 1933 and 1935 financed the building of more than fifty military airports, helped the army lay out seventy-four thousand miles of strategic highways, built a wind tunnel for plane designers, employed ten million dollars in renovating ordnance and improving arsenals, and under navy supervision used two hundred thirty-seven million dollars in constructing warships.*

In the summer of 1933 Roosevelt had little notion of either the Keynesian philosophy which would eventually appear to match his program so well, or of the monumental expense it would involve. But he did fret uneasily over the apparent conflict between his economy mood and relief spending. In July he went to the people with his third Fireside Chat to sell the magic of a dual budget—one balanced and the other unbalanced—to sell the mood of inspired experiment:

It may seem inconsistent for a government to cut down its regular expenses and at the same time to borrow and to spend billions for an emergency. But it is not inconsistent because a large portion of the emergency money has been paid out in the form of sound loans which will be repaid to the Treasury over a period of years; and to cover the rest of the emergency money we have imposed taxes to pay the interest and the installments on that part of the debt.

So you will see that we have kept our credit good. We have built a granite foundation in a period of confusion. That foundation of the Federal credit stands there broad and sure. It is the base of the whole recovery plan. . . .

. . . While we are making this great common effort there should be no discord and dispute. This is no time to cavil or to question the standard set by this universal agreement. It is time for patience and understanding

and cooperation. . . . I cannot guarantee the success of
this nationwide plan, but the people of this country can
guarantee its success. I have no faith in "cure-alls" but
I believe that we can greatly influence economic forces.
I have no sympathy with the professional economists
who insist that things must run their course and that
human agencies can have no influence on economic
ills. One reason is that I happen to know that professional economists have changed their definition of
economic laws every five or ten years for a very long
time, but I do have faith, and retain faith, in the
strength of the common purpose, and in the strength of
unified action taken by the American people.[10]

Early in May, 1933, Anne O'Hare McCormick wrote:

     . . . one is dazed by the dimensions of this
program, enacted or ready for enactment in the short
space of two months. Seen whole, however, it does not
appear so inconsistent as did the individual measures
as they issued hot, sometimes half-baked, from the
hopper. The strictly deflationary measures, such as the
cuts in pensions, salaries and government costs and the
closing of banks, are surgical measures for chronic
tumors in the political and financial systems. The inflationary measures are strong, perhaps dangerous, stimu-
lants to recovery. Whether they work or not, whether
the savings effected by the right hand are squandered by
the left, it is clear that the unhealthy growths had to be
pruned away before progress could be made in any
direction.

    But that is not all. The administration is not only
moving in two directions at once in the domestic field;
it charts two opposite roads in world policy and pro-
ceeds to follow them both. Mr. Roosevelt drafts tentative plans for a possible state of economic isolation in

which the United States will sustain itself and as far as possible contain itself. At the same time he has spent one month out of his two in conference with the representatives of other governments.

In a magnificent effort to turn back the tides into their natural channels, he has dramatically placed himself at the head of the world.[11]

But sometimes the disparate threads of policy were so far apart that not even Roosevelt could "weave them together." Stark decisions had to be made. Such was the case when F.D.R. faced a showdown in June, 1933, on this question: Would recovery be geared to international co-operation, or would the United States insulate itself to climb the hill alone? The occasion was the London Economic Conference which Roosevelt had inherited from Hoover. The incident was the conference's determination to stabilize the major currencies in terms of gold. At stake was the President's freedom to manipulate domestic currency in an attempt to raise prices. At stake also was the whole nationalistic orientation of AAA and NRA. The setting was a welter of confused instructions and lack of instructions, a planless and disorganized American delegation.

Forced to decide, the President chose the path of nationalism, and blasted the conference with a cable which repudiated gold stabilization. Drafted at sea, without State Department advice, it shocked London:

I would regard it as a catastrophe amounting to a world tragedy if the great Conference of Nations, called to bring about a more real and permanent financial stability and a greater prosperity to the masses of all Nations, should, in advance of any serious effort to consider these broader problems, allow itself to be diverted by the proposal of a purely artificial and temporary experiment affecting the monetary exchange of a few Nations only. Such action, such diversion, shows a singular lack of proportion and a failure to remember the larger purposes for which the Economic Conference originally was called together. . . .

The sound internal economic system of a Nation is a greater factor in its well-being than the price of its currency in changing terms of the currencies of other Nations.

It is for this reason that reduced cost of Government, adequate Government income, and ability to service Government debts are all so important to ultimate stability. So too, old fetishes of so-called international bankers are being replaced by efforts to plan national currencies with the objective of giving to those currencies a continuing purchasing power which does not greatly vary in terms of the commodities and the need of modern civilization.[12]

This message "torpedoed" the conference and aroused lingering hostilities in England and France. At home Roosevelt attempted during the fall to raise prices by devaluing the dollar. He and his close advisers set the price of gold each morning at breakfast, jumping about arbitrarily to discourage speculation but generally trending upward until the gold content of the currency had decreased by forty per cent. This resort to the "commodity dollar"—Al Smith called it the "baloney dollar"—was disappointing. Its chief result was to siphon gold into Fort Knox from abroad. The Silver Purchase Act of June, 1934, a victory for western inflationists, had a similar impact. The policy threatened to make the United States the "cemetery for the world's precious metals," Dixon Wecter has noted, but "a president who tried everything was bound to make mistakes."[13]

In fact, the President had approached inflation tentatively and uneasily. F.D.R. told his press conference in April, 1933:

So much of the legislation we have had this
spring is of a deflationary character, in the sense that it
locks up money or prevents the flow of money, that
we are faced with the problem of offsetting that in
some way. I would not say "inflation of the currency,"
because that is not the necessary meaning . . . we have
not yet caught up with the deflation that we have already caused.[14]

To Ickes Roosevelt confided: ". . . that there was an
agrarian revolt on in the country and that this was our
chief concern just now. . . . There is a burden of debt
weighing down upon everybody, especially the farmer,
and while cheap money doesn't buy much in the way
of goods, it does pay debts." [15]
To the people Roosevelt explained:

I do not hesitate to say in the simplest,
clearest language of which I am capable, that although
the prices of many products of the farm have gone up
and although many farm families are better off than
they were last year, I am not satisfied with the amount
or the extent of the rise, and that it is definitely a part
of our policy to increase that rise and to extend it to
those products which have as yet felt no benefit. If we
cannot do this one way we will do it another. Do it,
we will. . . .[16]

In January, 1934, the President sought broader inflationary powers and blamed the problem largely on
the alleged failure of business to co-operate:

Let me give you a little background on this
particular thing, because I think it is important. Last
spring things went up much too fast in this country.
Wheat went up to $1.25, which, undoubtedly, was al-
together too high. That was caused by speculation. A

great many manufacturers overproduced, all for various reasons, trying to get in under the wire before the Code went into effect.

The result was a perfectly natural one. There was quite a big drop in commodity prices of all kinds around the middle of July. That was a perfectly healthy thing. But a little bit later on, somewhere around September, there began a very definite drift of commodity prices downward. That was caused by a great many factors. It was caused by people who did not approve of the N.R.A. codes, it was caused by some of our foreign friends who were deliberately trying to increase the exchange value of the dollar and decrease the exchange value of the franc—there were a good many foreign elements that entered into it.

The result was that by the tenth or fifteenth of October we were in a definite downward drift which, if carried out, would have been a serious thing. . . .

That was when we took action on gold. . . .

It has, I think, been felt by people on the other side as well as here that if we had not pursued the gold-purchase policy, the actual exchange-value rate on gold would be four dollars instead of five dollars.[17]

AAA, NRA, work-relief spending and price manipulation were the core of the New Deal recovery program. But in the margins appeared a score or more of special acts to provide emergency aid. The Home Owners' Loan Corporation in the summer of 1933, and the Federal Housing Authority in 1934, brought relief to harried mortgage debtors. The Railway Transportation Act in 1933, and the Municipal and Corporate Bankruptcy Acts a year later, sought solutions for some of the most urgent problems faced by these institutions. The National Youth Administration in 1935 added a facet to the relief program designed to fill the gap between CCC and the adult-oriented WPA programs. 1934 saw the inauguration of the Export-Import Bank and the Reciprocal Trade Agreements Act to promote overseas markets along the lines sought by Cordell Hull and other devotees of free trade. From the spring of 1934 on the central emphasis was upon heavy deficit spending for work relief. Congress itself led the way when it refused Roosevelt's second "economy" bill for government operations.

In the confusion of politics and special interests it would prove all but impossible to appraise precisely the success of the recovery program. And the coming of war in Europe in 1939 would provide an artificial stimulus which would befog the ultimate impact.

On the surface results were impressive. National income rose from 40 billion in 1932 to 71.2 billion at its high in 1937. Even after the recession of 1938 it dropped only to 69.4 billion in 1939. But by ideal standards recovery was incomplete. There remained much unemployment, about seven and a half million early in 1938. Population had increased by 10 million since 1929, industrial productivity had improved and a higher national income might have been expected under normal conditions. Deficit spending had a direct impact, especially in offsetting the 1938 recession, but its "snowballing" effect was disappointing. Partly this grew from lack of business confidence; banks responded to cheap money less by extending new credit than by investing in stocks and bonds. The deficit itself was tiny by later standards, monumental by past precedents. The total government deficit between 1931 and 1938 was approximately 20 billion dollars, but about 12 billion of this was in new construction of permanent value or in loans that would be repaid.

The final balance must be struck in a broader context. In 1939, as war approached, the nation was not bankrupt—fiscally, politically or morally. As Arthur Schlesinger, Jr., has pointed out:

Much of the New Deal was imperfect, abortive, or ambiguous. Roosevelt's own administrative methods were insouciant, disorderly, and often demoralizing. But the shortcomings of the New Deal vanish in the general perspective of its supreme success: that is, in the restoration of America as a fighting faith, and in the restoration of democracy as a workable way of life.[18]

NOTES, *chapter 6*

1. Dexter Perkins, *The New Age of Franklin Roosevelt, 1932–1945*, 16-17.

2. Raymond Moley, *After Seven Years*, 184.

3. Samuel Rosenman, ed., *The Public Papers and Addresses of Franklin D. Roosevelt*, II, 251-252.

4. James M. Burns, *Roosevelt, the Lion and the Fox*, 192-193.

5. *Public Papers*, IV, 80-81.

6. M. D. Vincent and Beulah Amidon, "NRA: A Trial Balance," *Survey-Graphic*, XXIV (1935), 335, 364.

7. Leverett S. Lyon and Victor Abramson, *Government and Economic Life* (Brookings Institution, 1939–1940), II, 1056-1057, 1059-1061.

8. Arthur M. Schlesinger, Jr., *The Coming of the New Deal*, 176.

9. Dixon Wecter, *The Age of the Great Depression, 1929–1941* (Macmillan, 1948), 72-78.

10. *Public Papers*, II, 296, 302-303.

11. Anne O'Hare McCormick, *The World at Home: Selections from the Writings of Anne O'Hare McCormick*, 202.

12. *Public Papers*, II, 264-265.

13. Wecter, *Depression*, 69.

14. *Public Papers*, II, 119-120.

15. Harold Ickes, *The Secret Diary of Harold L. Ickes, The First Thousand Days, 1933–1936* (Simon and Schuster, 1953), I, 110.

16. *Public Papers*, II, 423.

17. *Public Papers*, III, 48-49.

18. Arthur M. Schlesinger, Jr., "The Broad Accomplishments of the New Deal," in Seymour Harris, ed., *Saving American Capitalism: A Liberal Economic Program* (Knopf, 1948), 80.

chapter 7 THE MOOD OF REFORM

The President's Annual Message to Congress on January 4, 1935, launched the Second New Deal. It announced a fresh start almost as if a new administration were being inaugurated. Achievements of the previous two years were dismissed perfunctorily: credit was taken for recovery only in the fields of agriculture, industrial production, and profits. Social justice was the new goal. Reform was declared to be inseparable from recovery. . . .

Security of the men, women, and children of the nation was named as the central objective. A program was submitted to Congress designed to establish three types of security—"a program which because of many lost years will take many future years to fulfill." Stranded populations in the city and country should be rescued by better use of natural resources and intelligent distribution of means of livelihood. Unemployment and old-age insurance, benefits for destitute children, mothers, sick and physically handicapped persons should provide security against the major hazards of life. Housing was the third part of the program. Each of these problems of security had already been the subject of experimentation and comprehensive studies. But the President now gave up expectation that unemployment would be solved immediately by private enterprise and the NRA, and asked that it be dealt with in ways which would carry out the program for security. Recovery would be stimulated by the federal government pouring purchasing power into the hands of the least privileged

groups, rather than by encouraging price rises which
would increase profits and "seep down" in the form of
higher wages to groups which would use their increased
purchasing power to stimulate recovery. The shift from
the latter program to the former, which was the shift
from the First to the Second New Deal, was neither
absolute nor sudden. The most practical justification
for the change was the failure of the First New Deal,
particularly NRA, to produce sound economic recovery,
and the security program of 1935 was launched only
after thorough experiment with the more conservative
methods of achieving recovery. . . .

The new work relief program [WPA] would super-
sede FERA and all but a few normal public building
operations of the PWA. Payment of the workers should
be at a security wage level, higher than the existing dole
but not so high as to discourage acceptance of private
employment. . . .

The broad political significance of the launching of
the security program of 1935 was that it ended the
period during which the administration had supported
economic policies of businessmen and established new
ties of mutual support between the administration and
all other groups of the population.[1]

Between January and June, 1935, there was a sharp
turn to the "left," and the charting of a second New
Deal. Roosevelt did gradually abandon the search for
co-operative balance among business, labor and agriculture. He did adopt a new tactic of making government
the protector of the weak, the make-weight against
economic concentration, the architect and engineer of
social planning.

But the intensity of the new departure concealed the
current of reform which ran through the Roosevelt
program from the beginning. In his September, 1932,
proposal for broad regulation of public utilities, F.D.R.
had said:

I believe that the "new deal," as you and I know it, can be applied to a whole lot of things. It can be applied very definitely to the relationship between the electric utilities on the one side, and the consumer and investor on the other.

True regulation is for the equal benefit of the consumer and the investor. The only man who will suffer from true regulation is the speculator, or the unscrupulous promoter who levies tribute equally from the man who buys service and from the man who invests his savings in this great industry.

I seek to protect both the consumer and the investor. . . . [2]

And he had seen the chief cause of the "railway problem" in ". . . the entire absence of any national planning for the continuance and operation of this absolutely vital national utility. The individual railroads should be regarded as part of a national transportation system." [3]

Nowhere was Roosevelt's deep commitment to reform and social planning more strikingly portrayed than in the Tennessee Valley Authority (1933). Here was a chance in one gigantic stroke to advance the cause of conservation, of publicly owned electrical power, of flood control and navigation improvement. Here was an opportunity to deepen the quality of rural life which Roosevelt so romantically idealized. In any event Roosevelt had no choice but action. His own peculiar contribution was in folding the many objectives into a single package, and in the concept of the public corporation to provide an integrated development. Arthur Schlesinger, Jr., has described the problem of the Valley:

The basin of the Tennessee River spilled over seven southern states—Tennessee, Alabama, Georgia, Mississippi, North Carolina, Kentucky, and

Virginia. The streams began high up in the mountains —in the Great Smokies and in the Blue Ridge, in the Iron Mountains and in the Unakas—and flowed into the valleys below. Near Knoxville the Holston and the French Broad Rivers joined to form the Tennessee; and for six hundred and fifty miles the Tennessee straggled and meandered across the state, now narrow and rushing, now wide and placid, curving south, then west, across northern Alabama to touch Mississippi, then turning north again through Tennessee and Kentucky to flow finally into the Ohio at Paducah. Together with its tributaries, it drained an area of forty thousand square miles.

There was a wide variety of life and landscape in the Valley, from the soaring trees of the Great Smokies through the bare, bleak hills of eastern Tennessee and the lazy cotton country of Alabama to the flat red lands of the west. But one condition united the Valley— poverty. Before the Civil War, a few great planters had lived in magnolia-scented affluence. These had been the exception; most people in the Valley had no slaves and scratched their living from a reluctant soil. After the war, northerners came into the region and eyed its stands of virgin timber. They set up logging mills, cut up the hardwood forests, changed a small farming country into a lumbering country, and then departed, leaving the natives stranded amidst abandoned lumber camps. This was the start of a pattern of exploitation and retreat. "Three fortunes had been taken off that country," said Arthur E. Morgan, an eminent civil engineer, with whom Roosevelt discussed the Tennessee problem, "—forests, oil and gas." Only poverty remained—poverty, with thousands on thousands of families who never saw $100 cash income a year; with meager industrial development and little investment capital; with the decay of schools and the deterioration of government; with the spread of tuberculosis and pellagra.

And there appeared no way out. Each year fifty-two inches of rain fell, swelling rivers into angry torrents, flooding the land and carrying away strength and fertility from the soil. The forests, so sadly thin and over cut, were further depleted by burning. Income was less than half the national average. Only two out of every hundred farms had electricity. In the fall of 1933, over half the families in the highland counties were on relief; in one county the rolls included 87 per cent of the families. There seemed no protection against flood, fire or erosion—no alternative to further descent into squalor. "The wreckage of rugged individualism," said Morgan, "has been handed to us with a request that we try to do something about it." *

Roosevelt's opportunity arose from the existence of the Wilson Dam at Muscle Shoals, begun during World War I to provide power for the manufacture of nitrates. Throughout the twenties a coterie of senators, led by George Norris of Nebraska, had held out for public operation of the dam. Against vetoes by Coolidge and Hoover they had been unable to do more, however, than prevent the give-away of the facilities to private interests. Now they flocked to the sympathetic man in the White House for fulfillment of their dreams.

David Lilienthal, for many years director of TVA, has summed up succinctly the philosophy of the program:

> For the first time since the trees fell before the settlers' ax, America set out to command nature not by defying her, as in that wasteful past, but by understanding and acting upon her first law—the oneness of men and natural resources, the unity that binds together land, streams, forests, minerals, farming, industry, mankind. . . .

The message of President Roosevelt urging approval of the Norris bill (which became a law with his signature on May 18, 1933) boldly proposed a new and fundamental change in the development of our country's resources. The words of the President's message were not only eloquent; there was in them a creativeness and an insight born of his New York State experience in establishing regional planning as a political reality. That understanding was matured at his Georgia home, in long days of thinking of the problems of the South and its relation to the whole nation.

It is clear [the message read] that the Muscle Shoals development is but a small part of the potential public usefulness of the entire Tennessee River. Such use, if envisioned in its entirety, transcends mere power development: it enters the wide fields of flood control, soil erosion, afforestation, elimination from agricultural use of marginal lands, and distribution and diversification of industry. In short, this power development of war days leads logically to national planning for a complete river watershed involving many states and the future lives and welfare of millions. It touches and gives life to all forms of human concerns.

The President then suggested

legislation to create a Tennessee Valley Authority— a corporation clothed with the power of government but possessed of the flexibility and initiative of a private enterprise. It should be charged with the broadest duty of planning for the proper use, conservation, and development of the natural resources of the Tennessee River drainage basin and its adjoining territory for the general social and economic welfare of the Nation. This authority should also be clothed with the necessary power to carry these plans into effect. Its duty should be the rehabilitation of the Muscle Shoals development and the co-ordination of it with the wider plan.

Many hard lessons have taught us the human waste that results from lack of planning. Here and there a few wise cities and counties have looked ahead and planned. But our Nation has "just grown." It is time to extend planning to a wider field, in this instance comprehending in one great project many States directly concerned with the basin of one of our greatest rivers.

The TVA Act was nothing inadvertent or impromptu. It was rather the deliberate and well-considered creation of a new national policy. For the first time in the history of the nation, the resources of a river were not only to be "envisioned in their entirety"; they were to be developed *in that unity with which nature herself regards her resources*—the waters, the land, and the forests together, a "seamless web"—just as Maitland saw "the unity of all history," of which one strand cannot be touched without affecting every other strand for good or ill.

Under this new policy, the opportunity of creating wealth for the people from the resources of this valley was to be faced as a single problem. . . .

What God had made one, man was to develop as one.

"Envisioned in its entirety" this river, like every river in the world, had many potential assets. It could yield hydro-electric power for the comfort of the people in their homes, could promote prosperity on their farms and foster the development of industry. But the same river by the very same dams, if they were wisely designed, could be made to provide a channel for navigation. The river could also be made to provide fun for fishermen and fish for food, pleasure from boating and swimming, a water supply for homes and factories. But the river also presented an account of liabilities. It threatened the welfare of the people by its recurrent floods; pollution from industrial wastes and public sewage diminished its value as a source of water supply and for recreation; its current carried to the sea the soil of the hills and fields to be lost there to men forever.

To a single agency, the TVA, these potentialities of the river for good and evil were entrusted. But the river was to be seen as part of the larger pattern of the region, one asset of the many that in nature are interwoven: the land, the minerals, the waters, the forests—and all of these as one—in their relation to the lives of the valley's people. It was the total benefit to all that was to be the common goal and the new agency's responsibility.

That is not the way public resource development had heretofore been undertaken in this country. Congress in creating TVA broke with the past. No single agency had in this way ever been assigned the unitary task of developing a river so as to release the total benefit from its waters for the people. . . .

How industry came to Ducktown in the mountains of eastern Tennessee a generation ago is one such a story [of unplanned exploitation]. Copper ore was discovered; mining began; a smeltery was built. One of the resources of this remote region was being developed; it meant new jobs, income to supplement farming and forestry. But the developers had only copper in their plans. The magnificent hardwood forests to a distance of seven miles were cut and burned as fuel for the smelter's roasting ovens. The sulphur fumes from the stacks destroyed the thin cover that remained; not only the trees but every sign of living vegetation was killed and the soil became poison to life.

The dead land, shorn of its cover of grass and trees was torn mercilessly by the rains; and the once lovely and fruitful earth was cut into deep gullies that widened into desolate canyons twenty and more feet deep. No one can look upon this horror as it is today without a shudder. Silt, swept from unprotected slopes, filled the

streams and destroyed fish life. The water was robbed
of its value for men, for animals, and for industry, while
farther down the stream a reservoir of a private power
company was filling with silt. One of Ducktown's resources, copper, had been developed. But all its other
resources had been destroyed in the process. The
people and their institutions suffered in the end. . . .

We have a choice. There is the important fact. Men
are not powerless; they have it in their hands to use
the machine to augment the dignity of human existence. . . .

Whether happiness or unhappiness, freedom or
slavery, in short whether good or evil results from an
improved environment depends largely upon how the
change has been brought about, upon the methods by
which the physical results have been reached, and in
what spirit and for what purpose the fruits of that
change are used. . . .

There is a . . . widely held objection to such an enterprise as we have seen in this valley. The hideous belief
has been spread over the earth that the price of material
progress and freedom from want must be the complete
surrender of individual freedom. . . .

In this one valley (in some ways the world in mi-
crocosm) it has been demonstrated that methods can be
developed—methods I have described as grassroots
democracy—which do create an opportunity for greater
happiness and deeper experience, for freedom, in the
very course of technical progress. Indeed this valley,
even in the brief span of a decade, supports a conviction
that when the use of technology has a moral purpose
and when its methods are thoroughly democratic, far
from forcing the surrender of individual freedom and
the things of the spirit to the machine, the machine
can be made to promote those very ends.[5]

By December, 1933, Roosevelt was thinking grandly

of a great national authority to promote similar work in all the major river valleys. By February, 1935, there were over twenty bills in Congress for such regional authorities, ranging from the Missouri to the Columbia, to the Merrimac and the Brazos. But all was not smooth. Expenditures would be enormous; there were conflicting vested interests in the Departments of Interior, War and Agriculture. There were arguments about purposes among the three original directors of TVA, and gradually the electrical power objective seemed to outrun the more idealistic and difficult concepts of social rehabilitation. While TVA flourished under the happy sponsorship of both New Dealers and Southern congressmen, other ambitious projects remained in the dream stage or were carried on by more limited techniques on the Columbia, the Colorado and the Missouri.

The focus of the opposition remained the competition between government and the private-power interests. Wendell Willkie, President of Commonwealth and Southern, whose local power company was being driven to the wall, spoke sharply for the utilities:

Like England's once famous military formation, the British Square, the TVA has had four fronts to present to the public, and it uses the front most suitable to the group which it is addressing. Before the courts it claims that it is not really a power enterprise, but primarily a conservation activity. . . . Only before a more sympathetic audience is it frankly an instrument for the electrification of America. . . .

Outside of the courtroom, the advocates of the TVA have been less guarded in their statements. . . .

And it seems likely that no one of the three Directors would today deny that the generation and sale of power constitute a major function if not the major function of the Tennessee Valley Authority. . . .

The American people, therefore, are paying more than half a billion dollars for eleven dams, chiefly designed to supply power to one area. But this power, as will shortly be demonstrated, is to be supplied to this area at *less than cost.* In other words, the TVA will operate annually at a deficit, and these annual deficits must, of course, be paid out of the pockets of the tax-payers.

The sponsors of the TVA maintained at the beginning that this vast program was not designed to create a competitive power system, but to set up a yardstick by which the rates of the private companies could be judged. The yardstick idea was undoubtedly attractive, since, after all, the average consumer did not understand much about electric rates and had no way of personally checking their relative highness or lowness.

Unfortunately, the yardstick is rubber from the first inch to the last.

From the generation of power at the beginning to its distribution to the ultimate consumer at the end, the TVA enjoys privileges and exemptions which are denied to the private utility, which conceal the true cost of TVA power, and the cost of which comes out of the pockets of you and me as taxpayers. . . .

Since the TVA is apparently selling its power at less than cost, it should say so. If people who live in New York City, for example, are to pay part of the electric bill of people who live in Corinth, Mississippi, the people in New York should know about it. . . .

Also, if the TVA is attempting to force the utilities into public ownership, it should employ means that will neither deceive nor injure the public and will not jeopardize the interest of utility investors.[6]

Roosevelt himself persisted in the broader view. In November, 1934, he told the newsmen accompanying him to Georgia:

Power is really a secondary matter. What we are doing there is taking a watershed with about three and a half million people in it, almost all of them rural, and we are trying to make a different type of citizen out of them, not what they would be under their present conditions. . . . So TVA is primarily intended to change and to improve the standards of living of the people of that Valley.

. . . You talk about a "yardstick of power." Harcourt Morgan is running the fertilizer end of it and at Muscle Shoals he is turning out, . . . a phosphate. . . . Now, at once the fertilizer companies . . . they say, "Are you going into the fertilizer business?" The answer is a very simple one. The plant is primarily an experimental plant. That is the primary purpose . . . if the farmers all through that area can be taught that that type of fertilizer at x number of dollars a ton is the best thing for them to use, then it is up to the National Fertilizer Association and its affiliated companies to meet that price. . . . We will know what the cost of manufacture is, and it is very easy to say what a reasonable profit is. Now, if those gentlemen fail to avail themselves of this perfectly magnificent opportunity to conduct a sound business and make a profit well, it is just too bad. Then somebody will get up in Congress and say, "These fellows are not meeting their opportunities and the farmers will have to have the fertilizer and of course we will have to provide it." But I, for one, hope that that day will never come. . . .[7]

The controversy over the yardstick dragged on. TVA carried many responsibilities which no private power company had to shoulder. There was no magic formula which could dictate how much of the overhead should be charged to power-production. Private interests, fighting incessantly what they thought to be a giant step toward government planning and the destruction of corporate free enterprise, insisted that costs were being hidden by assessing too much overhead to flood and navigation control. And TVA paid no taxes. The Valley Authority pointed to its payments in lieu of taxes to local governments and insisted that its bookkeeping allocations were accurate. In any case rates to the consumer through co-operatives and municipal light companies were often lower than before TVA. And the consumption of power mounted sharply; in some areas it nearly doubled by the outbreak of the War.

Meanwhile the broad program of co-ordinated valley development advanced along a ragged front. Some hastily conceived educational programs had to be given up. Some of the ambitions for industrial development were scaled down. Great strides were made in the conservation of resources and in the social and economic rehabilitation of the farming community. Whatever the arguments over fundamental theory, TVA set records for efficiency and freedom from political patronage. And the people of the valley became confirmed converts to the idea, as the new power began to reach their homes with the help of the Electric Farm and Home Authority and the Rural Electrification Administration.

TVA had deep roots and a well-planned future. But the great bulk of Roosevelt-reform in the first two years was the product of emergency, economic or political. This was the case with the Railroad Transportation Act of June, 1933, which wrote into law Roosevelt's campaign promise of co-ordinate planning and aid for the tottering transportation network. This was the case with the Indian Reorganization Act of June, 1934, compelled by the sheer desperation of the nation's most mistreated wards. The evident bankruptcy of traditional policy had opened the door to a new experiment in the reaffirmation of tribal independence and integrity under the inspired leadership of John Collier. And emergency accounted also for the creation of a United States Employment Service and the imposition of sharp controls on the air lines to prevent frauds which had become notorious in air-mail contracts.

Nowhere was the immediacy of crisis more apparent than in the extensive revision of the banking and securities laws. In fact, the public demand was overwhelming, fed as it was by the great crash and by the dramatic admissions of irresponsibility drawn from leading bankers by Ferdinand Pecora in a Senate Committee during the 1932 lame-duck session. Roosevelt had no alternative; indeed Congress itself took the initiative. As Denis Brogan has said:

. . . Senator Glass of Virginia, with the authority of a former Secretary of the Treasury and an author of the Federal Reserve System, was for drastic measures against the "little corner grocerymen who run banks." He wanted all banks integrated into the Federal Reserve System. He battled on the floor of the Senate the rising hope of the rural radicals, Senator Long of Louisiana, who defended the "State banks at the forks of the creeks of this country." The final Glass-Steagall Act of June 1, 1933, represented an uneasy compromise between the views of Glass and the much less conservative opinions of Representative Steagall and of that great body of American opinion which was profoundly suspicious of all banking orthodoxy.

The great novelty of the Glass-Steagall Act was the creation of a Federal corporation to insure small bank deposits. There were strong theoretical objections to such a course; the well-managed banks were made to pay for the badly managed banks over whose policies they had no control. State schemes of this type had been widely tried and had failed. But it was necessary

to restore faith in banking. The Act, too, forced a
separation of deposit from investment banking, an over-
due reform made imperative by the revelations of the
current investigation of various large banking houses.
. . . The Federal Reserve Board was given broad powers
in curbing speculative credit expansion by member
banks. But although no open system of Federal control of credit was enacted, even at the moment when the
low public standing of bankers was one of the current
ribald jokes all over the nation, the Glass-Steagall Act,
together with the control over the dollar given to
President Roosevelt, ended the old autonomy of the
American credit structure, and, largely unnoticed, began an extraordinary extension of the directing and
regulating powers of the Treasury Department. . . .[8]

As a friendly commentator noted: "The deposit
insurance system turned out, of course, to be one of the
most brilliant and successful accomplishments of the
Hundred Days. . . . In the end, the total bank sus-
pensions for the entire rest of the decade were less than
those in any year of the twenties—and were less than
8 per cent of those in the single year of 1933. . . ."[9]
Even more completely unavoidable in 1933 had
been the regulation of securities' sales. But here Roosevelt was caught in a welter of conflicting advice. He
finally turned aside varied plans for direct regulation
and chose the approach of Felix Frankfurter and his
protégés, James M. Landis and Benjamin Cohen. The
hastily drafted bill shelved for the moment the regulation of the stock exchanges and concentrated upon en-
suring to investors accurate and full information about
new securities issues. The White House explained this
"Truth-in-Securities" Act:

[8] D. W. Brogan, *The Era of Franklin D. Roosevelt.* Vol. 52, THE
CHRONICLES OF AMERICA, pp. 53-54, Copyright Yale University Press,
1950. Reprinted by permission of the publisher.

The plan is to protect the public by inform-
ing the investor, by requiring the issuer to lodge with
the Federal Trade Commission information which must
be true, before the securities can be offered for sale in
interstate commerce, and by providing that otherwise
the issuer will subject himself to a criminal penalty. It
requires all advertisements for the sale of such securities
in interstate commerce to carry definite informative
facts that will put the purchaser on notice. It changes
the ancient doctrine of caveat emptor to "let the seller
beware," and puts the burden on the seller rather than
the buyer.[10]

While financiers howled at this interference, advocates of regulation like Tugwell, Berle and William
O. Douglas, protested that it was a pale gesture, twenty-
five years out of date.

In the spring of 1934 the more violent battle was
fought over exchange regulation. In February Roosevelt
had posed the major problem himself, when he told
Congress:

. . . outside the field of legitimate investment, naked speculation has been made far too alluring
and far too easy for those who could and for those who
could not afford to gamble . . . it should be our national
policy to restrict, as far as possible the use of these exchanges for purely speculative operations.[11]

The bill which finally passed established a new
Securities Exchange Commission with broad powers to
control margins, to investigate, and to press for new
rules on the exchanges. Roosevelt moved to regain
business confidence with the appointment of a distinguished financier and Democrat as head of the new
Commission, Joseph P. Kennedy. But the measure
staked out a new era in finance.

It was a political as much as an economic crisis that cast Roosevelt in a prolabor role. Personally reluctant, he was forced to it by senators like Robert F. Wagner and Hugo Black. The particular crisis was Black's thirty-hour bill. Frances Perkins has described some of F.D.R.'s objections:

> The President, with his gift for the concrete, put his finger on a major difficulty. "What will they do in the dairy industry, the milk evaporating and canning industry? How can they put that on a thirty-hour week and still come out square?"
>
> He drew upon his experience as a farmer. "There is not a great shortage of jobs in my part of the country. There is bad unemployment in the great cities, but you can't take city men and put them in dairying. There have to be hours adapted to the rhythm of the cow."
>
> The "rhythm of the cow" became one of his favorite expressions when he talked about the Black bill at cabinet meetings and other conferences.
>
> Although sympathetic with the objective, he was doubtful that this bill would solve the unemployment problem. In fact, he was quite certain that it wouldn't. He was committed to the idea of a dynamic economy . . . rather than an economy of curtailment of production. He could not feel that a reduction to thirty hours a week was essential even for the health and welfare of the people. "Is there any harm," he would say, "in people working an eight-hour day and forty-eight hours a week?"
>
> The President also believed the Black Bill unconstitutional. . . .
>
> Finally we agreed that I should go before the congressional committee holding hearings on the bill. I would propose amendments to guarantee a floor under wages, that is, some kind of minimum wage machinery. I would point out the necessity for possibilities of varia-

tion from the strict application of the thirty-hour
week. . . .

. . . Roosevelt was fully committed. From that time
on, Congress, the newspapers, the people, knew he was
in favor of doing something by law to mitigate the hard-
ships of unemployment by techniques of control of
hours, wages, and working conditions. He was committed to the principle but not to this particular
program.[12]

Section 7 (a) of the NRA seemed at first an adequate
answer, providing as it did for labor participation in
code-making and inclusion of collective-bargaining
guarantees. Workers were at first enthusiastic. But the
specific administrative rulings soon assumed an anti-
union bias. By early 1935 union men were calling it
the "National Run Around," and A. F. of L. President
William Green was promising that labor would fight
Roosevelt in the next election.

As the President confronted Congress in January,
1935, there was more than labor's frustration to
strengthen his mood of reform. One force was the Congressional election itself, a sweeping Democratic victory.
William Allen White noted, "He has been all but
crowned by the people." There was reason for renewed
confidence here, but there was also a rankling compulsion to shift ground. The balance of his party in Congress had edged significantly to the left in the election.
And Roosevelt had faced the intemperate wrath of a
business community egged on by the Liberty League,
which spoke with Al Smith's voice. There seemed no
longer a politic reason to restrain reform in hope of
business support.

There was the natural momentum of the moment;
relief and recovery programs were well under way. The
next step was redress of the social imbalances. The
mushrooming problems of NRA cast doubts on indus-

trial self-government. And the momentum was strengthened by the wave of philosophical justification the New Dealers themselves had been producing. Roosevelt was immersed in an atmosphere of social planning. The National Planning Board reported to Roosevelt in 1934:

> Planning is not mechanical and organizational alone, but must rest within a set of general understandings, on values to which the nation is devoted, and for which it is willing to sacrifice lesser values. The general understanding on which our democratic system rests is that the happiness and interests of the people are paramount and that special privilege and personal ambition are subordinate to the larger national and popular purpose.
>
> Democracy assumes that the gains of civilization are essentially mass gains, and should be enjoyed by the whole people who created them, rather than by special classes or persons.
>
> Our government was set up for this purpose, and national planning should be directed toward this end. Ways and means of attaining these ends vary from time to time, but the general aim and purpose of our national endeavor is plain. Plans directed toward this end fall within the scope and spirit of the Constitution and of our American national goals. . . .
>
> Statesmanlike planning might prevent the vast losses caused by inattention, as in the case of soil erosion and flood and misuse of national resources. It might prevent the wastes arising from conflicting and clashing policies, as in the case of land reclamation and land retirement, the industrial wastes arising from lack of reasonable co-ordination, the still more tragic wastage of human material through inattention to the protection and security of productive labor. It might make possible the invention of new technological and managerial

devices for increasing the productivity of mankind and social devices for insuring the just participation of our people in their products.

. . . What stands between us and the realization of the hopes that gleamed before the eyes of our people from the earliest days are only our own attitudes and our social and political management.

. . . It is not our capacity to produce that fails us, but our capacity to plan the wisest use of our wealth of resources in materials and men.[13]

There had been changes in the thinking of the nation, too. Anne O'Hare McCormick reported in September, 1934:

. . . one striking fact emerges: no longer does everybody in America expect to grow rich. The young, especially, are deliberately facing a future in which they count on making no more than a living. Many do not even aspire to be rich. A lot of "front" has disappeared, and with it some stiffening ambition. In the strange America of today one hears the people apologizing for prosperity but not for poverty.

Beyond the material changes is a new mental attitude. . . . It does not take so much for granted and at the same time it accepts as a matter of course brand-new conceptions of social responsibility. In casual conversation we bandy terms we have but lately learned; whether or not the professors of the New Deal have altered our thinking, they have transformed our political and economic vocabulary.[14]

Roosevelt himself insisted:

Our task of reconstruction does not require the creation of new and strange values. It is rather the finding of the way once more to known, but to some degree forgotten, ideals and values. If the means and details are in some instances new, the objectives are as permanent as human nature.

Among our objectives I place the security of the men, women and children of the nation first. . . .

In a simple and primitive civilization, homes were to be had for the building. The bounties of nature in a new land provided crude but adequate food and shelter. . . . So, also, security was attained in the earlier days through the interdependence of members of families upon each other and of the families within a small community upon each other. The complexities of great communities and of organized industry make less real these simple means of security. Therefore, we are compelled to employ the active interest of the nation as a whole through government in order to encourage a greater security for each individual who composes it.[15]

In the spring of 1935, the momentum of reform moved in easily forseen channels: a sharp new program of work relief—WPA—a soil conservation act, new Resettlement and Rural Electrification Administrations to reinforce the work of the AAA and TVA. But Roosevelt's requests for public utilities regulation and Social Security suggested what lay around the bend. Throughout the spring and early summer two circumstances arose to confirm the shift to reform. The first was the action of the United States Supreme Court. In early January it declared unconstitutional the oil-production controls of the NRA. In May it knocked down the Railway Pension Act and the Frazier-Lemke Farm Mortgage Moratorium. And in late May it destroyed the NRA with an opinion which seemed to make impossible any future resort to such industrial self-regulation assisted by federal government power.

The second was the frightening popularity of certain extremists. The most dramatic was the "Kingfish"—

Senator Huey Long of Louisiana. Long was flamboyantly crude. On the Senate floor he called the President, "Prince Franklin, Knight of the Nourmahal," Henry Wallace "Lord Corn Wallace," Ickes "The Chicago Cinch Bug," and Hugh Johnson "Sitting Bull." He was perhaps the only legislator ever to keep his hat on in the President's office. But he had combined the tactics of the political machine and the dictator to give Louisiana a totalitarian regime unparalleled in American history. He was ambitious for the White House. And he was popular far beyond the boundaries of Louisiana. His "Share the Wealth" plan was a gigantic demagogic bluff, but it seemed believable: old-age pensions, free education through college, cheap food by distribution of surpluses, guaranteed annual income of at least $2,000 per family.

And there were others. From the Shrine of the Little Flower in Royal Oak, Michigan, Father Coughlin appealed all too successfully to class, ethnic and religious prejudice. He became one of the most effective radio speakers of his time, and he mixed politics and religion indiscriminately as he lashed out against the "godless capitalists, the Jews, communists, international bankers, and plutocrats." At first he supported Roosevelt, but late in 1934 he joined the clamor for nationalization of finance and industry and for a guaranteed "living wage." In California, an old man fell upon another delightfully simple solution—a $200-a-month pension for everyone over sixty. The money must all be spent; here was pump-priming enough to fill all the gaps. By early 1935 Dr. Francis E. Townsend could beam benevolently upon over two thousand of his clubs scattered throughout the country. Upton Sinclair, the progressive novelist and Socialist crusader, launched his movement to End Poverty In California. EPIC seemed to threaten the very existence of the old machines in the state. As the Okies stumbled westward from their dust-driven, bankrupt mid-western farms, the golden mecca of the Pacific Coast seemed a caldron of crisis. Watching the tragedy of surplus and starvation, John Steinbeck prepared to write, "There is a crime here that goes beyond denunciation. There is a sorrow here that weeping cannot symbolize. There is a failure here that topples all our success. The fertile earth, the straight tree rows, the sturdy trunks, and the ripe fruit. And children dying of pellagra must die because a profit cannot be taken from an orange. And coroners must fill in the certificates—died of malnutrition—because the food must rot, must be forced to rot . . . in the eyes of the hungry there is a growing wrath. In the souls of the people the grapes of wrath are filling and growing heavy, growing heavy for the vintage." [16]

NOTES, *chapter 7*

1. Basil Rauch, *The History of the New Deal, 1933–1938* (Creative Age Press, 1944) , 156-159.

2. Samuel Rosenman, ed., *The Public Papers and Addresses of Franklin D. Roosevelt*, I, 737.

3. *Public Papers*, I, 717.

4. Arthur M. Schlesinger, Jr., *The Coming of the New Deal*, 320-321.

5. David Lilienthal, *T.V.A., Democracy on the March* (Harper, 1944), 46-49, 53, 218-222.

6. Wendell Willkie, *This Is Wendell Willkie* (Dodd, Mead, 1940), 129, 132-134, 136-137.

7. Edgar Nixon, ed., *Franklin D. Roosevelt and Conservation*, I, 333-334.

8. Denis Brogan, *The Era of Franklin D. Roosevelt, A Chronicle of the New Deal and Global War* (Yale, 1950) , 53-54.

9. Schlesinger, *New Deal*, 443.

10. *Public Papers*, II, 94.

11. *Public Papers*, III, 90-91.

12. Frances Perkins, *The Roosevelt I Knew*, 194-196.

13. National Planning Board, *Final Report, 1933–1934* (Government Printing Office, 1934), 33-34.

14. Anne O'Hare McCormick, *The World at Home: Selections from the Writings of Anne O'Hare McCormick*, 234-235.

15. *Public Papers*, III, 288.

16. John Steinbeck, *The Grapes of Wrath* (Modern Library ed., 1941), 477.

There is no doubt that Roosevelt was tacking in the new direction long before the fateful NRA decision in the Schechter case on May 27, 1935. In fact, he had thrown his full support to the Wagner Labor Relations bill just three days before that ultimatum from the bench. But the mounting pressure of the demagogues and the sharp reprimand of the judges set his course firmly and gave him the weapons he needed to galvanize his congressional majority. The reform program, which had bogged sadly since January, rolled like a bulldozer in June, July and August. The turning point was the momentous press conference four days after the Schechter decision, in which he treated newsmen to a sharp dissenting opinion:

The whole tendency over these years has been to view the interstate commerce clause in the light of present-day civilization. The country was in the horse-and-buggy age when that clause was written. . . . They had in those days no problems relating to employment. They had no problems relating to the earning capacity of the people. . . . There were no social questions in those days. The question of health on a national basis had never been discussed. The question of fair business practices had never been discussed. The word was unknown in the vocabulary of the Founding Fathers. The ethics of the period were very different from what they are today. If one man could skin a fellow and get away with it, why, that was all right. . . .

The prosperity of the farmer does have an effect today on the manufacturer in Pittsburgh. The prosperity of the clothing worker in the city of New York has an effect on the prosperity of the farmer in Wisconsin, and so it goes. We are interdependent—we are tied together. . . . It has been our hope that under the interstate commerce clause we could recognize by legislation and by judicial decision that a harmful practice in one section of the country could be prevented on the theory that it was doing harm to another section of the country. . . .

. . . the implication of this opinion is that we have gone back, that the Supreme Court will no longer take into consideration anything that indirectly may affect interstate commerce. . . .[1]

F.D.R. went on to predict that the entire New Deal was in danger. There commenced almost at once what James M. Burns has called the "Second Hundred Days":

. . . Roosevelt threw himself into the legislative battle. No longer was he squeamish about putting the lash to congressional flanks. Now he was bluntly telling congressional leaders that certain bills must be passed. Administration contact men ranged amid the legislative rank and file, applying pressure. Late in the afternoon they would report back to the President. When they mentioned a balking congressman, the big hand would move instantly to the telephone; in a few moments the President would have the congressman on the wire, coaxing him, commanding him, negotiating with him. To scores of others, Roosevelt dictated one- or two-sentence chits asking for action. He and his lieutenants, working late into the night, acting in close concert with friendly leaders on Capitol Hill, stayed one or two jumps ahead of the divided opposition.

Congressmen complained, balked, dragged their heels, but in the end they acted. . . .

Nothing better showed Roosevelt's sudden change of direction than the tax bill. He had said nothing about such a measure in his January message; his budget message had suggested that no new taxes would be needed. He had toyed with a "share-the-wealth" scheme of the Treasury's in February, but as late as May 22 he seemed to be sticking to his January position. Unexpectedly on June 19 the President asked Congress for an inheritance tax as well as an estate tax, gift taxes to balk evasion of the inheritance tax, stepped-up income taxes on "very great individual incomes," and a corporation income tax graduated according to the size of corporations, with a dividend tax to prevent evasion. Leaving Congress "tired, sick, and sore, and in confusion," as one Senator said, the President then departed for the Yale-Harvard boat races.[2]

In addition to the "wealth tax," the essence of the second hundred days lay in the National Labor Relations Act, Social Security, and the Public Utilities Holding Company Act. The unions soon came to see the Wagner Act as labor's "charter of liberties." Based upon the presumption that strikes impeded interstate commerce and that strikes were caused by employers' refusing to bargain, it made the encouragement of collective bargaining and the protection of the right to organize a national policy. A Labor Relations Board was set up to enforce the act, both the union shop and the closed shop were authorized, and a series of "unfair" labor practices were banned. Among these were refusal to bargain collectively, interference with labor organizations or sponsorship of a company union, and discrimination against employees for union activities. Philip Murray's testimony in 1937, regarding one instance of the Steel Workers' Organizing Committee's success, illustrates the favorable reaction of labor leaders:

By May 1937 a distinct majority of Aliquippa's steel workers had become members of the S. W. O. C. In addition, a majority of the Jones & Laughlin Steel Corporation's twelve-thousand-odd employees in its Pittsburgh Works had also become members of the S. W. O. C. On behalf of these members the S. W. O. C. requested a conference with the corporation's officials early in May. The United States Steel Corporation had already recognized S. W. O. C. and signed a collective-bargaining contract with it. The same form of recognition was requested from Jones & Laughlin, which hesitated to grant it. Instead, Jones & Laughlin rushed plans to convert its company union, or employee representative plan, into a so-called independent union to compete with the S. W. O. C. This brought negotiations to a head, and in self-defense the Jones & Laughlin workers went on strike. The strike, at once, was successful; in fact, it was 100 percent. When the Jones & Laughlin officials saw their works completely closed down for the first time in their history, they reentered negotiations with the S. W. O. C. The corporation officials told me and my associates that they would sign a contract similar to the one between the S. W. O. C. and U. S. Steel, provided we could show that a majority of Jones & Laughlin's workers were S. W. O. C. members. . . .

Happily for the workers and the corporation, the National Labor Relations Board was in existence. Because of the existence of the Board, the Jones & Laughlin strike was one of the shortest on record, involving approximately 25,000 workers. It lasted just 36 hours.

In the past there would have been no other way out than a long-drawn-out battle, but here under the Wagner Act there was a definite, sane, constitutional, and democratic way of settling our differences. The company said we did not really represent its men. S. W. O. C. insisted that it did. The obvious way to settle it, therefore, was to hold an election.

. . . The result was a smashing victory—17,208 for the union and 7,207 against the union.

The Jones & Laughlin Steel Corporation thereupon signed a collective-bargaining contract with the S. W. O. C., recognizing it as the sole bargaining agency for all of its production and maintenance workers. This contract was the beginning of the extension of democratic principles and procedures into the operation of the Jones & Laughlin works. Twenty-five thousand workers who had been governed for years by the dictatorial rules that management arbitrarily promulgated elected their own representatives. These representatives sat around the conference table with management and negotiated fair democratic rules to govern the operations of the Jones & Laughlin mills. Here was an overt experiment in democratic ways. . . .

The Jones & Laughlin election is one of the largest conducted by the National Labor Relations Board. It represents a great victory of reason over strife in American industrial life. The Congress is to be congratulated for the enactment of the National Labor Relations Act, which has made this great achievement of democracy over autocracy possible.[3]

Management was outraged by the strongly prolabor bias of the act. There were cries that the employer's freedom of speech was being muzzled. Management dragged its heels for over a year and a half, fully expecting the Supreme Court to declare the Wagner Act unconstitutional under the narrow interpretation of the commerce clause suggested in the NRA decision. Meanwhile labor drove ahead, resorting to strikes in the face of resistance, 4,740 of them in 1937—twice as many as in any year since 1920. Many were jurisdictional disputes. The Wagner Act had cleared the way for a real struggle between the American Federation of Labor and the industrial unionists of the Committee for Industrial Organization. In 1935 and 1936 within the

A. F. of L., after 1937 outside it (as the Congress of
Industrial Organizations), the C. I. O. organized the
hitherto untouched great industries, such as steel and
automobiles. The competition proved disruptive to the
economy, but immensely productive in union memberships which rose from two and a quarter million in
1933 to fourteen million in 1945. It also brought a
wave of antilabor reaction.

But politically the Wagner Act was one of the New
Deal's great successes. In making unions legally—and,
as it turned out, popularly—acceptable, it cemented
organized labor into the Roosevelt coalition. The
liaison deepened as administrative decisions helped
labor extend its influence in numerous peripheral
areas: pensions, promotions, company insurance and
housing and other fringe benefits. In the process
struggling labor gradually became Big Labor, a new
family of dynamic pressure groups to join agricultural
and business interests in the battles over public policy.

It was difficult to rescue the wages and hours provisions of the NRA codes after the Schechter decision.
Frances Perkins brought out two bills which she had
kept locked in her desk for just such an emergency. One
evolved into the Walsh-Healey Public Contracts Act
which finally became law in June, 1936. It provided a
forty-hour week and minimum wages set by the Labor
Department, and it prevented child labor in industries
providing supplies for the government. The other—a
comprehensive maximum-hours and minimum-wage
bill—was buffeted about for three long years. The Fair
Labor Standards Act finally became law in June, 1938.

With Social Security, action was more timely, if not
nearly so comprehensive as labor and the reformers
wished. There had been a steady momentum for such
social insurance; twenty-seven states had already passed
old-age-assistance laws, and there was widespread fear
of the Townsend and Long plans. The bill which finally
emerged in the summer of 1935 was a compromise:

some security, for some people; it was an insurance
program, not a dole or handout; it combined both old-
age assistance and co-operative State-Federal Unemployment Insurance. It had taken over two years of
involved work by congressional and cabinet committees.
Roosevelt himself was entranced with the broad possibilities and was prepared to go much farther than
practical politics and disagreements allowed. Frances
Perkins paraphrased some of his informal remarks
about the developing program:

> At cabinet meetings and when he talked
privately with a group of us, he would say, "You want
to make it simple—very simple. So simple that everybody will understand it. And what's more, there is no
reason why everybody in the United States should not
be covered. I see no reason why every child, from the
day he is born, shouldn't be a member of the social
security system. When he begins to grow up, he should
know he will have old-age benefits directed from the
insurance system to which he will belong all his life. If
he is out of work, he gets a benefit. If he is sick or
crippled, he gets a benefit.
>
> "The system ought to be operated," this country
gentleman would go on, "through the post offices. Just
simple and natural—nothing elaborate or alarming
about it. The rural free delivery carrier ought to bring
papers to the door and pick them up after they are
filled out. The rural free delivery carrier ought to give
each child his social insurance number and his policy
or whatever takes the place of a policy. The rural free
delivery carrier ought to be the one who picks up the
claim of the man who is unemployed, or of the old lady
who wants old-age insurance benefits.
>
> "And there is no reason why just the industrial
workers should get the benefit of this. Everybody ought
to be in on it—the farmer and his wife and his family.
>
> "I don't see why not," he would say, as, across the

table I began to shake my head. "I don't see why not. Cradle to grave—from the cradle to the grave they ought to be in a social insurance system." . . .

When Roosevelt read the reports of the Beveridge Plan he jokingly said to me one day, "Frances, what does this mean? Why does Beveridge get his name on this? Why does he get the credit for this? You know I have been talking about cradle to the grave insurance ever since we first thought of it. It is my idea. It is not the Beveridge Plan. It is the Roosevelt Plan." . . .

The enactment of the Social Security Law was the beginning of a long public debate over the merits and methods of the policy. These came to a head finally with extensive revision of the law in 1939. On the whole Roosevelt could take pride in Social Security. The concept achieved wide acceptance and became a permanent monument to the New Deal. Further, under the leadership of John Gilbert Winant of New Hampshire, it became one of the most efficiently operated of all the governmental programs.

The Public Utilities Holding Company Act was a bit of unfinished business left over from the regulation of stock markets and banks, but it also marked the end of the uneasy marriage of business and the New Deal over which NRA had presided. Broadus Mitchell has explained the significance of the act:

The public-utility holding company was one of the fanciest financial erections—one could hardly call it a structure—of the New Economic Era. . . . In 1926 almost half the output of electricity was controlled by five companies; twenty companies dominated four-fifths of the power industry. The onset of the depression shook the holding companies, but soon was supplying further opportunities for concentration of control. The most conspicuous collapse was that of Samuel Insull's Middle West Public Utilities Company, in which large numbers of unsuspecting investors lost a stupendous aggregate, and which put Insull to ignominious flight.

One holding company, perhaps with a layer of several holding companies beneath it, may have been of use in coordinating the management and services of a number of otherwise disconnected operating properties. But the pyramids that were piled up, six, seven, eight, nine stories high, with special subsidiaries for promotional and engineering aid, were mostly inspired by nothing better than the cupidity and chicanery of their authors, the credulity of those who bought their securities, and the helplessness of consumers of gas and electricity who suffered under artificially high rates. It was the practice of the insiders to retain control of a majority or a sufficient block of the voting stock, unloading the remainder of the securities on the public; as one holding company was placed above another, the percentage of investment by the manipulators became less and less until it was trifling. Stock from top to bottom was abundantly watered, while fictitious charges of engineering and advertising affiliates and scandalous salaries ate up profits. . . .

The Public Utility Holding Company Act of August 26, 1935, contained the hotly debated "death sentence" against useless intermediate corporations. The Securities and Exchange Commission was directed, broadly, to limit each holding company to a single integrated system, corporate and geographic, and to require fair distribution of voting power among security owners. Acquisition of securities and assets by holding companies, payment of dividends, solicitations of proxies, intercompany loans, and service, sales, and construction contracts passed under the commission's supervision. . . . The giants of the industry were brought on the carpet.[5]

For the rest, the remarkable summer of 1935 saw the extension of Interstate Commerce Commission regulation to motor carriers, the Guffey Coal Act, and a new railway retirement law which sought to replace structures undercut by court decisions that spring. Strangely enough the long congressional session was hardly over before Huey Long, whose last gesture had been to filibuster to death the social security appropriation, moved off the stage. On September 8 he was assassinated in the State House at Baton Rouge.

Throughout the 1936 session, the Roosevelt reform program was quietly shelved as the partisans ranged themselves for the election. What was done, however, stamped in sharp relief the administration's determination to strike out against big business. The Revenue Act of 1936 featured a sharply progressive undistributed profits tax, to plug an important corporate tax loophole. The Robinson-Patman Price Discrimination Act gave the Federal Trade Commission the power to protect small retailers against cutthroat price policies of their chain competitors. Roosevelt supported Senator Wagner's slum-clearance bill, and the President's first antitrust suit was brought in June, 1936; during the campaign, F.D.R. began to step up his criticisms of monopoly practices.

Meanwhile the tension between White House and Supreme Court deepened. The Court invalidated the AAA in January, the Guffey Coal Act in May, and the New York state minimum wage for women in June. The one bright spot for F.D.R. was the Ashwander decision in mid-February which had, somewhat surprisingly, upheld the Tennessee Valley Authority.

But a change was permeating the Roosevelt administration in 1936 much more fundamental than an attempt to find a substitute for NRA, or a resort to new spending, or an attack upon the industrial giants. Roosevelt was shifting not only from right to left in

terms of the groups to which he appealed, but also from
an emphasis on collectivism to a stress on regulated
individualism. In June, 1936, he claimed:

> Today we restored democracy in govern-
ment.
> We are in the process of restoring democracy in
opportunity.[6]

Many years later, Rex Tugwell, who himself was a
casualty of this shift, speculated:

> It was . . . [Justice Louis D.] Brandeis who
was his intellectual guide and mentor during the
gestation of the New Deal; and Brandeis was a wolf in
sheep's clothing—more accurately, a doctrinaire parad-
ing as an instrumentalist. Brandeis very early drew
certain conclusions from his experience which hardened
into prejudices. These in time came to seem to him
axiomatic. And he applied them without scruple . . .
he had two means of enforcing his dogmas, and both
were used on Roosevelt with devastating effect.
> The first of these means was his disciples; the second
was the threat of unconstitutionality. The first apostle
in the Brandeis heirarchy was [Felix] Frankfurter. . . .
Through Frankfurter, mostly, the staffing of the New
Deal agencies was controlled and dissenters were got
rid of. And because Brandeis was, after Holmes's death,
the most influential member of the Court among intellectuals and liberals—and with Roosevelt—a word from
him was very nearly a command. And this was much
more true after the adverse decisions on the collec-
tivistic measures of the Hundred Days. In these
Brandeis joined with reactionaries to make a majority.
The Court disregarded entirely the effects of the measures and rested on principles—principles on which they
agreed.

Brandeis was an atomist. He believed in small social organizations, and this applied both to business and government. . . .

The succumbing of Roosevelt did not mean that he became a convinced atomist. It meant that he too was a pragmatist. . . . The ends he had in mind in New Deal days were comprehended in the phrase "recovery and reform." The Brandeis followers offered him an alternative to collectivism in both fields. Recovery could be had by spending without collectivizing; and reform could consist in filling out the progressive agenda—reorganizing the stock market, revising the banking laws, and the like. . . . Roosevelt judged that not only Brandeis but the country as a whole was still at the trust-busting mental age. The time to collectivize had not yet come.[7]

Roosevelt did not revert so completely to "atomism" as Tugwell has insisted. In February, 1936, for example, he wrote:

. . . with monopolies, Brandeis is one thousand per cent right in principle but in certain fields there must be a guiding or restraining hand of Government because of the very nature of the specific field. The British power network or gridiron is a good example—production, transmission and distribution owned by many small operators, private and municipal, yet tied together with Government assistance and supervision. But, then, the Britishers do not everlastingly rush to the Supreme Court but instead sit round the table with the Government in good faith—and get results.[8]

Whatever the concern of Roosevelt and his staff, the 1936 election was a ponderous vote of confidence. Roosevelt expanded this confidence into a monumentally ambitious program which was to bring him little but disappointment. The first step was the unprecedented attempt to reconstruct the United States Supreme Court. Even before Roosevelt's inauguration, Walter Lippmann had foreseen the necessity of constitutional reinterpretation:

> ... Of all the Western peoples the English-speaking nations have been the most successful in finding ways to preserve and yet to change. Their secret is their sense of the law, which in their great periods they have looked upon not as an iron frame, but as a garment which can be cut and altered so that it always covers them and yet allows them to move freely.
>
> It is the business of the Court in our political system to oversee this cutting and alteration of the garment that it may always fit comfortably and endure. ...'

But throughout 1935 and 1936 the Supreme Court had treated the Constitution as a rigid armor for traditional social philosophy. Much of the New Deal had been invalidated within a few months. The main blocks were four. Congress's power to regulate interstate commerce had been interpreted narrowly; it could not excuse, the court said, broad regulation of industry and agriculture. Separation of powers had been rigidly construed to prevent great delegation of legislative power to the President and his aides. The power to spend "for the general welfare" had been limited to the purposes for which Congress might legislate. Finally, the "due process of law" clause of the Fifth and Fourteenth Amendments had been understood to give the Supreme Court the responsibility of deciding when economic regulation by the states or the federal government had gone too far in the deprivation of economic "liberty."

Roosevelt's reaction to judicial impediment was strangely indirect. He asked Congress in February, 1937,

for a general reform of the federal courts. Claiming
that justice had bogged down, he proposed that the
Chief Justice be allowed to assign extra judges when
necessary to the Circuit Courts, that the Supreme
Court provide a supervisor to watch the courts for
overloaded calendars, and especially that the President
be empowered to appoint an additional judge to any
court in which an incumbent over seventy, who had
been on the bench for ten years, refused to resign. It
was evident that the President's real target was the
conservative bloc on the Supreme Court. Dexter Perkins
has sketched the fight:

The issue involved in this plan was a far-
reaching one . . . was it desirable by a new act of
legislation to swamp the so-called "reactionary" judges
and, by the addition of new members to the Court, insure a more hospitable reception to the New Deal
legislation of the future? That such a project was constitutional in the narrow sense of the term few could
question. . . . But were there deeper considerations involved? Was it fundamentally desirable to reshape the
Court and to undermine its independence as a result
of a political victory? . . . Opposition began to gather
from the day the message was read, and this opposition
came not only from the die-hard conservatives but from
many liberals who recognized the difficult situation . . .
and who, in some instances, were pondering upon some
way to meet the problem. . . . The indirection with
which Roosevelt approached the Court issue was
quickly capitalized by Chief Justice Charles Evans
Hughes. In Hughes the President met a foeman worthy
of his steel. . . . Hughes quickly seized the advantage
and in a famous letter tore to shreds the sophistical
argument that the Supreme Court was behind on its
work. But this in itself would not have been enough to
defeat the proposal. The crucial matter was that, shortly

after the Senate Committee began its hearings on the President's bill, the Court handed down two fateful decisions which demonstrated that the constitutional law of the United States was keeping pace with the times.

The first, the case of *West Coast Hotel v. Parrish*, found constitutional a minimum wage law enacted by the state of Washington. The vote was 5 to 4. Justice Roberts, who had voted against sustaining the New York law the year before on the ground that the state had failed to distinguish the statute from the minimum wage law invalidated in the Adkins case of 1932, now was ready frankly to overrule the previous decision. More important, a week later, the Court upheld the Wagner Act, again by a 5-to-4 vote. . . . The decision in this case was phrased in very broad terms. . . . it . . . foreshadowed the acceptance by the Court of such important statutes as the Social Security Act of the same year.

The decision of the Court in these two cases eviscerated the President's supporters. But more was to come. In June one of the four conservative judges, Justice Van Devanter, resigned. . . . Thus the argument for the bill was weaker than ever. Though the presidential pressure continued, in July the whole project was abandoned. . . .[10]

Roosevelt lost much in this battle, in party unity and in public support. His friends might claim it was really a court "unpacking" bill, but there was fuel here to feed the phony charge of "dictatorship."

Whatever the reason for Mr. Justice Roberts's "switch in time that saved nine," Roosevelt did win the campaign, for the moment. Although judicial review remained available for future use, the New Deal now found a sympathetic interpretation of the Constitution. Roosevelt himself kept a "before and after" tally sheet:

BEFORE THE COURT BILL
*(From beginning of October 1935 term
to introduction of Court Bill)*

A. AAA unconstitutional—limiting the federal spending power.
B. Guffey Act unconstitutional—limiting the federal commerce power.
C. New York Minimum Wage Law unconstitutional—limiting States through the due process clause.
D. Jones Case—crippling administrative procedure of Securities and Exchange Commission.
E. Washington Utility Case—limiting utility regulation by States under due process clause.

AFTER THE COURT BILL

A. Washington Minimum Wage Case—overruling New York Minimum Wage Case—a new interpretation of due process clause applied to the States.
B. Wagner Act Case—reversing the Guffey Act Case—a new interpretation of the federal commerce power.
C. Social Security Case—overruling AAA Case—a new interpretation of the Federal spending and taxing power.

The President has attained the most difficult of his *objectives,* i.e., the liberalization of the interpretation of the Constitution.

He has yet to obtain these two *objectives:*

(a) insurance of the continuity of that liberalism and
(b) a more perfect judicial mechanism for giving a maximum of justice in a minimum of time.[11]

The second step in the 1937 program slipped almost as badly. This was the attempt to revive the jaded spirit of reform. In fact only one measure of major proportions was passed during the regular session of the

1937 Congress—the Wagner Housing Act. In a special session that fall, Roosevelt submitted to Congress a package of pending reform legislation; but the second step was soon merged into the third—the harried evolution of a policy to deal with a new major recession. As James M. Burns tells the story:

Late in the summer stocks had slackened off. . . . Suddenly it seemed like 1929 all over again. Selling orders poured in from all over the country, transactions went to seven million shares in a single day, the ticker tape fell far behind. . . .

Roosevelt was in a paradoxical situation. He believed that economic conditions were fundamentally sound. . . . Yet the President dared not show his optimism in public. Above all he feared the dread parallel with Hoover, whose hopeful declarations month after month in the early 1930's had become a grim joke. . . .

Sitting tight worked no better for Roosevelt than it had for Hoover. Stocks kept on dropping; the whole economy was now showing a decline. . . .

. . . the special session was a shambles. The Senate at the start ran into a wrathful filibuster over Wagner's antilynching bill. In the House Roosevelt's leaders through a variety of trades squeezed out enough signatures on a petition to pry the wages and hours bill out of the Rules Committee; then the bill was dashed to pieces on the rocks of opposition from AFL factions and from Southern congressmen. The farm bill made faster progress but encountered a split between Secretary Wallace and President O'Neal of the Farm Bureau. The reorganization and regional planning bills simply made no progress at all. When Congress adjourned a few days before Christmas it had passed not one of Roosevelt's four proposals. . . .

During the fall and early winter Roosevelt's conservative advisers seemed to have the upper hand. . . . In his "budget seminar" with reporters shortly after the new year began Roosevelt said that the most important fact was the cut of over half a billion in estimated spending for the next fiscal year.

The President's caution did little to placate business. It served mainly to arouse the New Dealers around him. . . .

By the end of 1937 little knots of these . . . New Dealers had been meeting secretly and holding feverish discussions on how to salvage the New Deal. They were at odds, however, over economic strategy. The out-and-out Keynesians wanted Roosevelt to start a bigger and better spending program. Others called for an old-fashioned, slam-bang attack on the trusts. . . .

As it turned out . . . Roosevelt unwittingly decided the issue between the spenders and the trust busters for a time. His private complaints during the fall that certain business interests were ganging up on him showed which way the presidential mind was leaning. [Solicitor General Robert] Jackson . . . opened up the counterattack on business by blaming monopolists and profiteers for the recession. Ickes followed with a denunciation of the "sixty families" that, he cried, controlled the American economy. The New Dealers were not content to deplore the economic power of the monopolists. They flayed them for seeking political power, for trying to defy the popular mandate of 1936, even for leading the country toward fascism. Ickes waited anxiously for the President to back up the onslaughts. Roosevelt did, after a fashion—but he took care to reiterate that only a small minority of businessmen were guilty of "poor citizenship."

So trust busting was the order of the day. Nothing could have been better calculated to inflame the war between New Deal and business or to sharpen the alternatives facing Roosevelt. . . .

It was a condition, not a theory, that finally moved

the President. In March the stock market's halting decline turned suddenly into a panicky drop, and other indices slumped badly. Unemployment was still rising. In fact, the decline from the previous September was the sharpest the country had ever known. Even a number of business leaders were now calling guardedly for spending. . . . By now Hopkins was back in action, and, armed with memorandums from New Deal economists, he met Roosevelt at Warm Springs and urged on him a large-scale spending program.

Roosevelt knew that he must act. And he knew that he must act for the people—the people who loved him and who had sustained him. . . . Soon after arriving in Washington Roosevelt told Morgenthau that he had decided to scrap budget balancing and resume spending. . . . As usual, when the President shifted, there was little looking back. In mid-April he proposed to Congress a three-billion-dollar spending program, and in a long fireside chat took his new program to the people. Two weeks later he asked Congress to launch a thorough study of the concentration of economic power in American industry and the effect of that concentration upon the decline of competition. Congress responded enthusiastically to his proposals and passed the legislation by heavy majorities within a few weeks. Three billion was appropriated for spending and lending during the next fiscal year—[much of it mammoth increases in Hopkins' WPA], and the Temporary National Economic Committee, consisting of senators, representatives, and government officials, and staffed by scores of experts, was established under the chairmanship of Senator Joseph C. O'Mahoney to conduct a full-scale investigation of the economy. Within a few months business indices were edging up again, but a large lump of unemployment continued to weigh down the economy.[12]

Of the new policies, Richard Hofstadter has noted:

Roosevelt's sudden and desperate appeal to the ancient trust-busting device, together with his failure in the fall elections of 1938 to purge the conservative elements in his party, augured the political bankruptcy of the New Deal. The reform wave had spent itself, and the Democratic Party, divided by the Supreme Court fight and the purge and hamstrung by its large conservative bloc, was exhausted as an agency of reform. Always the realist, Roosevelt rang the death knell of the New Deal in his annual message to Congress on January 4, 1939. "We have now passed the period of internal conflict in the launching of our program of social reform," he declared. "Our full energies may now be released to invigorate the processes of recovery in order to preserve our reforms." Almost three years before Pearl Harbor his experimentation had run its course. "The processes of recovery" came only with war. "Our full energies" were never successfully released for peacetime production.[13]

The Temporary National Economic Committee did make its major impact upon American life. It took the people to school in the elaborate problem of corporation and industrial economics. TNEC told Americans:

. . . Today one company in each field controls all, or nearly all, of the nation's supply of aluminum, nickel, molybdenum, magnesium, shoe machinery, glass container machinery, and scientific precision glass, provides nearly all of the domestic telephone service and all of the trans-oceanic service, and operates all of the sleeping and parlor cars. Other concerns stand in a similar position with respect to important segments of the markets for international cable and radio communication, oil pipe-line, and railway freight transportation and trans-oceanic aviation. There are, in addition, numerous public utility corporations and innumerable small-town enterprises which enjoy complete monopolies in the local markets which they serve. . . .

In some fields two establishments together control the supply. Two companies provide all of the domestic telegraph service; two control all of the submarine cables between the United States and several foreign countries; two offer the only radio-telegraph service to many points abroad. Two companies, in each field, account for all, or nearly all, of the nation's supply of bananas, of plate glass and safety glass, of bulbs, tubing and rod, and bases for electric lamps, of electric accounting machines, of railroad air brakes, of oxyacetylene, of sulphur, and certain chemicals. In many local markets, on a smaller scale, two petty enterprises share a trade. Under circumstances such as these, formal or informal understandings governing price and production are readily attained. Each firm of a pair controlling the whole supply is likely to act as if it were a monopolist. In their effect upon the market, duopoly and monopoly tend to be substantially the same. . . .[14]

But the TNEC chairman, Senator O'Mahoney of Wyoming, made concrete suggestions which were pitifully superficial and general:

   1. National charters for national corporations, in order that these agencies may have a definite and a free place in our economy and local business may be differentiated and protected from national business;
   2. The effective and thorough enforcement of the antitrust laws to maintain competition and to prevent all combinations and agreements that destroy business;
   3. The encouragement of new business and small enterprise by revision of the tax laws for the purpose of encouraging new employment and new industry;
   4. A national conference called by Congress of the

various organizations, representative of business, labor, agriculture, and consumers which have for years been working on diverse phases of this central problem might concentrate public thought and action on the objectives on which there is general agreement instead of, as now, on the objectives concerning which there is only misunderstanding, suspicion, and disagreement.[15]

TNEC reported in 1941. Already the emphasis was upon production for war and the necessary industrial co-operation. Antitrust prosecutions dragged on interminably in the courts. In Congress and in the press there was a burgeoning reaction. And business pressure groups seemed increasingly more powerful in legislature and administration than even the President himself.

Strangely enough the New Deal, begun with decisive action, was buried in a swirling fog of confusion. Roosevelt himself probably never accepted the full logic of his last decision at the domestic crossroads. The "Roosevelt recession," and then the war, committed him to spending when he was prepared to accept "pump-priming" as a momentary expedient only. He believed in competition. But he maintained to the end his firm hopes for the balancing of interests, for government through co-operation, which had motivated much of the early New Deal. With spending he had been forced to an expedient which he was not willing to allow the dignity of being called a policy or experiment. With trust-busting, he found himself casting government in a negative role he did not relish. The war allowed him —forced him—to shrug the problem aside. But in six years of experimenting with it Roosevelt and his administration had altered permanently the context within which the future would face the old task again.

Personally, he was prepared to resume the challenge once peace had been won. In the midst of the war he explained to reporters that the New Deal had come about

> . . . because there was an awfully sick patient called the United States of America, and it was suffering from a grave internal disorder—awfully sick—all kinds of things happened to this patient, all internal things. And they sent for the doctor. And it was a long, long process—took several years before those ills, in that particular illness of ten years ago, were remedied. But after a while they were remedied. . . .

But since then, two years ago, the patient had a very bad accident—not an internal trouble. Two years ago, on the seventh of December, he was in a pretty bad smashup—broke his hip, broke his leg in two or three places, broke a wrist and an arm, and some ribs; and they didn't think he would live, for a while. And then he began to "come to"; and he has been in charge of a partner of the old doctor. Old Dr. New Deal didn't know "nothing" about legs and arms. He knew a great deal about internal medicine, but nothing about surgery. So he got his partner, who was an orthopedic surgeon, Dr. Win-the-War, to take care of this fellow who had been in this bad accident. And the result is that the patient is back on his feet. He has given up his crutches. He isn't wholly well yet, and he won't be until he wins the war. . . .

And when victory comes, the program of the past, of course, has got to be carried on, in my judgment, with what is going on in other countries—postwar program— because it will pay. . . .

. . . It seems pretty clear that we must plan for, and help to bring about, an expanded economy which will result in more security, in more employment, in more recreation, in more education, in more health, in better housing for all of our citizens, so that the conditions of 1932 and the beginning of 1933 won't come back again.[16]

NOTES, *chapter 8*

1. Samuel Rosenman, ed., *The Public Papers and Addresses of Franklin D. Roosevelt*, IV, 208-210.

2. James M. Burns, *Roosevelt, the Lion and the Fox*, 223-224.

3. U. S. Senate, 76th Congress, 1st. Sess., Committee on Education and Labor, "Hearings on . . . Bills to Amend the National Labor Relations Act," 4638-4639, 4657-4658, 4660-4661.

4. Frances Perkins, *The Roosevelt I Knew*, 282-283.

5. Broadus Mitchell, *Depression Decade: From New Era through New Deal, 1931–1941* (Rinehart, 1947), 174-176.

6. *Public Papers*, V, 211.

7. Rexford G. Tugwell, *The Art of Politics . . .*, 247-248.

8. Elliott Roosevelt, ed., *F.D.R., His Personal Letters, 1928–1945*, 561.

9. Walter Lippmann, *Interpretations, 1931–1932*, 323-324.

10. Dexter Perkins, *The New Age of Franklin Roosevelt*, 59-61.

11. *Personal Letters, 1928–1945*, 685-686.

12. Burns, *Roosevelt*, 319-321, 325-328.

13. Richard Hofstadter, *The American Political Tradition and the Men Who Made It*, 341-342.

14. Temporary National Economic Committee, *Final Report of the Executive Secretary* (Government Printing Office, 1941) , 7-9.

15. T.N.E.C., *Final Statement, March 11, 1941*, Senate Document #39, 77th Congress, 1st. Session, 686.

16. Samuel Rosenman, ed., *The Public Papers and Addresses of Franklin D. Roosevelt, 1941–1945* (Harper, 1950), *1943*, 570-571, 573-574.

chapter 9 MASTER POLITICIAN

Almost thirty years before Franklin Roosevelt entered the White House, George Washington Plunkitt, a Tammany district leader, recorded for posterity the classic distinction between the intellectual and the politician:

> If you are goin' to cast your first vote next November and want to go into politics, do as I did. Get a followin', if it's only one man, and then go to the district leader and say: "I want to join the organization. I've got one man who'll follow me through thick and thin." The leader won't laugh at your one-man followin'. He'll shake your hand warmly, offer to propose you for membership in his club, take you down to the corner for a drink and ask you to call again. But go to him and say: "I took first prize at college in Aristotle; I can recite all Shakspere forwards and backwards; there ain't nothin' in science that ain't as familiar to me as blockades on the elevated roads and I'm the real thing in the way of silver-tongued orators." What will he answer? He'll probably say: "I guess you are not to blame for your misfortunes, but we have no use for you here." [1]

..Roosevelt's techniques were different. But with Roosevelt, as with Plunkitt, the essence of success was ability to command a following. In retrospect the record, with all its ups and downs, is amazing:

	Popular Vote	% of Vote	Electoral Vote
1932			
Roosevelt	22,821,857	57.4	472
Hoover	15,761,841		59
1936			
Roosevelt	27,751,597	60.8	523
Landon	16,679,583		8
1940			
Roosevelt	27,244,160	54.9	449
Willkie	22,305,198		82
1944			
Roosevelt	25,602,504	53.4	432
Dewey	22,006,285		99 [2]

As the years rolled on, it would seem increasingly to be a Roosevelt record, rather than a party record. James Burns has summed up his essential techniques:

Grasp of Public Opinion. Roosevelt showed such a sure sense of popular moods and attitudes that some believed he had intuition or a sixth sense in this field. Actually, his understanding was rooted in solid, day-to-day accumulation of facts on what people were thinking. Roosevelt read half a dozen newspapers a day. He kept up a vast correspondence. Tens of thousands of letters came to the White House every week reporting people's views and problems. He got some understanding from crowds—the way they looked, how they reacted to certain passages in his speeches. As President he enjoyed special advantages. Through favored journalists he could put up trial balloons and test public reaction. He had special voting polls conducted, and he often received advanced information on other polls. Administrators in regional and state offices sent in a good deal of information, as did state and local party leaders. A huge division of press intelligence clipped hundreds of newspapers and compiled digests.

Timing. Roosevelt's timing also seemed intuitive, but it too was largely calculated. Essential in his timing was the care he took not to confront his political opposition when it was mobilizing and moving hard and fast; he believed, for example, that presidents could expect to lose some popular support during congressional sessions, and that the President should wait until Congress adjourned before seizing the offensive again. Sometimes he moved fast, before the opposition could mobilize. "I am like a cat," Roosevelt said once. "I make a quick stroke and then I relax." More often, he waited for the crest of the opposition wave to subside, then he acted. . . .

Attention to Political Detail. Roosevelt showed infinite patience in dealing with the day-to-day routine of politics, involving in most cases the ambitions, hopes, and desire for recognition of countless politicians. The White House establishment was carefully organized for this purpose. . . .

. . . take the case of David E. Fitzgerald, a Democratic leader in New Haven. In 1935 the White House sent him an autographed picture of the President. Fitzgerald traveled with Roosevelt's entourage during the New England tour in 1936; his note of congratulations brought a "Dear Dave" reply from the President. Each of three Fitzgerald letters in 1940 was answered by a warm little note from Roosevelt; a postelection wire of congratulations brought a Presidential letter in which "Dear Mr. Fitzgerald" was crossed out and "Dear Dave" substituted. When Fitzgerald caught cold campaigning, the White House sent him flowers. In 1941, another "Dear Dave" letter; a year later Fitzgerald died, and a warm Presidential letter went to his widow, who replied, in a widow's tremulous handwriting, "Mr. Fitzgerald was always an ardent admirer of yours. . . ."

Attention to Intragroup Factions. The White House

checked carefully on the political situation within groups, in order both to keep on friendly terms with all the factions and to avoid being compromised by some faction of politically suspect leanings. Splits among Negroes, Jews, labor groups, bankers, veterans, and the like were followed with care. . . .

Separating Opposition Leaders from Rank and File. Splitting enemy leaders from their followers is an old political tactic, but few politicians have used it as persistently or as meticulously as Roosevelt. Almost invariably he attacked "Republican leaders" or "Republican spokesmen," never the Republican party or Republicans generally. "There are thousands of people," Roosevelt had said to Rosenman as far back as 1930, "who think as you and I do about government. They are enrolled as Republicans because their families have been Republicans for generations—that's the only reason; some of them think it is *infra dig* to be called a Democrat; the Democrats in their village are not the socially 'nice' people the enrolled Republicans are. So never attack the Republicans or the Republican party—only the Republican *leaders.* Then any Republican voter who hears it will say to himself: 'Well he doesn't mean me. . . .' "

Fighting on Your Own Battleground. Offensively this meant attacking the opposition at its weakest point in an effort to force it to accept the gage of battle on the worst ground for it. Defensively it meant answering the opposition's most extreme or absurd attacks. In 1930 Roosevelt ignored Republican charges against his handling of the New York City situation until almost the end of the campaign. In his Madison Square Garden speech in 1936 he skillfully converted Landon's effort to put him on the defensive into a superb defense of the New Deal on his own terms.

Personal Charm and Political Craft. No political technique is effective unless employed with skill in a given situation. Immensely strengthening all Roosevelt's

tactics were the calculated flattery he could use in
winning over critics and the sheer astuteness with which
he outmaneuvered rival leaders. An example of the
latter was his handling of John L. Lewis's campaign
donation in 1936. The CIO chief came into Roosevelt's
office one day with a check for $250,000 and with a
photographer to record the ceremony. Roosevelt was all
smiles, but he would not take the check.

"No John," he said. "Just keep it, and I'll call on you
if and when any small need arises."

Lewis left, grumbling that he had been outsmarted.
He had been. During the next few weeks requests for
money flowed in from Farley and from independent
Roosevelt groups. In vain Lewis tried to stem the torrent
by insisting on a written order from the President.
Roosevelt backed up such requests with orders or with
telephone calls. In the end Lewis's treasury was drained
of almost half a million dollars—and without undue
notice in the press.[3]

*The campaigns themselves brought to the test his
more specific skills. Like a champion salesman, his
major asset was enthusiasm. Moley once wrote:*

> Campaigning, for him, was unadulterated
> joy. It was broad rivers, green forests, waving corn, and
> undulating wheat; it was crowds of friends, from the
> half dozen who, seated on a baggage truck, waved to
> the cheery face at the speeding window to perspiring
> thousands at a race track or fairground; it was hands
> extended in welcome, voices warm with greeting, faces
> reflecting his smile along the interminable wayside.
> These are the things that ever and ever renew the life
> of the troubadour. . . .[4]

Part of his secret was his slogans: "Good Neighbor," "Four Freedoms," "Forgotten Man," "The Four
Horsemen—Destruction, Delay, Despair and Deceit."

He could steal the enemy's own phrases. In 1936, as criticism of "make-work" programs mounted, he could say:

There is a grand word going around—boondoggling. It is a pretty good word. If we can boondoggle ourselves out of the depression, that word is going to be enshrined in the hearts of the American people for years to come.[5]

Yet there was more to this than a voice, a smile and a basket full of slogans. Roosevelt identified superbly with his audience. He placed himself and the voters on the side of the good and the true and singled out their common enemies for attack and ridicule. These isolates naturally detested him, but Roosevelt came to revel in their opposition. He loved to tell the story of the four millionaires in Philadelphia's Rittenhouse Club who heard him say in a radio speech, "I wonder what is being said by my rich friends in their over-stuffed armchairs in their well-stocked clubs." "All four men . . . recoiled," F.D.R. said, "and one of them finding his voice, exclaimed, 'My God, do you suppose that blankety blank could have overheard us?' "[6]

The Fireside Chats were particularly successful. While the more sophisticated found them patronizing and vacuous, most Americans were captivated by the warm, personal rapport he established.

People wrote him because they saw him as their friend, deeply and personally responsive to their troubles. They cut his picture out of the paper, framed it in gilt cardboard and put it on their tables. When he spoke, they clustered around the radio, nodding in agreement and relief. Martha Gellhorn, writing from North Carolina in 1934, found the President's portrait in every house; he was "at once God and their intimate friend; he knows them all by name, knows their little town and mill, their little lives and problems. . . . He is there; and will not let them down." Lorena Hickock reported from New Orleans: "People down here all seem to think they know the President personally!" [7]

No such sorcerer could have worked without an enormous team of apprentices. But Roosevelt kept the guide lines firmly in his own hands. He spent much time mediating among Jim Farley's regulars and the rapier-fighting idea men of the Brain Trust. He concerned himself with the most specific matters of tactics and organization. And the essence of his approach remained identification with the rank-and-file politicians and their constituents. Tugwell has commented of the local leaders, "They went through the Roosevelt machinery like so much sea water through a big fish's gills. From them he got the political plankton that nourished victory." [8] He made it very nearly a fetish to draft speeches to reach his own tenant farmer, Moses Smith. And there was little condescension in this. Its secret lay in his own habits of mind. Bored by statistics and elaborate analyses, he insisted always on the simple, personalized explanation.

A remarkable number of the crucial decisions were made by F.D.R. alone. Consequently the faults were often his. One was his misjudgment of his opponents. He underestimated badly both Willkie and Dewey. Another was his tendency to handle political problems in personal terms. Sometimes he became unduly bitter at those against whom he had turned. More often, his genial friendliness was interpreted as agreement and he seemed later to have been dishonest or misleading.

He recognized some of his limitations. As Arthur Schlesinger, Jr., has pointed out:

> Though Roosevelt played both high and low politics with equal skill, he really did not play them with equal relish. He greatly enjoyed low politics as a

game—but only up to a point. . . . The rather simple-hearted idealism which lay so near the core of Roosevelt's personality could not indefinitely support the experiments in smart-aleckness and trickiness. "When he did something cheap," Tom Corcoran once said, "he was basically ashamed of himself. He would never admit it—but he would show it instead in his attitude toward something else." . . .

What he really cared about was high politics—not politics as intrigue, but politics as education. Nothing government could do mattered much, he deeply believed, unless it was firmly grasped by the public mind. He once said, "I want to be a preaching President —like my cousin." . . . And the future possibilities of leadership similarly depended on what the people thought and wanted—or could be induced to think and want. As Roosevelt said to Upton Sinclair, "I cannot go any faster than the people will let me." [9]

This reciprocity between politician and people led Roosevelt to use his talents in many directions and in differing dimensions throughout the long twelve years in Washington.

The President was confident as he approached 1936. A year before the election he told Harold Ickes, "We will win easily next year but we are going to make it a crusade." He had nevertheless read the signs. By February, 1936, he would tell Ickes ". . . that the next four years would be very tough ones, with a crisis in 1941. . . . He said that he believed there would be a realignment of parties, and he pointed to the defection of Al Smith and Governor Talmadge as indicating a trend of that sort." [10]

The President's decision, gradually evolving throughout 1935, was to make the most of the conservative defection. There was the shift in legislation to emphasize the concerns of labor and the urban middle class. In Raymond Moley's bitter terms, "He was . . . bartering acreage for population." [11] And there was a campaign tactic designed to isolate the conservative opposition. Even in the summer of 1934 F.D.R. had written a friend abroad:

> All the big guns have started shooting—Al Smith, John W. Davis, James W. Wadsworth, du Pont, Shouse, etc. Their organization has already been labeled the "I CAN'T TAKE IT CLUB." [12]

This Liberty League proved itself, as Farley has said, "a huge bass drum, impressive to look at and noisy to hear, and yet nothing else but a hollow shell. . . ." [13] Meanwhile the farmers were actively courted. Tugwell describes Roosevelt's remarkable "non-political" tour that drought-ridden summer of 1936:

> For hundreds of miles in each direction from the center of North and South Dakota, Colorado, Oklahoma, and Texas, reaching west to the mountains and east almost to the Mississippi, the land was bare as a desert. The cattle and sheep had even dug up and consumed the roots of the dead grasses. . . . Morale might be reestablished if confidence was restored; and confidence might come from a promise that the help now being given would be sustained into reconstruction. The President saw the opportunity.
>
> Pity and sympathy for people in distress, even when they were genuine, might as well be capitalized on. The government—the New Deal—was going to the rescue. . . . Roosevelt had a feeling for the land and for the people who worked it. He shared their victories and defeats. But he could do something for them only when he moved at the head of a widespread generous impulse among those who were far from the particular scene. The dramatization of drought might put Roosevelt in a favorable light, but also it might bring adequate relief to the drought-stricken farmers. . . .

On the morning of the President's arrival it was rain-ing. It had not rained before, they said, in seven months. It was a miracle! The politicians on the plat-form nearly cried with joy. Even the reserved and scientific-minded Henry Wallace, Secretary of Agri-culture, beamed with satisfaction.

Presently, however, the President made something clear. It was a "non-political" trip. Americans in a wide area of the land were in trouble. The President had come to see what more could be done for them than was already being done, and to assure them that their government would stand by. . . .

There was no newspaper in the nation, even the most disaffected, that could resist the drama of a President in a farmyard. None did. It was the most effective political trip I ever knew or heard of. The campaign of '36 might well have been called off right there.

To emphasize its non-political nature, Jim Farley and all his henchmen were left worrying in the East while the President entertained in his car squads of local officials, Republican and Democratic alike. . . .

The technique infuriated the local Democrats, and presently Farley's Washington people were protesting stridently. But this only emphasized the President's master stroke—one of the most amusing incidents I can recall from my political years—the so-called "non-political" drought conference in Des Moines, attended by all the midwestern Governors. And Alf Landon, who had already been nominated by the Republicans for the presidency, was one of them. Was he going to help Alf Landon be elected? we asked him. He laughed and laughed. "He won't come," we said. "You'll see," he answered. "He'll have to come." And he did.

I think Landon was the most embarrassed candidate I ever saw. He came to Des Moines, of course, as Governor of a state needing help from the federal es-tablishment. But there was never an instant when the hordes of watchers present could forget that he was the candidate suggested by the Republicans as a substitute for the confident and majestic Roosevelt. It was absurd and pathetic. The reporters saw him as "Little Alf," and a whole nation was looking over the reporters' shoulders.[14]

Landon warned of regimentation. Roosevelt privately sneered that the Republicans had planned to campaign on the Ten Commandments and to discard all the real issues. Publicly he answered the charges by quoting the record, by associating himself with the Founding Fathers and the people, by insisting that it was really the Democrats who were saving American capitalism. And he used ridicule with stunning impact. He warned:

There will be—there are—many false issues. . . . Partisans, not willing to face realities, will drag out red herrings—as they have always done—to divert attention from the trail of their own weaknesses.

This practice is as old as our democracy. Avoiding the facts—fearful of the truth—a malicious opposition charged that George Washington planned to make himself king under a British form of government; that Thomas Jefferson planned to set up a guillotine under a French Revolutionary form of government; that Andrew Jackson soaked the rich of the Eastern seaboard and planned to surrender American democracy to the dictatorship of a frontier mob. They called Abraham Lincoln a Roman Emperor; Theodore Roosevelt a Destroyer; Woodrow Wilson a self-constituted Messiah.

In this campaign another herring turns up. . . . This year it is Russian. Desperate in mood, angry at failure, cunning in purpose, individuals and groups are seeking to make Communism an issue in an election where Communism is not a controversy between the two major parties. . . . I repudiate the support of any advocate of Communism or of any other alien "ism" which would by fair means or foul change our American democracy. . . .

In the spring of 1933 we faced a crisis which was the ugly fruit of twelve years of neglect of the causes of economic and social unrest. . . .

Most people in the United States remember today the fact that starvation was averted, that homes and farms were saved, that banks were reopened, that crop prices rose, that industry revived, and that the dangerous forces subversive of our form of government were turned aside.

A few people—a few only—unwilling to remember, seem to have forgotten those days.

In the summer of 1933, a nice old gentleman wearing a silk hat fell off the end of a pier. He was unable to swim. A friend ran down the pier, dived overboard and pulled him out; but the silk hat floated off with the tide. After the old gentleman had been revived, he was effusive in his thanks. He praised his friend for saving his life. Today, three years later, the old gentleman is berating his friend because the silk hat was lost.[15]

The ridicule alternated with stark and angry name-calling. Of the "reactionary" opposition, for example:

Never before in all our history have these forces been so united against one candidate as they stand today. They are unanimous in their hate for me—and I welcome their hatred.

I should like to have it said of my first Administration that in it the forces of selfishness and of lust for power met their match. I should like to have it said of my second Administration that in it these forces met their master.[16]

In town after town throughout the West, his back-platform remarks related national problems to the im-

*mediate community. In Chicago he read the long record
of the administration and noted:*

> I have talked to farmers, I have talked to
> miners, I have talked to industrial workers; and in all
> that I have seen and heard one fact has been clear
> as crystal—that they are part and parcel of a rounded
> whole, and that none of them can succeed in his
> chosen occupation if those in the other occupations
> fail in their prosperity. . . .

Tonight, in this center of business, I give the same
message to the business men of America. . . .

To them I say:

Do you have a deposit in the bank? It is safer today
than it has ever been in our history. . . .

Are you an investor? Your stocks and bonds are up to
five- and six-year high levels.

Are you a merchant? Your markets have the precious
life-blood of purchasing power. . . .

Are you in industry? Industrial earnings, industrial
profits are the highest in four, six, or even seven
years! . . .

Are you in railroads? Freight loadings are steadily going up. Passenger receipts are steadily going up—have in
some cases doubled—because your Government made
the railroads cut rates and make money.

Are you a middleman in the great stream of farm
products? The meat and grain that move through your
yards and elevators have a steadier supply, a steadier
demand and steadier prices than you have known for
years. . . .

The struggle against private monopoly is a struggle for,
and not against, American business. It is a struggle to
preserve individual enterprise and economic freedom.

I believe in individualism. . . .

Believing in the solvency of business, the solvency of
farmers and the solvency of workers, I believe also in

the solvency of Government. Your Government is solvent....

The people of America have no quarrel with business. They insist only that the power of concentrated wealth shall not be abused.

We have come through a hard struggle to preserve democracy in America. Where other Nations in other parts of the world have lost that fight, we have won.

The business men of America and all other citizens have joined in a firm resolve to hold the fruits of that victory, to cling to the old ideals and old fundamentals upon which America has grown great.[17]

In Madison Square Garden, at the close of the campaign, he promised:

Of course we will continue our efforts for young men and women so that they may obtain an education and an opportunity to put it to use. Of course we will continue our help for the crippled, for the blind, for the mothers, our insurance for the unemployed, our security for the aged. Of course we will continue to protect the consumer against unnecessary price spreads, against the costs that are added by monopoly and speculation. We will continue our successful efforts to increase his purchasing power and to keep it constant.

For these things, too, and for a multitude of others like them, we have only just begun to fight.[18]

Strangely the remarkable 1936 vote of confidence led to the most politically disastrous years of the Roosevelt leadership. The President launched two major attacks: the Supreme Court fight and the attempt to "purge" anti-Roosevelt Democrats in the 1938 congressional primaries. Both were miserable failures.

F.D.R. had come to rate too highly the power of his personal leadership. He was also toying with one of his ancient, but hopeless, ideals: the realignment of the parties. He had forgotten for the moment the massive power of the Southern conservatives in the Democratic party, the immense advantage of the local leader over the national figure in dominating the specific processes of nomination, the deep conservatism of the American people about their institutions. And he slipped badly at his own game of political tactics. The purge could be made to seem an attack on the security of all congressmen; the "court-packing" bill, an assault on the independence of the judiciary. The two maneuvers gave every disenchanted conservative, every resentful congressman, a banner to which he could rush.

The task Roosevelt undertook in the purge was difficult because he had to manage it somehow within the framework of party loyalty. He explained the matter at Denton, Maryland, in attacking Senator Tydings: "The Democratic Party will live and continue to receive the support of the majority of Americans just so long as it remains a liberal party. . . . As the leader of that party, I propose to try to keep it liberal." [19] But, in assailing Senator Walter F. George of Georgia, F.D.R. hastened to demonstrate the limits that bound his campaign:

> Let me make it clear that he is, and I hope always will be, my personal friend. He is beyond question, beyond any possible question, a gentleman and a scholar; but there are other gentlemen in the Senate and in the House for whom I have a real affectionate regard, but with whom I differ heartily and sincerely on the principles and policies of how the Government of the United States ought to be run. . . .

The test lies . . . in the answer to two questions: first, has the record of the candidate shown, while differing perhaps in details, a constant active fighting attitude in favor of the broad objectives of the party and of the government as they are constituted today; and, secondly, does the candidate really, in his heart, deep down in his heart, believe in those objectives? I regret that in the case of my friend, Senator George, I cannot honestly answer either of these questions in the affirmative.[20]

Only one of Roosevelt's victims went under, a New York Congressman who was beaten really by Ed Flynn and not by the President. The congressional elections brought some setbacks for the party, but Roosevelt insisted that much good had been done:

> Frankly, I think we will have less trouble with the next Congress than with the last. I think the idea is slowly getting through the heads of people like Tydings and George and Bennett Clark that even if they control the 1940 Convention they cannot elect their ticket without the support of this Administration —and I am sufficiently honest to decline to support any conservative Democrat.[21]

The defeats of 1937 and 1938 neither dulled Roosevelt's conviction of his party's liberal role nor of his own destiny. Perhaps, indeed, they reaffirmed both as he prepared to break one of the most sacred traditions of American politics, the two-term limit on the Presidency. Although he hesitated long over the decision, its context was clear in Roosevelt's mind. He had not groomed a successor; he did not find around him a liberal who could win; the burgeoning crises of foreign policy and war enlisted his sense of duty; the potential repudiation of the New Deal by his own party or at the polls enlisted both his feeling of obligation and his regard for his own historic repute. He knew that he could not dictate his successor; he knew that he could not have the nomination for himself; he knew that the nomination must seem a genuine draft, but he knew that such a draft must be arranged. Meanwhile, he played his cards close to the vest, and a score of candidates began to lay foundations for their own nominations—Jim Farley, John Garner, Cordell Hull, Harry Hopkins, among them. Some thought they had his personal approval. What made it even more confusing was the fact that Roosevelt was at least half prepared to retire to Hyde Park and leave the party to welter in its confusion if things did not go precisely right in Chicago.

Frances Perkins has caught the situation aptly:

> . . . men who would not have attempted to win the nomination against Roosevelt felt they had been left out on a limb. The indignation began to be clear when we got to the convention. By this time [Frank] Walker was telling those who had a right to know that the candidate was Roosevelt, and the lines were being laid for the nomination, which would have to be made to appear a universal demand. Indeed, as far as the people were concerned, it was a universal demand. But it is in the nature of political parties and delegates to like a change. With change there is a chance for new people. . . . They were angry because of the patronage that had been denied them for eight years. They were angry that so many strangers and amateurs had come into political life. They were angry about the purge, which had hurt some of them and some of their friends. Some were deeply disturbed over the Supreme Court fight. . . . Some thought that we had had enough of the New Deal, and that it was time to call a halt.[22]

Harold Gosnell explains what happened:

> France's fall three weeks before the Democratic National Convention carried great weight with FDR. By this time he had apparently convinced himself that the world situation required him to defy the no-third-term tradition. . . .

Harry Hopkins, with a private wire to the White House in the bathroom of his suite in the Blackstone Hotel, was the President's self-appointed convention manager. This was a most unusual situation for a man who was not even a delegate to the convention. Edward Flynn was at Hopkins's side to soften the blow, and they passed the word along that Roosevelt would run again if drafted. Many of the party regulars were jealous of Hopkins's power, and they resented the way in which the convention was run.

The delegates went about their business in a sullen mood. . . .

It was plain that FDR was a coy candidate who would like to see the initiative for his nomination come from the outside. The Roosevelt managers urged Farley to withdraw his candidacy in order to preserve harmony in a time of national crisis. Farley would not budge. The roll call gave Roosevelt 946, Farley 72, Garner 61, Tydings 9, and Hull 5.

To add bitterness to the cup the delegates were forced to drink, word came from the White House that the Boss's choice for Vice President was Henry Wallace, Secretary of Agriculture. This was too much for some of the delegates and their followers in the galleries. There were rumblings and catcalls.

Frances Perkins telephoned to the President to come to the convention and calm the delegates. FDR would not move. He did not have to run. If they didn't like Wallace, then he, FDR would bow out. He added that the "Missus" might go to the convention.

Eleanor Roosevelt did go to the convention, and she did a masterful job. She lifted the sights of the hot and tired delegates. The world was on fire. The man in the White House was doing his best to protect the country. It was no time for petty political squabbles.

Eleanor's speech turned the tide.[23]

The nomination was only half the battle. Roosevelt proposed to rest on his laurels, but the Republican Convention was swept by Wendell Willkie, a figure almost as dramatic as the old master himself. President of a great utility which had been wounded by TVA, Willkie was also a rumpled, folksy, smiling personality who could be made into a man of the people—"poor little barefoot Wall Street boy," Harold Ickes derisively called him. Willkie was an amateur. He had so recently joined the G.O.P. that Who's Who still listed him as a Democrat; he once forgot and said to a party audience, "You Republicans." He was so close to Roosevelt's own brand of liberalism that he seemed to be saying only "me too.":

It is clear now that the system of 1929 could not be permitted to stand. Democracy in this third phase needed more social controls. These the New Deal supplied, in a vast network of regulation. The liberal cannot object to these reforms in principle. He realizes the national character of the great American corporations and of many business and financial operations; he realizes that an extension of Federal authority is necessary to establish adequate control over these matters. . . .

. . . [but] the liberal does not see in the present Administration any will to leave men free. He sees only an attempt to increase the powers of government. For the old American principle that government is a liability to be borne by the citizens for the sake of peace, order and security, the New Deal has substituted the notion that government is an asset without which none of us can survive. . . .[24]

This was a ground on which Roosevelt could boast performance against promise. But the tactic was to let Willkie wear himself out. When Roosevelt did start *his campaign at Philadelphia on October 23, Willkie had already made over twenty major addresses. And F.D.R. turned to ridicule again:*

The tears, the crocodile tears, for the laboring man and the laboring woman now being shed in this campaign come from those same Republican leaders who had their chance to prove their love for labor in 1932—and missed it.

Back in 1932, those leaders were willing to let the workers starve if they could not get a job. . . .

Back in 1932, they met the demands of unemployed veterans with troops and tanks.

Back in 1932, they raised their hands in horror at the thought of fixing a minimum wage or maximum hours for labor; they never gave one thought to such things as pensions for old age or insurance for the unemployed.

In 1940, eight years later, what a different tune is played by them! It is a tune played against a sounding board of election day. It is a tune with overtones which whisper: "Votes, votes, votes." [25]

If Roosevelt caught the G.O.P. in a deep dilemma on domestic issues, he ridiculed relentlessly the Republican isolationists who hated Willkie almost as much as they did F.D.R.:

What did the Republican leaders do when they had this chance to increase our national defense almost three years ago? You would think from their present barrage of verbal pyrotechnics, that they rushed in to pass that bill, or that they even demanded a larger expansion of the Navy.

But, ah! my friends, they were not in a national campaign for votes then.

In those days they were trying to build up a different kind of political fence.

In those days they thought that the way to win

votes was by representing this Administration as extravagant in national defense, indeed as hysterical, and as manufacturing panics and inventing foreign dangers. . . .

On the radio these Republican orators swing through the air with the greatest of ease; but the American people are not voting this year for the best trapeze performer. . . .

Great Britain and a lot of other nations would never have received one ounce of help from us—if the decision had been left to Martin, Barton and Fish. . . .[26]

The magic rhythm of Martin, Barton and Fish caught on at once—a slogan of a campaign rescued from near disaster. Binkley describes the result:

The collapse of France and the deadly peril in which it threw Britain apparently reversed a current trend in Roosevelt's declining strength. During the summer the Gallup Poll had indicated a strong probability of the election of Willkie. As late as August 4 the President's strength was only 51 per cent . . . the balloting in the November election gave the President 54.9 per cent of the popular vote. . . . It did not help Willkie when a presidential campaign parade routed through the New York financial district was greeted by the prolonged boos of its denizens . . . the same day, Roosevelt quoted one of Willkie's rash proponents as saying that the President's supporters were "paupers, those who earn less than $1,200 a year and aren't worth that, and the Roosevelt family." . . . No comparable blunder had been made since a slave holding Senator had called laborers the "mudsills of society," a term of contempt of which Lincoln kept reminding his audiences. . . .

It was the great cities . . . that wiped out Willkie's lead in the rural precincts, the villages, towns, and smaller cities, and gave Roosevelt the electoral votes of

New York, Missouri, Ohio, Wisconsin, and Illinois. Illuminating the conclusions of the statistical analyses are the comments of William J. Galvin, Democratic leader in a Charlestown ward of metropolitan Boston. The ward is inhabited by longshoremen, packers, waitresses, and minor city employees, who supported Roosevelt four to one. "Probably no section of the country gained more under the New Deal," said Galvin, and he then proceeded to enumerate specific benefits received: "Hundreds got pay raises under the wage-hour law; more hundreds of seasonal workers are having slack months cushioned by unemployment-insurance benefits. The NYA is helping from 300 to 500 youths; at the worst of the depression thousands held WPA jobs; of 1500 persons past sixty-five in the ward, more than 600 received old-age assistance; another 600 cases are on direct relief and get aid for dependent children. Charlestown is a food-stamp area; the WPA improved its bathing beach; a new low-cost housing project will relieve some of the ward's congestion." For the first time in anybody's memory the Boston Irish are being appointed to Federal district judgeships. Indicative of this ethnic group's loyalty elsewhere is the comment of a Detroit Catholic priest: "If I ever attacked Roosevelt from the pulpit it would be the end of me here." [27]

The coming of war revolutionized the terms of the 1944 campaign. The Republican party nominated New York's Governor, Thomas E. Dewey. Dewey proved himself a regular, but a liberal and an internationalist, thorough in planning, sharp and relentless in attack. But Roosevelt had phenomenal assets. With the war still on, his party could not refuse him the nomination; Dewey was immensely inhibited in his criticism of war administration and foreign policy. The C.I.O.'s Political Action Committee gave Roosevelt a more efficient election machine than the party itself had ever mustered. Even the colorless nomination of Harry S. Truman for Vice-President and Roosevelt's obvious ageing did not deter the electorate. When Roosevelt himself began to fear Dewey's relentless pounding, a mere handful of appearances served to sharpen the old stereotype and arouse the old confidence.

Two incidents revealed clearly the advantages of the "old champ" against the competent but stuffy challenger. One was the Teamsters' Union speech, perhaps the ablest, politically, he ever made: On Dewey's "New Dealism" he said:

The whole purpose of Republican oratory these days seems to be to switch labels. . . .

Can the Old Guard pass itself off as the New Deal? I think not.

We have all seen many marvelous stunts in the circus but no performing elephant could turn a handspring without falling flat on his back. . . .

What the Republican leaders are now saying in effect is this: "Oh just forget what we used to say, we have changed our minds now—we have been reading the public opinion polls about these things and now we know what the American people want." And they say: "Don't leave the task of making peace to those old men who first urged it, and who have already laid the foundations for it, and who have had to fight all of us inch by inch during the last five years to do it. Why, just turn it all over to us. We'll do it so skillfully—that we won't lose a single isolationist vote or a single isolationist campaign contribution.[28]

And on Dewey's talk about the "Roosevelt Recession":

Now, there is an old and somewhat lugubrious adage that says: "Never speak of rope in the house of a man who has been hanged." In the same way,

if I were a Republican leader speaking to a mixed
audience, the last word in the whole dictionary that I
think I would use is that word "depression." [28]

*In reply to the criticism of his family F.D.R. pro-
duced the response which has become a classic:*

> These Republican leaders have not been con-
tent with attacks on me, or my wife, or my sons. No,
not content with that, they now include my little dog,
Fala. Well, of course, I don't resent attacks, and my
family doesn't resent attacks, but Fala *does* resent
attacks. You know, Fala is Scotch, and being a Scottie,
as soon as he learned that the Republican fiction writers
in Congress and out had concocted a story that I had
left him behind on the Aleutian Islands and had sent a
destroyer back to find him—at a cost to the taxpayers
of two or three, or eight or twenty million dollars—his
Scotch soul was furious. He has not been the same dog
since. I am accustomed to hearing malicious falsehoods
about myself—such as that old, worm-eaten chestnut
that I have represented myself as indispensable. But I
think I have a right to resent, to object to libelous
statements about my dog. [28]

*The second incident to reveal his continued mastery
was F.D.R.'s epic four-hour ride through the cold
October rain in New York. His outraged secretary, Bill
Hassett, wrote down that night:*

> The drizzle increased to a full-fledged rain
almost immediately after the President left the train
for his long tour through four of the five boroughs of
New York: Brooklyn, Queens, Bronx, and Manhattan.
He rode in an open car, wholly exposed to the cold rain.
But the ardor of the populace was not dampened and
the sidewalk crowds increased with the rain. . . .

From the Navy Yard through the rain-drenched
streets we sped, the crowds increasing, through Park
Avenue and Tillar Street, Washington and Fulton
Streets, to Bedford Avenue and Ebbetts Field. The
rain was beating down steadily when we reached Ebbetts
Field. Undismayed, the President threw off his Navy
cape and, standing bareheaded in the storm, captured
the enthusiasm of the crowd in the rain-drenched
grounds by declaring that this was his first visit to
Ebbetts Field although he had often rooted for the
Brooklyn Dodgers.

There the Boss stood in the rainstorm, bareheaded and
without his cape, and while the rain beat down upon
him he waved his greeting to the crowd—with his best
smile, too, dynamic, radiant—his very presence in the
storm giving the lie to his detractors who have carried
on unremittingly a whispering campaign, a vendetta,
against his health. By an irony of fate and of fact, the
columnist who has been the bellwether in this unholy
crusade is himself a sick man. Ironically, too, his malady
is a diseased spleen. I'll bet the Boss survives the bulk of
these detractors and calumniators—some of them pretty
puny specimens, though large of mouth. They have
without ceasing fostered the propaganda that the Boss
is old, ill tempered, tired, and worn out—aided and
abetted by photographers who supply, on order, re-
touched pictures putting him in the worst possible
light. Well, the Ebbetts Field appearance has made
plain, everyday liars out of this species of vermin. . . .

On we went from Ebbetts Field to the Borough of
Queens, thence to the Bronx and the United States
Naval Station of the Waves at Hunter College. . . .

From the Naval Training Station we went on through
Harlem and thence eventually to Broadway and through
the garment workers' area, where despite increasing
rain the crowds were thicker than in any other section
along the fifty-mile-plus route. From Seventh Avenue

we went via 34th Street to Fifth Avenue and thence to Washington Square. There the thoroughly drenched President went to Mrs. Roosevelt's apartment—for his first visit—to dry himself and rest in preparation for his address at the Waldorf-Astoria this evening. He had ridden for four hours in an open car under a continuous downpour of rain. . . .[29]

In a sense Roosevelt passed the politician's test with his colors flying smartly. He did win four times. But there were limits to these victories. In broader terms the test of Roosevelt leadership must be the state in which he left the American party system. It will be another generation before anything like a firm estimate can be made. But James M. Burns has raised some serious questions:

Roosevelt did not bother to organize the party for the long run. As a politician eager to win, Roosevelt was concerned with his own political and electoral standing at whatever expense to the party. It was much easier to exploit his own political skill than try to improve the rickety, sprawling party organization. . . .

Roosevelt was less a great creative leader than a skillful manipulator and a brilliant interpreter. Given a big, decisive event—depression at home or naked aggression abroad—he could dramatize its significance and convey its import to the American people. But when the crisis was less striking but no less serious, and when its solution demanded a union of intellectual comprehension and unified and continuing strategic action, Roosevelt saw his efforts turn to dust. . . . He was always a superb tactician, and sometimes a courageous leader, but he failed to achieve that combination of tactical skill and strategic planning that represents the acme of political leadership. . . .[30]

NOTES, *chapter 9*

1. William L. Riordan, *Plunkitt of Tammany Hall. . . .* (Knopf, 1948), 13-14.

2. *Historical Statistics of the United States 1789–1945* (U.S. Government Printing Office, 1949).

3. James M. Burns, *Roosevelt, the Lion and the Fox*, 284-287.

4. Raymond Moley, *After Seven Years*, 52.

5. Samuel Rosenman, ed., *The Public Papers and Addresses of Franklin D. Roosevelt*, V. 58.

6. Elliott Roosevelt, ed., *F.D.R., His Personal Letters, 1928–1945*, 1006-1007.

7. Arthur M. Schlesinger, Jr., *The Coming of the New Deal*, 571-572.

8. Rexford G. Tugwell, *The Art of Politics . . .*, 7.

9. Schlesinger, *New Deal*, 557-558.

10. Harold Ickes, *The Secret Diary of Harold L. Ickes, The First Thousand Days, 1933–1936*, I, 465, 533.

11. Raymond Moley, *27 Masters of Politics in a Personal Perspective* (Funk and Wagnalls, 1949), 40.

12. *Personal Letters, 1928–1945*, 417.

13. James A. Farley, *Behind the Ballots: The Personal History of a Politician*, 304.

14. Tugwell, *Art*, 10-14.

15. *Public Papers*, V, 383-385.

16. *Public Papers*, V, 568-569.

17. *Public Papers*, V, 480-481, 488-489.

18. *Public Papers*, V, 572.

19. Samuel Rosenman, *The Public Papers and Addresses of Franklin D. Roosevelt, 1937–1940* (Macmillan, 1941), *1938*, 517.

20. *Public Papers, 1938*, 469-470.

21. *Personal Letters, 1928–1945*, 827.

22. Frances Perkins, *The Roosevelt I Knew*, 128-129.

23. Harold Gosnell, *Champion Campaigner, Franklin D. Roosevelt* (Macmillan, 1952), 175-178.

24. Wendell Willkie, *This Is Wendell Willkie*, 223-224.

25. *Public Papers, 1940*, 489.

26. *Public Papers, 1940*, 504, 506.

27. Wilfred Binkley, *American Political Parties, Their Natural History* (Knopf, 1947), 382-384, with quotations

214 FRANKLIN D. ROOSEVELT

from Samuel Lubell, "Post Mortem: Who elected Roosevelt?" *Saturday Evening Post,* January 24, 1941.

   28. *Public Papers, 1944–1945,* 285-286, 289-290.

   29. William D. Hassett, *Off the Record with F.D.R., 1942–1945* (Rutgers, 1958), 278-280.

   30. Burns, *Roosevelt,* 380, 403-404.

chapter **10** IN THE SHADOW OF THE
DICTATORS

Relief, Recovery, Reform—and Politics—jostled each
other on a crowded stage throughout the thirties, but
their act was played out to the accompaniment of
rumbling discontent and violent war-mongering abroad.

Just a month before Franklin Roosevelt's first inauguration, Adolph Hitler climaxed fourteen years of
maneuver, murder and mockery by seizing power as
Chancellor of Germany. Mussolini was already well-
established as Fascist dictator of Italy. On March 27,
1933, Japan resigned from the League of Nations; in
December, 1934, she renounced her naval limitation
treaties with France, Great Britain, Italy and the
United States. As Japan stepped up her unconscionable
war on the Chinese, Hitler preached the dogma of hate:
for England, Russia, and France against whom he armed
apace; for the Jews, whom he butchered. And Mussolini,
casting about for the first stone in his new Roman
Empire, attacked hapless Ethiopian spearmen with
machine guns, bombs and poison gas. Early in May,
1936, Italy annexed Ethiopia. That summer unstable
Spain exploded in a Fascist rebellion against her weak
and liberal Republican regime. Spain became a laboratory of modern war: Mussolini and Hitler hastened to
aid Franco with tanks, planes and men; Stalin eagerly
sent "volunteers," matériel, and organizers to the Republican defenders. In October the German-Italian Axis
was formed; in November Japan and Germany linked
arms. By 1937, there was no mistaking the intent of the

new imperialists. The League was bankrupt. Europe, Asia and Africa abounded with underdeveloped nations, large in resources and manpower, helpless to defend themselves, easy picking for pirates. And the old great powers stood divided, reluctant, indecisive. They feared Soviet Russia as much as Hitler and more than Mussolini. They distrusted each other. They were hobbled by the same world depression which had paved the highway for demagogues and dictators elsewhere.

As the crisis burgeoned, the American people continued to look backward and inward. The great withdrawal from world affairs was a blend of bitterness and reluctance. The generation which had fought in America's first modern war remembered the brutality, the mud, the death—and it remembered the glorious crusade of Wilson's symbols, and the disillusioning spectacle of power politics at the peace table. It was difficult to believe that war could come to the western hemisphere. It was almost impossible to divorce the domestic politics of Europe—against which Washington and Jefferson had so urgently warned—from the growing threats to world peace. Why should Americans endanger their hard-won freedom and prosperity in a hopeless campaign to save the world from itself? After 1929, why should they endanger their own recovery? They haggled over unpaid war debts and revived ancient prejudices against the British.

In this mood Republican leadership had hammered out a strange foreign policy, partly adopting the ostrich concept of the people, partly pushing hesitantly beyond it. The League of Nations and the World Court were shunned like the Black Plague. The Smoot-Hawley tariff of 1930 produced the highest trade barriers in American history. As Harding's Secretary of State, Charles Evans Hughes had hopefully pegged American defense on treaties for naval limitation, for the neutralization of Pacific Islands, for the protection of China's integrity. Their fatal faults were the lack of machinery for enforcement, and—as it proved—the unwillingness of the United States to accept their emptiness when they had been violated, in fact, by Japan.

There were hopeful notes within the limits public opinion allowed. One was the Stimson Doctrine, the Hoover administration's refusal to recognize the Japanese puppet regime in Manchuria. Another was the Clark Memorandum of 1930 which repudiated the right to police the western hemisphere, claimed and enforced by the United States since the era of Theodore Roosevelt. Thus F.D.R. inherited not only the mood of isolationism, but also a few, faltering steps toward responsibility in world affairs, and a firm commitment to a new policy in Latin America. He inherited also a World Monetary Conference, which Hoover was helping to arrange, and a World Disarmament Conference which was about to reconvene after earlier frustrations.

Roosevelt moved at once to strengthen the internationalist thread of Hoover's policies. In April, 1933, at the Pan American Union he affirmed the "Good Neighbor" policy which he had forecast in his Inaugural Address:

> The essential qualities of a true Pan Americanism must be the same as those which constitute a good neighbor, namely, mutual understanding, and, through such understanding, a sympathetic appreciation of the others' point of view. It is only in this manner that we can hope to build up a system of which confidence, friendship and good-will are the cornerstones.
> In this spirit the people of every Republic on our continent are coming to a deep understanding of the fact that the Monroe Doctrine, of which so much has been written and spoken for more than a century, was and is directed at the maintenance of independence by the peoples of the continent. . . .
> In this spirit of mutual understanding and of co-

operation on this Continent you and I cannot fail to be disturbed by any armed strife between neighbors. . . .

We all of us have peculiar problems, and, to speak frankly, the interests of our own citizens must, in each instance, come first. But it is equally true that it is of vital importance to every Nation of this Continent that the American Governments, individually, take, without further delay, such action as may be possible to abolish all unnecessary and artificial barriers and restrictions which now hamper the healthy flow of trade between the peoples of the American Republics.[1]

A month later he made an "Appeal to the Nations" and to his own Congress for disarmament:

It is high time for us and for every other Nation to understand the simple fact that the invasion of any Nation, or the destruction of a national sovereignty can be prevented only by the complete elimination of the weapons that make such a course possible today. . . .

The way to disarm is to disarm. The way to prevent invasion is to make it impossible.

I have asked for an agreement among Nations on four practical and simultaneous steps.

First, that through a series of steps the weapons of offensive warfare be eliminated;

Second, that the first definite step be taken now;

Third, that while these steps are being taken no Nation shall increase existing armaments over and above the limitations of treaty obligations.

Fourth, that subject to existing treaty rights no Nation during the disarmament period shall send any armed force of whatsoever nature across its own borders.[2]

By July some of the illusions were shattered. The London Economic Conference had been "torpedoed"

—by Roosevelt. The Disarmament Conference was just as sad. F.D.R.'s "Appeal to the Nations," the day before Hitler's militant speech to the Reichstag in mid-May, had re-echoed emptily. England and France feared that offensive weapons could not be distinguished from defensive weapons. The Senate Foreign Affairs Committee insisted that any Presidential embargo of warring parties must be applied to all participants, and not merely to the aggressors. Hitler was willing to make propaganda by seeming to go along, despite his rapid rearming. When Germany withdrew from the Conference in the fall of 1933, Roosevelt brought home his own delegation quietly—but not quietly enough to stop Hitler's press from claiming that it was F.D.R. who had landed a "knock-out blow" on the League of Nations.

All of this has led one scholar to label it "Foreign Policy by Makeshift," though in fact, once Roosevelt had made up his mind during the summer of 1933, there was a consistent opposition to totalitarian expansion. There would always be two limits, however. If real conflicts of interest appeared, foreign policy must bend to domestic recovery. And Roosevelt the policymaker would not move more rapidly than could Roosevelt the salesman. He would tell Sam Rosenman, "It's a terrible thing to look over your shoulder when you are trying to lead—and to find no one there." [8]

Even in the summer and fall of 1933 there were significant areas in which the liberal Roosevelt could work without fundamental conflict. One was the recognition of Soviet Russia which had been so persistently feared and so studiously ignored by the State Department throughout the twenties.

Another was the Good Neighbor policy. Hoover had already laid the groundwork by withdrawing Marines from Nicaragua in January. In August Roosevelt signed a treaty with Haiti providing for the departure of the Marines there by October, 1934. Hull's permissiveness at the Montevideo Inter-American Conference in

December made a good impression. The United States agreed easily to an Argentine-inspired treaty which committed American powers to nonintervention in the affairs of others. During the summer of 1933 Roosevelt had himself pointed the way by refusing to intervene in the Cuban revolution against the dictatorial Machado regime. In May, 1934, a treaty was concluded with Cuba which made formal the abrogation of the Platt Amendment which had given the United States the right to intervene there since 1898. The first Reciprocal Trade Agreement was signed with Cuba in August, 1934, and the creation of a transitional Commonwealth of the Philippines served as further assurance that the old imperialism was dying. In 1936 a treaty with Panama ended the protectorate there. By then the foundation had been well laid for the hemispheric co-operation which would turn the Monroe Doctrine into an inter-American article of faith, and which would make the defense of the Americas against the Axis a nearly unanimous venture.

It had also become a major boast of the Roosevelt administration. At Chautauqua in August, 1936, he summarized the policy and claimed:

> To a measurable degree it has succeeded; the whole world now knows that the United States cherishes no predatory ambitions. We are strong; but less powerful nations know that they need not fear our strength. We seek no conquest; we stand for peace. . . .

Throughout the Americas the spirit of the good neighbor is a practical and living fact.[4]

By December, 1936, when he had journeyed to Buenos Aires to open the Inter-American Conference, Roosevelt was already thinking of hemispheric solidarity as a weapon against the dictators. The Conference adopted a machinery to implement the promises of peace which had been exchanged since 1933, a mechanism of mutual consultation which married the broadly differing ambitions of Argentina for absolute nonintervention and the United States for maintaining the Monroe Doctrine.

Hull's Reciprocal Trade Agreements program was the partner of the Good Neighbor policy. But it was held off for a year by Roosevelt's lapse into economic nationalism and by his fear of a battle in Congress for which full preparation must be made. By the 1934 session he was ready for the bill. Henry Wallace, in his best-selling pamphlet, America Must Choose, staked out the argument for reciprocity:

> . . . I see the seeds of war alike in laissez-faire accumulating pressing surpluses at home, and in seeking by hook or crook to thrust such surpluses abroad. Whether such a system is permitted freely to secrete and discharge its own poison within national borders or about the world at large, the pressure of ungoverned surpluses seems to me an equal stimulant to ruination and slaughter, before and during wars. . . .
>
> It comes to this: If we insist upon selling without buying, we have to lend our surplus to foreign countries, and never take it back. It stays abroad. But we think we still own it, and that makes us figure out ways and means of keeping the investment safe. We must have some security that transcends the good faith of the borrower. There is no surer path to war.
>
> The method of reciprocal trade, on the other hand, leads to peace. It makes no sales without providing opportunities for the buyers to pay the bill. Since the bill does not remain outstanding indefinitely, and does not have to be collected at the point of a gun, it makes new business easy to get and profitable. . . . [5]

Roosevelt himself could personalize the issue more dramatically. Faced with complaints from New York dairy farmers about the impending agreement with Canada, he explained:

> Now, here is the theory: There are a great many items but we can take them all together. If I give the Canadian farmers a chance to ship in a million and a half more gallons [of cream] than they ship in today, it means our people are going to be able to sell a very large amount of other goods—automobiles, shoes, etc. That is our theory; the more trade, the more employment.[6]

After twelve years of the agreements, economist Broadus Mitchell would conclude:

> Twenty-six reciprocal trade agreements (including four supplementary ones) were signed under this act and its extensions in 1937 and 1940 to the end of our period, beginning with the agreement with Cuba, effective September 3, 1934, and embracing, as the last, that with Argentina, effective only three weeks before Pearl Harbor, November 15, 1941. It is impossible to say what the history of the nation's foreign trade program would have been in these seven years in the absence of the agreements program. As it was, the rate of improvement did not increase, except for the year 1936, which was countered by a corresponding decline in 1937, until the effect of armaments orders became conspicuous with the outbreak of war. Even then, until 1940 the rate of gain was not as great as in 1936, after which the curve was steeper. By the end of 1941 the nation's foreign trade was above that of 1929 and equal to that of the middle of 1920. . . .
> The act empowered the President, in order to obtain from other countries concessions on American exports, to reduce existing United States tariff rates up to 50 per cent, to bind existing rates against increase, and to

guarantee continued duty-free entry of products on the free list. Nearly two thirds of the nation's total foreign trade, and a higher percentage of that with Latin America, was carried on with countries covered by reciprocal trade agreements. Perhaps of equal importance with the direct concessions obtained was inauguration or confirmation by the agreements of the most-favored-nation provision. This protected American exporters against subsequent lowering of import duties by an agreement country to producers elsewhere, generalized the concessions to all countries which did not discriminate against the United States, and tended to break down the constricting system of quotas, exchange control, and purchases by government monopolies which had grown up in the world and was at that moment serving the military purposes of countries with which the United States was soon to be at war.[7]

When Roosevelt turned to the problems of Europe, he was inhibited by both the broad acceptance of isolationism and his own confusion. Especially important was the key position isolationists occupied in Congress. Many of the old progressives who supported his domestic program—George Norris for example—were rigidly suspicious of all things European. Many a New Dealer was also an idealistic pacifist. Even the Cabinet was badly divided. On the problem of war debts Roosevelt was neither willing nor able to move for their cancellation or even for another moratorium such as Hoover had granted. He thought much but did little. In the vacuum the isolationists took the lead with an act to ban the sale of securities of any nation which had defaulted on a war-debt payment. This bill punished American bondholders as well as foreign governments, discouraged token payments, which some nations might have made, and raised another block to world trade.

It was easily forgotten that the ability of nations to pay their debts depended upon their ability to earn gold or dollars. Little Finland became the pet of American public opinion when she alone continued payments. No notice was taken of the tiny size of her debt, or her favorable balance of trade with the New World. Meanwhile, Roosevelt felt that the best he could do was to put the problem on the shelf.

Roosevelt continued to see disarmament as the essential prerequisite to peace. Early in 1936 he wrote to Jesse Straus in Paris, "The Armament race means bankruptcy or war—there is no possible out from that statement." [8] As the Axis powers proved obdurate, Roosevelt cast about for new expedients. When Great Britain refused to agree to make public notice of all arms purchases, Roosevelt's irritation was sharp. In March, 1935, he complained:

> . . . the only practical way of keeping German armaments down to an agreed-on level . . . [is] to inspect German armament supplies. England dashes this hope by declining to be inspected herself. The last paragraph is a frank admission that the British decline to accept detailed publicity as to armament orders on the ground that it would prejudice their armament trade.
>
> At some future time it may be advisable to pull this rabbit out of our hat as proof that the present British Government is not sincere in seeking limitation or reduction of present world armaments or present world trade in warlike weapons.
>
> I am much discouraged. [9]

As late as the spring of 1937, when disarmament was a lost cause, he would still insist that the only hope was to stop the race somehow:

The more I study the situation, the more I am convinced that an economic approach to peace is a pretty weak reed for Europe to lean on. . . . How do we make progress if England and France say we cannot help Germany and Italy to achieve economic security if they continue to arm and threaten, while simultaneously Germany and Italy say we must continue to arm and threaten because they will not give us economic security. [10]

Even in minor matters Roosevelt was excessively worried about the isolationists. But in 1935, he did dust off his old crusade for American membership in the Permanent Court of International Justice. The fight in the Senate degenerated into a squabble over "reservations" reminiscent of the debate on the League of Nations fifteen years before; the World Court measure was lost under a deluge of hostile letters and telegrams.

The President was angry. He wrote to Senate leader Joe Robinson:

As to the thirty-six Senators who placed themselves on record against the principles of a World Court, I am inclined to think that if they ever get to Heaven they will be doing a great deal of apologizing for a very long time—that is if God is against war—and I think He is. [11]

But F.D.R. must share the blame. On this issue he had been unwilling to exert the kind of leadership which had proved so effective on the domestic program. More important, while inaction was bringing him defeat, a group of senators was mobilizing the nation for a retreat from the world. As James M. Burns has written:

In the white marble caucus room of the

Senate Office Building late in 1934 sat the stage managers of a carefully planned, elaborately staged drama. In the center behind the long table was the hero of the drama, a stern, hard-faced young senator named Gerald P. Nye; flanking him were other idols of American isolationism—Arthur H. Vandenberg, Bennett Champ Clark, Homer T. Bone. Of villains in this drama there were many: evil, bloodsucking "merchants of death," who paraded before the committee day after day to confess their sins. Of heroines there was only one: an ethereal being, always appealed to but never seen, a figure named Peace. Crowded behind the villains was the chorus, the spectators who craned their necks and muttered with indignation as the play unfolded.

Such was the Nye Committee investigating the munitions industry. Like many other famous Senate investigations, the Nye probe was less a search for data than a dramatization of things already known or rightly suspected. But the charges were dramatic and shocking. Arms makers had bribed politicians, shared patents, divided up business, reaped incredible profits, evaded taxes—all in the sordid trade of death weapons. Even worse, munitions makers helped foment wars to boost their profits.

Rarely have Senate hearings fallen with such heavy impact on the stream of American opinion. . . . Writers were busy showing that 1917 was not due to German submarines or a conception of neutral rights, but to a few greedy capitalists. Germany was not so guilty after all. The Americans had been saps and suckers.

With war clouds piling up again in Europe, millions of Americans vowed, "Never again." Women organized peace societies. College students formed the "Veterans of Future Wars" to collect their bonuses now, before they had to fight and die. Isolationism was strong everywhere, but especially in the Midwest, Northwest, and Rockies. . . .

At this crucial juncture Roosevelt offered little leadership . . . only one outcome was possible—a national stampede for a storm cellar to sit out the tempests ahead. During the second Hundred Days, isolationists on Capitol Hill were pressing for legislation requiring the President, in event of war abroad, to embargo export of arms to all belligerents. Roosevelt and Hull favored such embargo authority, but they wanted to empower the President to discriminate between aggressor and victim. . . .

But the isolationists would have none of it. Such discretion, they shouted, would mean sure entanglement in alien quarrels. Pittman was hostile and surly. The President was riding for a fall, he warned. . . .

The President did get licked. Mandatory arms embargo legislation passed both chambers by almost unanimous votes [August 31, 1935]. Roosevelt dared not stand against the tide; he had urgent domestic bills to get through and the isolationists were threatening to filibuster. The President signed the measure, but he warned that the inflexible provisions might drag us into war instead of keeping us out.[12]

Actually, Roosevelt had been neither blind nor inactive. He had been searching for months for the weapons which the executive might use without resort to Congress. In April, 1935, he had written Colonel Edward M. House:

It seems to me that if France, Italy, England and the "Little Entente" decide on positive action they would be far wiser not to invade Germany but rather to establish a complete blockade of Germany. . . . Such a blockade would raise for us the question of its effectiveness. If we found it was an effective blockade, as a matter of fact, recognition of the blockade by us would obviously follow. This, after all, is not a boycott nor an economic sanction, but in effect it is the same thing. A boycott or sanction could not be recognized by us without Congressional action but a blockade would fall under the Executive's power after establishment of the fact.[13]

He was worried by the decline of United States prestige. To Ambassador Bullitt he complained that spring: "I gather that no European Capital in the present confusion cares a continental damn what the United States thinks or does." [14]

He tried direct persuasion on Mussolini. But when the Fascist legions poured over the Ethiopian boundary, his public statement to the Nation contained only a moralistic homily which implied mild disapproval but promised inaction:

> Our national determination to keep free of foreign wars and foreign entanglements cannot prevent us from feeling deep concern when ideals and principles that we have cherished are challenged. In the United States we regard it as axiomatic that every person shall enjoy the free exercise of his religion according to the dictates of his conscience. Our flag for a century and a half has been the symbol of the principles of liberty, of conscience, of religious freedom and of equality before the law; and these concepts are deeply ingrained in our national character. . . .
>
> As President of the United States I say to you most earnestly once more that the people of America and the Government of those people intend and expect to remain at peace with all the world. . . .[15]

Roosevelt's embarrassment was intensified by what happened in Ethiopia. Given the Senate's attitude, Hull did not dare to support the League's proposal for sanctions against Mussolini. The Neutrality Act did not cover the raw materials of war. Hull attempted to fill the breach with a demand for a "moral embargo" by Americans, particularly on oil. But American exports to Italy mounted sharply. Confusion became worse when attempts of Sir Samuel Hoare and Pierre Laval to appease Il Duce by partitioning Ethiopia undermined the sanctions program. In the fog of inaction, Mussolini crushed his antique opponent.

The President oscillated with events. In January, 1936, he wrote his ambassador in Warsaw: "Everywhere people ask me—'If there is a European War can you keep us out of it'—and I tell them that I can and will if the people of the Nation back me up." [16]

February, 1936, saw the assassination of the Japanese Premier by militarists, and on March 7 Hitler bluffed his way into the demilitarized Rhineland. Now Roosevelt confided to William E. Dodd in Berlin:

> All the experts here, there and the other place say "There will be no war." They said the same thing all through July, 1914. . . . In those days I believed the experts. Today I have my tongue in my cheek. This does not mean that I am become cynical; but as President, I have to be ready just like a Fire Department! [17]

Meanwhile the Senate steadfastly refused Hull's pleas that the executive be given discretion in the new neutrality legislation and that it be extended to cover the items on his "moral embargo" list. Walter Lippmann described the policy aptly: "I see two thugs about to start an assault on my honest neighbor next door. As he may expect me to hand him a stick to help beat them off, I am signaling the thugs to go ahead and I'll keep clear. I am neutral." [18]

Nevertheless, when the Spanish army rebellion broke out in July, Roosevelt applied the neutrality spirit with force. He did not need to; the act did not technically apply to civil wars. He did not feel neutral himself; he could write to Claude Bowers in Berlin: "Over here the Hearst papers and most of the conservative editors are playing up all kinds of atrocities on the part of what they call the Communist government in Madrid—nothing about atrocities on the part of the rebels." [19]

But Roosevelt and Hull agreed with London and Paris that it was more urgent to avoid giving Hitler an excuse to move than it was to save the Spanish Republic. They announced another "moral embargo." It was substantially successful, although approximately three thousand Americans did go to Spain to fight for the Republic. It helped Franco immensely; since England and France held their embargoes firm while Italy and Germany sent troops and weapons and officers to El Caudillo.

When Roosevelt did speak on foreign policy as the 1936 campaign approached, he underlined the mood of isolationism. At Chautauqua in August, he said:

> We shun political commitments which might entangle us in foreign wars; we avoid connection with the political activities of the League of Nations; but I am glad to say that we have co-operated wholeheartedly in the social and humanitarian work at Geneva. . . .

We are not isolationists except in so far as we seek to isolate ourselves completely from war. Yet we must remember that so long as war exists on earth there will be some danger that even the Nation which most ardently desires peace may be drawn into war.

I have seen war. I have seen war on land and sea. I have seen blood running from the wounded. I have seen men coughing out their gassed lungs. I have seen the dead in the mud. I have seen cities destroyed. I have seen two hundred limping, exhausted men come

out of the line—the survivors of a regiment of one
thousand that went forward forty-eight hours before.
I have seen children starving. I have seen the agony of
mothers and wives. I hate war.

I have passed unnumbered hours, I shall pass unnumbered hours, thinking and planning how war may
be kept from this Nation.[20]

In January, 1937, the President requested, and got,
a congressional embargo against both parties in the
bloody Spanish War which was to stretch out for two
more years. Privately, however, he betrayed his uneasiness to an old friend:

What a confusion it all is. Every week
changes the picture and the basis for it all lies, *I think*,
not in communism or the fear of communism but in
Germany and the fear of what the present German
leaders are meeting for or being drawn toward.

For all these reasons, I am "watchfully waiting. . . ."
I would not dare to say this out loud because sometimes it is better to appear much wiser than one really
is.[21]

His uneasiness grew with the rigid new neutrality
law of May 1, 1937. He had lost his battle for executive
discretion, and he had lost his battle for embargo of
raw materials. The Herald-Tribune labeled the bill:
"An Act to Preserve the United States from Intervention in the War of 1914–1918." To the existing barriers
the Congress had added bans against raising contributions to help belligerents, American citizens' traveling
on belligerent ships, the arming of American merchant-
men, and dealing in the securities of belligerent nations. The one measure of flexibility grew from the unwillingness of Congress to attack directly the great
mining and manufacturing interests in the raw-materials

area. It was left to the President to list from time to
time the raw materials which were to be embargoed.
But these might still be bought in the United States by
belligerents if they paid cash and carried them in their
own ships. There were limits to neutrality, it appeared.
The Congress was perfectly willing to sell oil, steel,
copper to any belligerent provided only that things were
arranged so that no American could possibly suffer,
physically or financially.

1937 proved to be a year of decision. For the United
States it dramatically displayed the defects of neutrality.
The French and British began to lose confidence in their
prospective Russian ally, as the Soviet blood purges
shocked the world and as rumors abounded of a Stalin-
Hitler flirtation. Meanwhile in July, the Japanese army
broke out of Manchuria into North China and Chiang
Kai-shek decided to make his stand. The administration's concern was reflected in Hull's and Ambassador
Grew's sharp warnings to Tokyo and in Hull's vague
demands for world co-operation. But the neutrality act
spoke a hundred times more clearly than anything the
Secretary of State could say. Roosevelt could only refuse
to apply it, taking advantage of Japan's failure to make
a formal declaration of war. It was all too evident that
the rigid embargoes would play into the hands of the
Nipponese warlords and strangle the already starved
Chinese armies. Meanwhile British and American
offers to mediate were sharply rejected in Tokyo.

Roosevelt's refusal to invoke the law in the Asian
crisis brought no massive criticism. Encouraged, he now
planned a speech to test what seemed a public change
of heart. It was timed to coincide with the opening of
the Nine Power Conference in Brussels, where the
United States and other signatories of the treaty to
guard China's integrity would decide what to do about
Japanese aggression. It was delivered October 5, 1937, in
Chicago at the heart of the isolationist domain. This

"Quarantine" speech was the turning point of Roosevelt's foreign policy:

> Innocent peoples, innocent nations, are being cruelly sacrificed to a greed for power and supremacy which is devoid of all sense of justice and humane considerations.

To paraphrase a recent author "perhaps we foresee a time when men, exultant in the technique of homicide, will rage so hotly over the world that every precious thing will be in danger, every book and picture and harmony, every treasure garnered through two millenniums, the small, the delicate, the defenseless—all will be lost or wrecked or utterly destroyed."

If those things come to pass in other parts of the world, let no one imagine that America will escape, that America may expect mercy, that this Western Hemisphere will not be attacked and that it will continue tranquilly and peacefully to carry on the ethics and the arts of civilization. . . .

If those days are not to come to pass—if we are to have a world in which we can breathe freely and live in amity without fear—the peace-loving nations must make a concerted effort to uphold laws and principles on which alone peace can rest secure. . . .

The overwhelming majority of the peoples and nations of the world today want to live in peace. . . . The peace, the freedom and the security of ninety percent of the population of the world is being jeopardized by the remaining ten percent. . . . Surely the ninety percent . . . can and must find some way to make their will prevail. . . .

It seems to be unfortunately true that the epidemic of world lawlessness is spreading.

When an epidemic of physical disease starts to spread, the community approves and joins in a quarantine of the patients in order to protect the health of the community against the spread of the disease. . . .

War is a contagion, whether it be declared or undeclared. It can engulf states and peoples remote from the original scene of hostilities. We are determined to keep out of war, yet we cannot insure ourselves against the disastrous effects of war and the dangers of involvement. We are adopting such measures as will minimize our risk of involvement, but we cannot have complete protection in a world of disorder in which confidence and security have broken down. . . .

America hates war. America hopes for peace. Therefore, America actively engages in the search for peace.[22]

Charles Beard summarized the mixed reactions:

Internationalists greeted the speech as revealing a definite reversal of policy on the part of the President and applauded it; but they were cautious and uncertain in respect of suggesting to the President ways and means of "implementing" his new policy. In general they laid stress on the effectiveness of collective action if vigorously applied to the governments designated as aggressors; but they were diffident, and refrained from emphasizing the primary point of their doctrine: "moral" and "economic" sanctions are futile unless backed by adequate armed force and, if necessary, by war against the designated aggressors.

Some internationalists, even so, maintained that the United States could apply moral and economic sanctions to "aggressors," on its own motion or in conjunction with other "peace-loving" nations, without incurring the risk of war, without assuming an obligation to go to war in case these measures failed to overcome the aggressors against whom they were directed. . . .

As a rule, . . . members of the anti-war bloc maintained that there was no middle ground, that the United States could not depart from neutrality as recognized in international law without a definite risk of war, and that the quarantine doctrine, if actually applied, meant nothing more nor less than setting out on the road to war. Hence they spoke and wrote in unequivocal language against it. Public opinion at the time appeared to be arrayed on their side. On the basis of various popular polls taken in the preceding months, it had been reported that about three fourths of the people were opposed to getting into another world war. Indeed in April, 1937, 71 per cent of the persons polled had answered that they thought it had been a mistake for the United States to become embroiled in the first World War.[23]

The President was stung by the studied silence of party leaders. Hull made clear privately his disapproval of the strong language, and there was no genuine mobilization of public opinion. Roosevelt prepared to retreat. Only to an old friend did he try to explain:

> As you know, I am fighting against a public psychology of long standing—a psychology which comes very close to saying "Peace at any price."
> I have felt, however, that there will be a growing response to the ideal that when a few nations fail to maintain certain fundamental rules of conduct, the most practical and most peaceful thing to do in the long run is to "quarantine" them. I am inclined to think that this is more Christian, as well as more practical, than that the world should go to war with them.[24]

When a Japanese commander deliberately sank an American gunboat, the Panay, on the Yangtze River that December, there was a moment of shock, but no great wave of feeling. The matter was settled within ten days by Japan's obsequious apologies. In January, 1938, when Representative Louis Ludlow proposed a constitutional amendment to require a popular referendum on any declaration of war, it was defeated by only thirty-one votes in the House. As Japan stepped up her murderous bombing of crowded Chinese cities, the feeling grew that the United States should withdraw from Asia completely.

But Roosevelt's determination had hardened. Committed to isolation for the moment, with collective security a pathetic memory and England and France cowering before Hitler, he moved to expand the defense establishment apace. During the debate on the Ludlow amendment he had written his oldest son:

> On the Pacific Coast especially, the defense of the Coast lies not on the Coast, but between three and four thousand miles from the Coast.
> Once the defense of the Coast is withdrawn to the Coast itself, no government can give adequate security to Portland or any other city within two hundred miles of the Pacific Ocean.[25]

At the end of January, Roosevelt warned Congress that American cities could be bombed, that both coasts could be attacked. He got appropriations for two battleships and two cruisers, as well as general increases for both Army and Navy. Meanwhile, Secretary of the Treasury Henry Morgenthau used the powers at his disposal to stock-pile strategic materials and to aid the British and French purchasing missions in their search for scarce equipment.

That March Hitler grabbed Austria. By summer tension was growing over Der Fuehrer's ambitions in Czechoslovakia. On August 18, Roosevelt announced that the United States would not stand by as a neutral if Canada should be attacked. In September, he confided to Ambassador Phillips in Rome:

> ... we do not easily lose our heads, but if we get the idea that the future of our form of government

is threatened by a coalition of European dictators, we might wade in with everything we have to give.

If war starts now the situation here will be very different from 1914. . . . Today I think ninety-nine per cent of our people are definitely anti-German and anti-Italian in sentiment—and incidentally, I would not propose to ask them to be neutral in thought. I would strongly encourage their natural sympathy while at the same time avoiding any thought of sending troops to Europe. . . .[26]

But there were dangers at home. Roosevelt was only half joking when he wrote:

Did you know that Phil La Follette started his Third Party with a huge meeting in Wisconsin, the chief feature of which was the dedication of a new emblem—a twenty foot wide banner with a red circle and a blue cross on it? While the crowd present was carried away with the enthusiasm of the moment, most of the country seem to think this was a feeble imitation of the Swastika. All that remains is for some major party to adopt a new form of arm salute. I have suggested the raising of both arms above the head, followed by a bow from the waist. At least this will be good for people's figures![27]

When Roosevelt did act in the European crisis it was as a neutral broker. In mid-September Hitler mobilized Germany in support of his claims that the Sudeten Germans within Czechoslovakia were being abused. Britain and France were weak in both arms and leadership. Two pathetic trips to Hitler taught Neville Chamberlain, the British Prime Minister, the taste of humiliation. When Chamberlain made a last desperate plea to Hitler, Roosevelt and Hull supported it with their own personal appeal to the Germans and the Czechs to avoid war. When Hitler refused to con-

238 FRANKLIN D. ROOSEVELT

tinue negotiations, Roosevelt sent a second appeal and then, simultaneously with the British, asked Mussolini to intervene. Il Duce did. The result was an immediate conference at Munich, held while German troops were massed on the Czech frontier and German ships were being ordered into neutral ports.

For the moment the decision to take Sudetenland away from the Czechs was hailed as a moderate price for peace. Chamberlain announced on his return from Munich, "I believe it is peace in our time." Hitler promised, "Germany has no more territorial problems in Europe." Many guessed, but few wanted to admit, that it had been a blackmailer's deal. No one knew that Hitler had turned at once to his Chief of Staff to request information on what military action would be required to destroy Czechoslovakia completely.

By late October, Roosevelt was ready to warn his radio audience: "It is becoming increasingly clear that peace by fear has no higher or more enduring quality than peace by the sword. There can be no peace if the reign of law is to be replaced by a recurrent sanctification of sheer force. There can be no peace if national policy adopts as a deliberate instrument the threat of war." [28]

In November, the Nazis triggered a frenzied wave of pillage, rape and murder against the Jews. Roosevelt and Hull had long since taken the initiative in trying to solve the problems of the nearly two hundred thousand refugees who had already escaped Germany. They had been able to do little as it became clear that Americans were no more willing than others to break down their immigration barriers in an era of depression. Now public opinion began to shift sharply. Roosevelt recalled his ambassador from Germany. An unofficial boycott of German goods began to catch on. Newspapers condemned the Nazi brutality. Secretary Ickes took to the radio to pillory Henry Ford and Charles A.

Lindbergh for accepting German decorations. Meanwhile, concerned about German infiltration in Latin America, Hull worked hard to perfect the Declaration of Lima, which was adopted the day before Christmas. This strengthened the machinery for hemisphere solidarity in the face of "all foreign intervention or activity."

In his Annual Message on January 4, 1939, Roosevelt finally made his commitment:

> There comes a time in the affairs of men when they must prepare to defend, not their homes alone, but the tenets of faith and humanity on which their churches, their governments and their very civilization are founded. The defense of religion, of democracy and of good faith among nations is all the same fight. To save one we must now make up our minds to save all. . . .
> . . . the world has grown so small and the weapons of attack so swift that no nation can be safe in its will to peace so long as any other powerful nation refuses to settle its grievances at the council table. . . .
> At the very least, we can and should avoid any action, or any lack of action, which will encourage, assist or build up an aggressor. We have learned that when we deliberately try to legislate neutrality, our neutrality laws may operate unevenly and unfairly—may actually give aid to an aggressor and deny it to the victim. The instinct of self-preservation should warn us that we ought not to let that happen any more.
> And we have learned something else—the old, old lesson that probability of attack is mightily decreased by the assurance of an ever ready defense. . . ."[29]

Roosevelt asked for repeal of the compulsory embargo provisions of the Neutrality Act. On January 5 he presented an unprecedented nine-billion-dollar budget,

and a week later another request for a half billion more
for defense. When he was quoted by a senator as having
said that the American frontier was on the Rhine,
Roosevelt denied it, but he explained to an old friend:

> . . . I did point out that there are fifteen or
> sixteen independent nations in Europe whose con-
> tinued independent political and economic existence
> is of actual moment to the ultimate defense of the
> United States. . . . And I pointed out that Czechoslo-
> vakia, a year ago, could very properly be called a link
> in American defense against German and Italian ag-
> gression in the future: that Czechoslovakia no longer
> constituted such a link.
> All of which was, of course, not only true but proper.
> The howls and curses that have continued to come from
> Berlin and Rome convince me that the general result
> has been good even if a few silly Senators reported the
> conversation in a wholly untruthful way.[30]

The budget was substantially passed.

The hard-fought battle for revision of neutrality legislation was lost. The administration ran into a rock wall
with senators like William E. Borah who announced
that his sources of information were more reliable than
the State Department's and that he knew there was no
danger of war in Europe "this year." "All this hysteria,"
he said, was "manufactured and artificial." Meanwhile
the world burned.

On March 14 Hitler tore up the Munich Pact, rolled
across prostrate Czechoslovakia and then grabbed the
territory of Memel from tiny Lithuania. Franco finally
mashed the last of the loyalist resistance in Spain. Il
Duce took advantage of the moment to attack Albania.
On April 14 Roosevelt turned suddenly to personal
diplomacy again with an appeal to Hitler and Mussolini
to negotiate their problems and assure the peace for

ten years. Their answers were bombastic charges that they were being "encircled" and impoverished, that their people must expand or die.

In all these bitter weeks, while Congress was thwarting Roosevelt's efforts abroad and pinching off the New Deal at home, there was one radiantly magnificent interlude. This was the visit of the British king and queen in June. Attending to every detail, Roosevelt set the stage for their reception with the care and gusto of a Broadway director. The royal pair played their parts brilliantly, the queen winning everyone's heart with her gracious bonnie ways, the king looking young, strong and earnest. Scene after scene came off perfectly: the reception by half a million Washingtonians in sweltering Washington heat; the well-schooled king even remembering to remark "Cotton Ed Smith?" when he met South Carolina's senior Senator; the state dinner in the White House climaxed with an eloquent presidential toast and with songs by Kate Smith and Marian Anderson; the inevitable wreath laying at Arlington Cemetery; the drive through New York City's crowds to the World's Fair; the picnic at Hyde Park that featured hot dogs, baked beans, and strawberry shortcake; the long tête-à-tête between president and monarch ending at 1:30 in the morning when Roosevelt put his hand on the royal knee and said, "Young man, it's time for you to go to bed!"; the final good-by at the Hyde Park station, with the crowds bursting spontaneously into "Auld Lang Syne" and the President calling after the moving train, "Good luck to you! All the luck in the world!" [81]

King George and Queen Elizabeth returned to a Europe awaiting disaster. In July Roosevelt again requested the repeal of the embargo. He even toyed for a moment with ignoring it. While Hitler stepped up his demands on Poland to relinquish its corridor to the sea, Hull abrogated, finally, the United States Trade Treaty with Japan. But in Europe it was too late. On August 23, Hitler's pact with Stalin was announced. The next day Roosevelt urged Italy, Germany and Poland to submit to arbitration. At dawn on September 1, the Nazi hordes swept across the border of Poland. Two days later England and France declared war on Hitler

NOTES, *chapter 10*

1. Samuel Rosenman, ed., *The Public Papers and Addresses of Franklin D. Roosevelt,* II, 130-131.

2. *Public Papers,* II, 192-193.

3. Samuel Rosenman, *Working with Roosevelt,* 167.

4. *Public Papers,* V, 286-287.

5. Henry Wallace, *America Must Choose,* 19-20.

6. *Public Papers,* IV, 448.

7. Broadus Mitchell, *Depression Decade: From New Era through New Deal, 1931–1941,* 357-358.

8. Elliott Roosevelt, ed., *F.D.R., His Personal Letters, 1928–1945,* 555.

9. *Personal Letters, 1928–1945,* 462.

10. *Personal Letters, 1928–1945,* 680.

11. *Personal Letters, 1928–1945,* 450.

12. James M. Burns, *Roosevelt, the Lion and the Fox,* 253-255.

13. *Personal Letters, 1928–1945,* 472-473.

14. *Personal Letters, 1928–1945,* 476.

15. *Public Papers,* IV, 410-411.

16. *Personal Letters, 1928–1945,* 547.

17. *Personal Letters, 1928–1945,* 571.

18. Quoted in Allan Nevins, *The New Deal in World Affairs, A Chronicle of International Affairs, 1933–1945* (Yale, 1950), 96.

19. *Personal Letters, 1928–1945,* 614.

20. *Public Papers,* V, 288-289.

21. *Personal Letters, 1928–1945,* 656.

22. U. S. State Department, *Peace and War: United States Foreign Policy, 1931–1941* (Government Printing Office, 1943), 384-387.

23. Charles A. Beard, *American Foreign Policy in the Making, 1932–1940* (Yale, 1946), 196-198.

24. *Personal Letters, 1928–1945,* 716-717.

25. *Personal Letters, 1928–1945,* 751.

26. *Personal Letters, 1928–1945,* 810-811.

27. *Personal Letters, 1928–1945,* 785.

28. *Public Papers, 1938,* 564.

29. *Public Papers, 1939,* 2-4.

30. *Personal Letters, 1928–1945,* 862-863.

31. Burns, *Roosevelt,* 393.

chapter **11** THE UNDECLARED WAR

Hitler had done what Roosevelt could not. He had
aroused beyond recall sympathies among the American
people for his victims and for Britain and France. This
did not mean, however, that they were ready to endanger their own security. Roosevelt knew this well
when he delivered his Fireside Chat on September 3,
1939:

> You must master at the outset a simple but
> unalterable fact in modern foreign relations between
> nations. When peace has been broken anywhere, the
> peace of all countries everywhere is in danger. . . .
> Let no man or woman thoughtlessly or falsely talk
> of America sending its armies to European fields. . . .
> . . . We seek to keep war from our own firesides by
> keeping war from coming to the Americas. For that
> we have historic precedent that goes back to the days
> of the Administration of President George Washing-
> ton. . . .
> This Nation will remain a neutral Nation, but I
> cannot ask that every American remain neutral in
> thought as well. Even a neutral has a right to take
> account of facts. Even a neutral cannot be asked to
> close his mind or his conscience. . . .
> As long as it remains within my power to prevent,
> there will be no black-out of peace in the United
> States.[1]

When he called a special session of Congress on
September 21 to repeal the embargo provisions of the

neutrality act, he based his plea, not on aid to the allies, but on the need to make the nation really "neutral."

Beginning with the foundation of our constitutional Government in the year 1789, the American policy in respect to belligerent nations, with one notable exception, has been based on international law. . . .

The single exception . . . was the policy adopted by this nation during the Napoleonic Wars, when, seeking to avoid involvement, we acted for some years under the so-called Embargo and Non-Intercourse Acts. That policy turned out to be a disastrous failure. . . .

Our next deviation by statute from the sound principles of neutrality and peace through international law, did not come for one hundred and thirty years. It was the so-called Neutrality Act of 1935. . . .

I regret that the Congress passed that Act. I regret equally that I signed that Act. . . .

These embargo provisions . . . prevent the sale to a belligerent by an American factory of any completed implements of war, but they allow the sale of many types of uncompleted implements of war, as well as all kinds of general material and supplies. They, furthermore, allow such products of industry and agriculture to be taken in American flag ships to belligerent nations. There in itself—under the present law—lies definite danger to our neutrality and our peace.

From a purely material point of view what is the advantage to us in sending all manner of articles across the ocean for final processing there when we can give employment to thousands by doing it here? . . .

It has been erroneously said that return to that policy might bring us nearer to war. I give you my deep and unalterable conviction, based on years of experience as a worker in the field of international peace, that by the repeal of the embargo the United States will more probably remain at peace than if the law remains as it stands today. I say this because with the repeal of the embargo, this Government clearly and definitely will insist that American citizens and American ships keep away from the immediate perils of the actual zones of conflict. . . .

The enactment of the embargo provisions did more than merely reverse our traditional policy. It had the effect of putting land powers on the same footing as naval powers, so far as sea-borne commerce was concerned. A land power which threatened war could thus feel assured in advance that any prospective sea-power antagonist would be weakened through denial of its ancient right to buy anything anywhere. This, four years ago, began to give a definite advantage to one belligerent against another. . . .[2]

He went on to request other adjustments which would "require all purchases to be made in cash, and all cargoes to be carried in the purchasers' own ships, at the purchasers' own risk. . . ."[2]

The major result of the fourth Neutrality Act was to legalize cash-and-carry sales of munitions as well as raw materials and unfinished products. The whole country knew that this could favor only Great Britain, France— and Japan.

During the autumn the blitz swept across Poland with unprecedented speed. On September 17 Russia had invaded her from the east, anxious to make good on the deal arranged with Hitler. On September 28 the unhappy nation was partitioned by the two pirates. On October 14 war broke out between Russia and tiny Finland, the hero of the war-debts controversy. In private Roosevelt called it "this dreadful rape of Finland."[3] There was little he could do aside from approving the ten-million-dollar agricultural credit which Congress voted for the tiny republic on the Baltic. Meanwhile American ships were warned out of Euro-

pean waters; American ports were closed to belligerent
warships. And Albert Einstein quietly informed Roosevelt of the possibilities of an atomic bomb. During the
fall a secret advisory committee on uranium was set up.

Even before Congress had acted, however, it had
become clear that American neutrality would be friendly
whenever possible to the western allies. But isolationism
was by no means dead, and a great national debate
shaped up as Europe moved into the "phony" war that
winter. The pressure was off for the moment as France
and England lay, presumably safe, behind the gargantuan Maginot Line and the Channel; Poland was
smashed, but Hitler seemed stalled, and the world had
only the stubborn resistance of the Finns to Russian
attacks to watch. In October, under pressure from its
carpenter Vice-President William L. Hutchinson, the
A. F. of L. took its position against American involvement in the war. In the course of the embargo debate,
Senator Borah warned, ". . . you will send munitions
without pay and you will send your boys back to the
slaughter pens of Europe." [4]

The debate would continue to the morning of Pearl
Harbor. Soon there would be an America First Committee, handsomely financed, sporting the support of a
varied stable: rabid Roosevelt-haters, old mid-western
isolationists, anti-Semites, pacifists, Anglophobes, Fascist sympathizers, and idealist Christians. Father Coughlin lined up. And so did Wisconsin's Philip La Follette: ". . . if we go to war to save democracy in Europe,
we shall wind up by losing democracy at home." [5]
Until Germany invaded Russia America First would
have a hard time dissociating itself from the Communists who wanted to help. After June, 1941, however,
they would add to their ranks many who feared Communism more than Fascism. Senator Charles Tobey of
New Hampshire would predict: "Today we ally ourselves with Russia in her war with Germany, but it is

possible that ten years from now we might ally ourselves with Germany to halt the menace of Communism sweeping Europe. . . ." [6]

The darling of the America Firsters was Charles A.
Lindbergh, the hero of the twenties, whose gentle and
cultured wife had written one popular book after another about their air jaunts around the world. Lindbergh was more than an idol or a front; he was articulate
and shyly charming. More important, he was immensely
sincere and he spoke again and again with the emotion
of deep concern as he watched his country move toward
what he thought was national suicide. He was no Nazi-
sympathizer. But as late as April, 1941, he could tell a
congressional committee:

> I know I will be severely criticized by the
> interventionists in America when I say we should not
> enter a war unless we have a reasonable chance of win-
> ning. That, they will claim, is far too materialistic a
> standpoint. They will advance again the same argu-
> ments that were used to persuade France to declare war
> against Germany in 1939. But I do not believe that our
> American ideals, and our way of life, will gain through
> an unsuccessful war. And I know that the United
> States is not prepared to wage war in Europe success-
> fully at this time. . . .
> When history is written, the responsibility for the
> downfall of democracies of Europe will rest squarely
> upon the shoulders of the interventionists who led
> their nations into war uninformed and unprepared. . . .
> . . . War is not inevitable for this country. . . . No
> one can make us fight abroad unless we ourselves are
> willing to do so. No one will attempt to fight us here if
> we arm ourselves as a great nation should be armed. [7]

America First had been formally organized in September, 1940. Four months earlier its opposition had
already coalesced in the Committee to Defend America

by Aiding the Allies. One of the Committee founders was William Allen White, the progressive Kansas newsman. As early as December, 1939, the President had written to White:

> As you know, I do not entertain the thought of some of the statesmen of 1918 that the world can make, or we can help the world achieve, a permanently lasting peace—that is a peace which we would visualize as enduring for a century or more. On the other hand, I do not want this country to take part in a patched up temporizing peace which would blow up in our faces in a year or two. . . .
>
> If . . . Germany and Russia win the war or force a peace favorable to them, the situation of your civilization and mine is indeed in peril. Our world trade would be at the mercy of the combine and our increasingly better relations with our twenty neighbors to the south would end—unless we were willing to go to war in their behalf against a German-Russian dominated Europe.
>
> What worries me, especially, is that public opinion over here is patting itself on the back every morning and thanking God for the Atlantic Ocean (and the Pacific Ocean). We greatly underestimate the serious implications to our own future and I fear most people are merely going around saying:
>
> "Thank God for Roosevelt and Hull—no matter what happens, they will keep us out of war. . . ."
>
> The Lord and you know perfectly well that Roosevelt and Hull fully expect to keep us out of war—but, on the other hand, we are not going around thanking God for allowing us physical safety within our continental limits.
>
> Things move with such terrific speed, these days, that it really is essential to us to think in broader terms and, in effect, to warn the American people that they, too, should think of possible ultimate results in Europe and the Far East.
>
> Therefore, my sage old friend, my problem is to get

the American people to think of conceivable conse-
quences without scaring the American people into
thinking that they are going to be dragged into this
war.

Think it over and do come down to Washington
soon. . . .⁸

Throughout the winter Washington buzzed with
defense preparations. In January, 1940, another mammoth budget was approved. In February Sumner Welles
left for the European capitals to survey prospects for
peace. But at the end of March Japan set up her puppet
régime in Manchukuo and demanded recognition; days
later Denmark and Norway were invaded. Roosevelt and
Hull could do little aside from freezing Danish and
Norwegian assets in the United States and issuing a
general warning that the status of the Netherlands
East Indies must not be changed. As the phony war
became intensely real, F.D.R. made four last-minute
personal appeals to Mussolini to intervene with Hitler
for peace.

On May 10 Hitler moved into Belgium, Holland and
Luxembourg. On June 5 the Battle for France began.
The French collapse was abrupt, almost unbelievable at
the time. With the Maginot Line outflanked, they
reeled under the punches of Hitler's panzer troops.
British forces were cut off and sealed against the sea at
Dunkirk, where an epic withdrawal commenced under
the pounding of German guns and bombs. The French
armies rolled back on Paris, and then beyond. The
capital fell on June 14. Meanwhile, Mussolini jumped
into the war headlong on June 10, as if he feared that
it would end before he had had his chance. And Russia
quietly annexed Latvia, Lithuania and Estonia while
the world was watching Paris. On June 22 the new Vichy
French government, headed by Marshal Henri Pétain,
sued for peace.

The effect in Washington was electric. All kinds of preparations were speeded up. At the end of May the President had created an Office of Emergency Management and a National Defense Advisory Commission, headed by General Motors executive William Knudsen, and he requested another billion and a quarter for defense. Congress provided the new naval and military appropriations at once.

On June 18, Admiral Harold Stark called for a four-billion-dollar expansion for a two-ocean Navy. On June 20—two days before the French Armistice—four days before the Republican National Convention—Roosevelt shrewdly announced the appointment of Henry L. Stimson as Secretary of War, and Frank Knox as Secretary of the Navy. Both were Republicans: Stimson a former Secretary of State, Knox the Republican Vice-Presidential candidate in 1936 and a publisher of great influence in the Midwest. As the month of June came to an end, Congress passed a new revenue act, a supplementary defense appropriation, an Espionage Act and an Alien Registration Act.

Hull later wrote: "Of one point the President and I had not the slightest doubt; namely, that an allied victory was essential to the security of the United States." [*]

In two notable radio addresses Roosevelt sought to grasp the initiative. In a Fireside Chat on May 26 he had served notice that the government would finance new factories to speed up production, and then he attacked the isolationists without naming them:

There are some among us who were persuaded by minority groups that we could maintain our physical safety by retiring within our continental boundaries. . . . Obviously a defense policy based on that is merely to invite future attack.

And, finally, there are a few among us who have deliberately and consciously closed their eyes because they were determined to be opposed to their government, its foreign policy and every other policy, to be partisan, and to believe that anything that the Government did was wholly wrong.

To those who have closed their eyes for any of these many reasons, . . . to all of them the past two weeks have meant the shattering of many illusions. . . .

In some quarters, with this rude awakening has come fear, bordering on panic. . . .

I did not share those illusions. I do not share those fears. . . .

Today's threat to our national security is not a matter of military weapons alone. We know of new methods of attack.

The Trojan Horse. The Fifth Column that betrays a nation unprepared for treachery.

Spies, saboteurs and traitors are the actors in this new strategy. With all of these we must and will deal vigorously.

But there is an added technique for weakening a nation at its very roots, for disrupting the entire pattern of life of a people. It is important that we understand it.

The method is simple. It is, first, a dissemination of discord. A group—not too large—a group that may be sectional or racial or political—is encouraged to exploit its prejudices through false slogans and emotional appeals. The aim of those who deliberately egg on these groups is to create a confusion of counsel, public indecision, political paralysis and, eventually, a state of panic. . . .

As a result of these new techniques . . . The unity of the State can be so sapped that its strength is destroyed. . . .

These dividing forces are undiluted poison.[10]

Roosevelt did not impute treason to the isolationists.

It was easy for the public to assume that he meant them as well as foreign agents.

On June 10, as Mussolini hastened into the war, Roosevelt abandoned all the cautions of his State Department. At Charlottesville, Virginia, he said distinctly, and slowly for emphasis:

> On this 10th day of June, 1940, the hand that held the dagger struck it into the back of its neighbor. . . .

In our unity, in our American unity, we will pursue two obvious and simultaneous courses; we will extend to the opponents of force the material resources of this nation and, at the same time, we will harness and speed up the use of those resources in order that we ourselves in the Americas may have equipment and training equal to the task of any emergency and every defense.

All roads leading to the accomplishment of these objectives must be kept clear of obstructions. We will not slow down or detour. Signs and signals call for speed—full speed ahead." [11]

Three days later he answered Premier Reynaud's call for aid with a personal note of encouragement. But Churchill sought to force his hand by seeking permission to publish the message and telling Reynaud that "the United States is committed beyond recall to take the only remaining step, namely becoming a belligerent in form as she already has constituted herself in fact." [12] Roosevelt hastily refused and pointed out that only Congress could declare war.

Speech, even though it be decisive and courageous, is cheap. Action was pitifully limited. With both France and England crying desperately for help on the high seas, particularly for destroyers to fight the Nazi submarines, Roosevelt had to confess that his hands were tied.

As Hermann Goering threw his air force against the British Isles to soften them up for invasion, Harry Hopkins hurried off to Chicago to grease the wheels for the third-term "draft." If Roosevelt sometimes seemed remote from both fights, it was partly because he was deep in plans for specific action that would unfold that fall. Despite the coming election, Congress voted for the four-billion-dollar naval expansion, empowered the President to call up the National Guard if necessary; and an executive order slapped an embargo on the sale of aviation gasoline outside the western hemisphere. Congress even faced up to the first peace-time Selective Service Act and to an excess profits tax, at the very beginning of the national campaign. Although his advisers wanted him to wait until after election Roosevelt insisted that the first "draft" numbers be drawn on October 28. On August 18 a United States–Canada Joint Defense Board had been set up by Roosevelt and Mackenzie King at Ogdensburg, New York. On July 30 the hemisphere defenses had been further strengthened by the Declaration of Havana.

All of this was of little help to beleaguered Britain. Cordell Hull has described the elaborate maneuvering which led to the first substantial act of aid, the destroyer-air-base swap which was announced early in September:

When [the British Ambassador, Lord] Lothian came to my office on August 4 I could appreciate Britain's dangers as fully as he could depict them. . . . Britain vitally needed the destroyers at that very moment, to cover a period of low strength in smaller types of warships until a number of such ships she now had on the ways could be ready in the first part of 1941. As Churchill said in a message to the President on August 15: "The worth of every destroyer that you can spare to us is measured in rubies." . . .

Lord Lothian came in to see me at the office early

Sunday afternoon so that we could go over the situation prior to his conversation with the President that evening [August 25]. He brought up certain objections. . . . He said his Government did not like the American proposal that we have exclusive authority to locate and select the bases we needed, with no voice whatever on the part of Britain. His Government also objected to the proposed exchange of the destroyers for the bases, and desired to put the matter in the form of gifts back and forth. . . .

We had difficulties on our side as well, however. The Attorney General, Robert H. Jackson, believed there was legal authority for the President, as Commander in Chief of our armed forces, to sell the destroyers to Britain. But if the President were to do so without special Congressional authority, he should be able to satisfy Congress that, in return for the destroyers, we were obtaining facilities to bases which would clearly give us greater security than would the retention of the fifty destroyers. . . .

More important still was the fact that the President had no authority to make a gift of Government property. . . .

. . . Green H. Hackworth, Legal Adviser of the State Department . . . suddenly suggested that there might be a compromise after all between Churchill's desire for reciprocal gifts and our own legal position that the President could not give away the destroyers but had to get something in return.

Since the British had not stated precisely what bases they intended to lease to us, why not divide them into two parcels? The first would comprise the bases in Newfoundland and Bermuda. These Britain could lease to us as an outright gift. The second would comprise the bases around the Caribbean, strategically more valuable to us because of their nearness to the Panama Canal. These could be leased to us in consideration of the cession of the fifty destroyers. . . .

Churchill was ready to give assurances that the British fleet would not be scuttled or surrendered. . . .

With his usual indomitable spirit, he said he did not wish this . . . to be published because "I think it is much more likely that the German Government will be the one to surrender or scuttle its fleet or what is left of it. In this, as you are aware, they have already had some practice. You will remember that I said some months ago in one of my private cables to you that any such action on our part would be a dastardly act, and that is the opinion of everyone of us." . . .

Thus were concluded within a week negotiations among the most momentous in our history.[18]

Almost immediately a similar shift in policy came in regard to Japan. Early in September Ambassador Grew warned:

Whatever may be the intentions of the present Japanese Government, there can be no doubt that the army and other elements in the country see in the present world situation a "golden opportunity" to carry into effect their dreams of expansion; the German victories have gone to their heads like strong wine; . . .

Now, however, I sense a gradual change in the outburst of exhilaration which greeted the new Government on its inception. The Japanese Government, the army and navy and the public are beginning to see that Germany may not defeat Great Britain after all, . . . and now to add to that dawning realization, they see the United States and Great Britain steadily drawing closer together in measures of mutual defense with the American acquisition of naval bases in British possessions in the Atlantic and with our support of the British fleet by the transfer of fifty destroyers. They hear reports of our haste to build a two-ocean navy and of our considering the strengthening of our naval bases

in the Pacific and even rumors of our eventual use of
Singapore. These developments and rumors are having
their logical effect on Japanese consciousness. On the
one hand they tend to emphasize the potential danger
which Japan faces from eventual positive action by
the United States and Great Britain acting together
. . . or by the United States alone. On the other hand
they furnish cogent arguments for those elements in
Japan who seek economic and political security by
obtaining markets and sources of raw materials wholly
within the control of Japan. . . .

High-pressure diplomacy, especially in the Netherlands East Indies, will continue . . . The "nibbling
policy" appears likely to continue until the world situation, and especially the attitude of the United States,
becomes clearer. [14]

Grew went on to sketch the alternative dangers.
Strong sanctions against Japan might bring retaliation.
But American weakness in the Pacific could only en-
courage her to continue on south. Above all the United
States must preserve the status quo in the Pacific until
the British had won out in Europe.

On September 4 Hull had warned Japan that further
expansion into Indo-China would be viewed with concern by the United States. On October 16 an executive
order embargoed scrap and steel exports to an unbend-
ing Japan.

Roosevelt explained his reluctance to go further when
his wife asked for help in answering campaign criticisms:
"The real answer which you cannot use is that if we
forbid oil shipments to Japan, Japan will increase her
purchases of Mexican oil and furthermore, may be
driven by actual necessity to a descent on the Dutch
East Indies. At this writing, we all regard such action
on our part as an encouragement to the spread of war
in the Far East." [15]

Yet he did say at Dayton on October 12:

> Our course is clear. Our decision is made. We will continue to pile up our defenses and our armaments. We will continue to help those who resist aggression, and who now hold the aggressors far from our shores. . . .
> The people of the United States, the people of all the Americas, reject the doctrine of appeasement. They recognize it for what it is—a major weapon of the aggressor nations. . . .[16]

In rebuttal Willkie could only protest that Roosevelt must share the responsibility for Munich—and then that Roosevelt's election would mean war in six months. Worried about Willkie's Gallup poll increases, worried whether he had guessed right on the public temper and the pace of rearmament, the destroyer deal, the draft and the Japanese embargo, Roosevelt slipped into an error that was to plague him for the rest of his life. In Boston, the day after the draft-drawing, he proclaimed:

> I have said this before, but I shall say it again and again and again:
> Your boys are not going to be sent into any foreign wars.[17]

The election victory removed the last uncertainty for Roosevelt, although the argument as to what he had promised would rage indefinitely. As Samuel Rosenman saw the President's job now, it lay in four areas:

> It was Roosevelt's first and primary task to convince the American people of the great peril which they faced if Britain were to fall as had the rest of Europe. . . .
> His second great task was to find a way to enable the

allies in Europe and Asia to hold on until more help could come to them. . . .

Third, to ensure that there would be equality of sacrifice by every citizen, he had to condition the American people willingly to accept restrictions and controls to which they had never been accustomed. . . .

Roosevelts' fourth great task during the next four years was to act as the chief propaganda agent of democracy both at home and abroad.[18]

Roosevelt picked up the challenge in December, as British Field Marshal Wavell began his advance against the Italians in North Africa and as the Gallup poll reported a significant drop in the number of Americans who thought America's role in World War I had been a mistake. In a press conference on December 17 he suggested an imaginative new concept of aid to the western allies. Rosenman has explained how this Lend-Lease idea developed:

Several weeks after his re-election, Roosevelt left on a cruise on the *Tuscaloosa*. In the course of this cruise, he had an opportunity to consider various expedients to continue the flow of American war materials to Britain.

He concluded that . . . neither Congress nor American public opinion would support an outright repeal of the provisions of the neutrality act. He felt that even if legislation could be enacted that would permit direct loans to Britain, it would be only a temporary stopgap and would raise the same diplomatic frictions which accompanied the war-debt-settlement discussions following the first World War. Outright gifts of munitions and war matériel would be politically difficult if not impossible.

During his cruise, the President received a remarkable 4,000-word letter from Prime Minister Churchill, reviewing in some detail the British military position and financial situation. . . . But the letter—which Churchill has called one of the most important he ever wrote—offered no solution to the problem of how to alleviate Britain's financial squeeze. . . .

Toward the end of his cruise, the President one evening disclosed to Harry [Hopkins] the answer he had arrived at—bold, ingenious, imaginative. It was his own device. What remained was to reduce the concept to legislative terms, and, much more important, to explain it to the country with simplicity and in a way that would capture its imagination—and obtain its approval. The former was accomplished with the aid of resourceful lawyers like Ben Cohen, Edward H. Foley, Herman Oliphant and Oscar Cox; the latter could only be done, and was done, by Roosevelt himself.

He first publicly mentioned the subject at his press conference on December 17. . . .

"What I am trying to do is to eliminate the dollar sign," he said, and continued extemporaneously, "Suppose my neighbor's home catches fire, and I have a length of garden hose four or five hundred feet away. If he can take my garden hose and connect it up with his hydrant, I may help him to put out his fire. Now, what do I do? I don't say to him before that operation, 'Neighbor, my garden hose cost me $15; you have to pay me $15 for it.' What is the transaction that goes on? I don't want $15. I want my garden hose back after the fire is over."

After the fire is out, the President went on, he gets his garden hose back, and if it is damaged beyond repair in putting out the fire, "he [my neighbor] says, 'All right, I will replace it.'"

"Now, if I get a nice garden hose back, I am in pretty good shape." [19]

On December 29 the President went to the nation with his "Arsenal of Democracy" speech: "There will be no 'bottlenecks' in our determination to aid Great

Britain. No dictator, no combination of dictators, will weaken that determination by threats of how they will construe that determination. . . ." [20]

On January 6 he went to Congress with his request for Lend-Lease and with the classic statement of the Four Freedoms:

> In the future days, which we seek to make secure, we look forward to a world founded upon four essential human freedoms.
>
> The first is freedom of speech and expression—everywhere in the world.
>
> The second is freedom of every person to worship God in his own way—everywhere in the world.
>
> The third is freedom from want—which, translated into world terms, means economic understandings which will secure to every nation a healthy peace-time life for its inhabitants—everywhere in the world.
>
> The fourth is freedom from fear—which, translated into world terms, means a world-wide reduction of armaments to such a point and in such a thorough fashion that no nation will be in a position to commit an act of physical aggression against any neighbor—anywhere in the world.
>
> That is no vision of a distant millennium. It is a definite basis for a kind of world attainable in our own time and generation. That kind of world is the very antithesis of the so-called new order of tyranny which the dictators seek to create with the crash of a bomb. . . .
>
> Freedom means the supremacy of human rights everywhere. Our support goes to those who struggle to gain those rights or keep them. Our strength is in our unity of purpose. . . ." [21]

The Lend-Lease battle was not easily won. Friends and foes both recognized that this was the decisive point. Despite constant pleas from Churchill, Roosevelt felt it necessary to be patient with a Congress which had settled down to a Great Debate. Only on March 11 was he finally able to sign the bill.

Meanwhile, Hitler had called off the cross-channel invasion for the winter, but he had turned at once to the task of cutting Britain's lifeline to America. On March 24 the "Desert Fox," Erwin Rommel, began his German counterattack in North Africa, and Hitler's legions soon poured into Yugoslavia on their way to save Il Duce's crumbling forces in Greece. Russia guarded her rear with a nonaggression treaty with Japan in April. As the inspired Greek resistance finally melted, and Rommel rolled back the British in Libya, Hitler began to mass his troops in the east. On June 22 the Nazi armored columns swept across the Russian border from Poland to the Ukraine. Britain had been given respite for the moment, but the war at last assumed a global scale.

Action in Washington was quick. Roosevelt's January budget request had stood at over 17 billions. United States-British staff talks had begun secretly six weeks before Lend-Lease was passed. Roosevelt promised "all material aid possible" to harried Yugoslavia, sent United States officers to confer with the Dutch and the British at Singapore in mid-April, and opened the Red Sea to American shipping. There was no question of American sentiments. On June 10 Mussolini charged that the United States was in fact at war. Roosevelt's reaction was the freezing of Axis funds four days later, and the closing of German and Italian consulates in another week. When the invasion of Russia came, the President promised immediate aid and refused to apply the neutrality statutes.

Meanwhile, the governmental machinery was being overhauled to meet the new demands. But the extent of American commitment was best illustrated in the Battle of the Atlantic. The Administration saw it as the key to the war, certainly as the key to American defense.

Early in the spring United States forces had occupied Greenland. The Government of Denmark protested, under the watchful eyes of German officials, but Roosevelt instructed the State Department to write the Danish king:

> Of necessity it must be considered that the acts of the Government of Denmark are under the duress of German occupation. . . .

The United States, therefore, finds it necessary to hold Greenland in trust for Denmark with the objective that full control will be restored to Denmark just as soon as the Government of Denmark ceases to labor under any form of duress on the part of any other nation.[22]

On May 4 F.D.R. wrote to Churchill:

> . . . the outcome of this struggle is going to be decided in the Atlantic and unless Hitler can win there he cannot win anywhere in the world in the end. . . .

Our patrols are pushing farther out into the Atlantic. I have just added all of our heavier units of the Coast Guard to the Navy for the purpose of implementing that patrol. Other steps to strengthen that patrol will be taken soon.[23]

By May 27 he felt sufficiently sure of his ground to tell his radio audience:

> The blunt truth is this . . . the present rate of Nazi sinkings of merchant ships is more than three times as high as the capacity of British shipyards to replace them; it is more than twice the combined British and American output of merchant ships today.

We can answer this peril by two simultaneous measures: first, by speeding up and increasing our great shipbuilding program; and second, by helping to cut down the losses on the high seas.

. . . Nazi occupation of Iceland or bases in Greenland would bring the war close to our continental shores. . . .

Equally, the Azores and the Cape Verde Islands, if occupied or controlled by Germany, would directly endanger the freedom of the Atlantic and our own physical safety. Under German domination those islands would become bases for submarines, warships, and airplanes raiding the waters that lie immediately off our own coast and attacking the shipping in the South Atlantic. . . .

. . . Our Bunker Hill of tomorrow may be several thousand miles from Boston.

Our national policy today, therefore, is this.

First, we shall actively resist wherever necessary, with all our resources, every attempt by Hitler to extend his Nazi domination to the Western Hemisphere, or to threaten it. We shall actively resist his every attempt to gain control of the seas. We insist upon the vital importance of keeping Hitlerism away from any point in the world which could be used and would be used as a base of attack against the Americas.

Second, from the point of view of strict naval and military necessity, we shall give every possible assistance to Britain. . . . Our patrols are helping now to insure delivery of the needed supplies to Britain. . . .

I say that the delivery of needed supplies to Britain is imperative. I say that this can be done; it must be done; and it will be done.[24]

On July 7 American troops occupied Iceland to relieve the British. Harry Hopkins left at once for London and Moscow as the President's personal agent in working out supply and diplomatic problems. And early in August the President slipped quietly out of Washington for a vacation. A few days later the world knew that he and Winston Churchill had met aboard ship off Newfoundland. Their main concern had been the tactics of immediate defense. But out of this Atlantic Conference came a general statement of war objectives which rang round the world, with an idealism which might answer Hitler's ranting about the perfidy of the old imperial bandits:

Joint declaration of the President of the United States of America and the Prime Minister, Mr. Churchill, representing His Majesty's Government in the United Kingdom, being met together, deem it right to make known certain common principles in the national policies of their respective countries on which they base their hopes for a better future for the world.

First, their countries seek no aggrandizement, territorial or other;

Second, they desire to see no territorial changes that do not accord with the freely expressed wishes of the peoples concerned;

Third, they respect the right of all peoples to choose the form of government under which they will live; and they wish to see sovereign rights and self-government restored to those who have been forcibly deprived of them;

Fourth, they will endeavor, with due respect for their existing obligations, to further the enjoyment by all states, great or small, victor or vanquished, of access, on equal terms, to the trade and to the raw materials of the world which are needed for their economic prosperity;

Fifth, they desire to bring about the fullest collaboration between all nations in the economic field with the object of securing, for all, improved labor standards, economic advancement, and social security;

Sixth, after the final destruction of the Nazi tyranny, they hope to see established a peace which will afford to all nations the means of dwelling in safety within their own boundaries, and which will afford assurance that all the men in all the lands may live out their lives in freedom from fear and want;

Seventh, such a peace should enable all men to traverse the high seas and oceans without hindrance;

Eighth, they believe that all of the nations of the world, for realistic as well as spiritual reasons, must come to the abandonment of the use of force. Since no future peace can be maintained if land, sea, or air armaments continue to be employed by nations which threaten, or may threaten, aggression outside of their frontiers, they believe, pending the establishment of a wider and permanent system of general security, that the disarmament of such nations is essential. They will likewise aid and encourage all other practicable measures which will lighten for peace-loving peoples the crushing burden of armaments.[25]

The German's answer was increasing fury in the North Atlantic. In May the American ship Robin Moor had been sunk. On August 17 the Panamanian Sessa was torpedoed off Greenland. In September the American Steelfarer was sunk in the Red Sea. On September 4 the destroyer Greer was attacked off Iceland. Roosevelt called it "piracy"; he did not explain that the Greer was at the moment radioing the German's position to the British. Roosevelt had announced on August 18 that the United States would ferry planes for the British to the Middle East; on September 1 he had promised every effort to beat Germany; now, on September 11, he announced that United States ships would "shoot on sight" in the western Atlantic. He explained, ". . . when you see a rattlesnake poised to strike, you do not wait until he has struck before you crush him." [26]

By the middle of the month the Attorney-General had ruled that the United States could legally carry arms to the British in the Near East, Far East and western hemisphere; the Secretary of the Navy explained that he was convoying all ships carrying lend-lease matériel as far as Iceland. When the destroyer Kearney was torpedoed off Iceland, Roosevelt announced on October 27, ". . . the shooting has started. . . . America has been attacked." Three days later her sister ship, the Reuben James, was sunk.

As the war became hot, Roosevelt grew more and more restive under criticism. In May he had protested to a leader of the Anglophobes:

> When will you Irishmen ever get over hating England? Remember that if England goes down, Ireland goes down too . . . do stop thinking in terms of ancient hatreds and think of the future.[27]

When an isolationist senator broke out in July with a demand that the Good Neighbor policy be abandoned and American troops be used to set up puppet governments in Latin America, the President wrote him in wrath:

> It is as I expected. . . . A dispatch from Rome quotes the Italian press as alleging that your statement ends the Good Neighbor Policy and represents the real opinion of the President and of the State Department. It goes on to say that your remarks amount to a frank statement made out of turn and that the Statements of the President and the Acting Secretary of State are mere camouflage because they are not yet ready to assume the role of the aggressor in South America. Finally, the Italian papers plead with the Latin-American countries to take warning and abandon all cooperation with this country.

Simultaneously the German newspapers are "congratulating Senator Clark" on his "touching frankness in letting the cat out of the bag and that the real aim of the United States is not that of the Good Neighbor but of the Big Stick."[28]

There was little time for recrimination—or for much thought. For, as the shooting war broke out in the Atlantic, the Japanese began to push with relentless purpose toward southeast Asia. On December 14, 1940, Ambassador Grew had warned Roosevelt:

> . . . unless we are prepared, with General Hugh Johnson, to withdraw bag and baggage from the entire sphere of "Greater East Asia including the South Seas" (which God forbid), we are bound eventually to come to a head-on clash with Japan. . . .
> . . . Only if they become certain that we mean to fight if called upon to do so will our preliminary measures stand some chance of proving effective and of removing the necessity for war— . . .[29]

In January, 1941, Grew had confided to his diary: "There is a lot of talk around town to the effect that the Japanese, in case of a break with the United States, are planning to go all out in a surprise mass attack on Pearl Harbor. I rather guess that the boys in Hawaii are not precisely asleep."[30]

Roosevelt and the State Department hesitated as spring wore on. Action might force the Japanese; inaction might encourage them. Their advance in French Indo-China at the height of the Atlantic crisis in July cast the die. The United States denounced the move; Roosevelt froze Japanese assets the next day. On August 1 an embargo on aviation oil to Japan was announced. For the moment Roosevelt was encouraged. He wrote to Harry Hopkins in London on July 26:

> Tell Former Naval Person [Churchill] our concurrent action in regard to Japan is, I think, bearing fruit. I hear their government much upset and no conclusive future policy has been determined on. Tell him also in great confidence that I have suggested to Nomura that Indo-China be neutralized by Britain, Dutch,

Chinese, Japan and ourselves, placing Indo-China some-what in status of Switzerland. Japan to get rice and fertilizer but all on condition that Japan withdraw armed forces.[31]

This was as far as the United States would go. For Japan it was not far enough. On October 18 the militar-ists ousted the last of the democratic liberals and General Tojo became head of the government. Early in November Hull warned the Cabinet that Japanese relations were critical. A special envoy, Saburo Kurusu, arrived to help Ambassador Nomura in the constant dis-cussions with Hull. While Congress finally voted to arm merchant ships and allow them to sail into the war zones, Tojo told the world that his aim was peace in East Asia, and Grew warned that he might not be able to give advance notice if an attack came.

Though both sides claimed peace, the formal pro-posals of Kurusu and Hull betrayed how far apart they were. The Japanese would agree to move out of French Indo-China only when the war with China ended. Meanwhile the United States must restore commercial relations with Japan, meet her requirements for oil and co-operate with her in obtaining needed resources from the Netherlands East Indies. The United States pro-posal insisted on the withdrawal of all Japanese forces from both Indo-China and China, the recognition of Chiang Kai-shek's regime, and the renunciation of all preferential treatment in trade as well as all extrater-ritorial rights. There must also be a nonaggression pact among the Pacific powers and the development of a reciprocal trade agreement between the United States and Japan.

Roosevelt wrote to Churchill: "This seems to me a fair proposal for the Japanese but its acceptance or re-jection is really a matter of internal Japanese politics. I am not very hopeful and we must all be prepared for real trouble, possibly soon." [32]

Negotiations continued. Clearly the United States could have had peace—for the moment—at the price of giving Japan a completely free hand in China, of providing without limit the oil and materials she needed from the United States and from southeast Asia. Roosevelt and Hull insisted that east Asia must not be made a Japanese Czechoslovakia. Three days after the United States proposals were made, Tojo served notice that the United States and British imperialisms in the east must be destroyed. On December 3 the Japanese diplomats in the United States began to burn their documents and codes. On December 6 Roosevelt sent a long-postponed, personal appeal to Emperor Hirohito.

Walter Millis has described the answer which had been preparing for days as a Japanese fleet steamed across the North Pacific:

The first plane, a dive bomber, streaked in low over Pearl Harbor at 7:55 A.M., coming in from the south with its consorts close behind it. Two reconnaissance float planes had been catapulted from the Japanese cruisers before them, but if they reached Oahu they were not observed. The first wave of the main body, 189 aircraft in all, had been flown off the carrier decks at 6:00 A.M., Hawaiian time. As they sighted the north point of Oahu, at ten minutes before 8, they split up. In accordance with sound air warfare doctrine, the first objective was the American defensive aviation. One dive bomber unit, swerving only a little to the right, went in from the north over the ranked and helpless Army fighters on Wheeler Field. Another, swinging wide around the west coast of the island, came up from the south against the Army bombers on Hickam Field and the Navy PBY's on Ford Island. Immediately behind these were 40 torpedo bombers, launching their deadly missiles from a low altitude at the "sitting ducks" in Battleship Row. Fifty horizontal bombers were on the heels of the torpedo planes, in case the first should fail against nets or baffles; and after them all there came 45 fighters, to put down any opposition which might get into the air or, failing that, to polish off the remains at Wheeler and Hickam, at Ford Island, Kaneohe, and the Marine base at Ewa.

The whole of this massive force was flung within the space of a few minutes at virtually every prominent naval and air installation on Oahu. The Japanese pilots knew that an hour behind them a second wave of 171 aircraft—54 horizontal bombers, 81 dive bombers, and 36 fighters—was on its way in support. But most of the damage was done within the first quarter of an hour. . . .

. . . the net result was that in the first fifteen minutes of the action the Japanese had successfully destroyed or paralyzed virtually the entire air strength of Oahu. In the same space of time they had gone far toward the accomplishment of their main objective, the destruction of the United States Pacific Fleet.

Seven of Kimmel's eight battleships were moored along the southeasterly face of Ford Island, at big concrete bollards or mooring posts set just off the shore line. . . .

Over this great fleet the 40 Japanese torpedo bombers broke like a storm just before 8 o'clock. They came from every direction, each pilot carefully briefed on the particular angle from which to launch his torpedo in order to get the best run and cause the maximum confusion in the defense. Taking the gunners by complete surprise, they were almost impossible to hit; in a few moments the harbor was crisscrossed by the white wakes of their missiles, and tremendous explosions were leaping up against the steel sides of the battleships. The horizontal and dive bombers were immediately behind them; and the bombs were landing even as the torpedoes went home. Every one of the five outboard battleships took one or more torpedo hits in the first few minutes, and the two inboard ships, *Maryland* and *Tennessee*, were hit by bombs. Other torpedo planes and bombers were at the same time attacking the ships moored along the northwest face of the island. The old target ship *Utah*, lying in a berth often used by the aircraft carriers, took two torpedoes, turned over, and sank at 8:13, the first total casualty. The light cruiser *Raleigh*, lying just ahead of her, received one torpedo and later a bomb hit, and only heroic measures kept her from turning turtle.

In Battleship Row, the repair ship *Vestal*, lying alongside of *Arizona*, had afforded the latter slight protection. Two torpedoes streaked past the smaller vessel to reach the battleship, while a heavy armor-piercing bomb found its way to *Arizona*'s forward magazine, and she blew up with a terrific detonation. The whole forward half of the ship was a total wreck, through which tremendous oil fires now poured up their flames and great billows of smoke. Just south of her *West Virginia* had taken four or five torpedo and bomb hits. Enormous rents had been torn in her plating; there was a fierce fire amidships, and she was settling now to the bottom, fortunately on an even keel. *Tennessee*, lying inboard, was not too badly damaged; but she was pinned against the bollards by the sinking *West Virginia* and was imperiled by the oil fires raging in the *Arizona* and across the water between them. South of this pair, the old *Oklahoma*, lying outboard of *Maryland*, had received four torpedo hits in the first minutes; she was soon listing extravagantly, and at 8:32 she rolled completely over and lay, like an immense whale, with her bottom and propellers showing to the now densely smoke-filled sky. . . .

All this had been accomplished in the first half hour of the attack, and most of it in the first ten or fifteen minutes. The torpedo planes, their missiles expended, faded away. There were still horizontal and dive bombers ranging unhindered over the scene, but for another fifteen or twenty minutes there was something like a "lull" in the action. . . .

Then at 8:50 the second great wave of Japanese horizontal and dive bombers (there were no torpedo planes in the echelon) sighted Oahu, split up like the first, and swept in to finish the kill. The anti-aircraft fire was better now; there were a few American fighters in the air, and there was not a great deal left for the support wave to do. But though the second attack was consequently less effective than the first, it put in some further heavy blows. . . .

. . . by 9:45 the last of the raiding planes had faded into the silent skies. . . .

Twenty-four hours before the admiral had at his command eight great battleships, "the backbone of the fleet." He now had none. Two, *Pennsylvania* and *Maryland*, could be restored to service fairly quickly and a third, *Tennessee*, was not very much worse off, although before she could be repaired it would be necessary to blast away the massive concrete bollards against which she had been wedged by the sinking *West Virginia*. Two of the remaining five, *Oklahoma* and *Arizona*, were total losses. The three others were ultimately salvaged and restored to service. . . .

Three cruisers—*Raleigh*, *Helena* and *Honolulu*—had been more or less seriously damaged and three destroyers wrecked; the lives of 2,086 naval officers and men had been lost. The subsequent history of the war was to suggest that the battleships were actually, perhaps, of less critical importance than both we and the Japanese supposed at the time. . . .

Yet one cannot overcome the fact that the Japanese had, in one hour and fifty-five minutes, knocked the heart out of the United States Pacific Fleet. Morally as well as materially, they had paralyzed American naval action in the Pacific for a period of many weeks, which was exactly what they had set out to do. And they had accomplished it at a cost to themselves of just 29 aircraft, five midget submarines, and one fleet submarine.[33]

NOTES, *chapter 11*

1. Samuel Rosenman, ed., *The Public Papers and Addresses of Franklin D. Roosevelt, 1939*, 461-464.

2. *Public Papers, 1939*, 515-516, 518.

3. Elliott Roosevelt, ed., *F.D.R., His Personal Letters, 1928–1945*, 961.

4. *Vital Speeches*, VI, 23.

5. *Vital Speeches*, VII, 265.

6. *Vital Speeches*, VII, 750.

7. *Vital Speeches*, VII, 424-425.

8. *Personal Letters, 1928–1945*, 967-968.

9. Cordell Hull, *The Memoirs of Cordell Hull* (Macmillan, 1948), 766.

10. *Public Papers, 1940*, 231, 238-239.

11. U. S. State Department, *Peace and War: United States Foreign Policy, 1931–1941*, 548-549.

12. Winston Churchill, *Their Finest Hour* (Houghton, Mifflin, 1949), 185.

13. Hull, *Memoirs*, 832, 834-835, 837, 839, 841.

14. Joseph C. Grew, *The Turbulent Era, A Diplomatic Record of Forty Years, 1904–1951* (Houghton, Mifflin, 1952), II, 1225-1226.

15. *Personal Letters, 1928–1945*, 1077.

16. *Public Papers, 1940*, 466.

17. *Public Papers, 1940*, 517.

18. Samuel Rosenman, *Working with Roosevelt*, 266-267.

19. Rosenman, *Roosevelt*, 257-258.

20. *Public Papers, 1940*, 644.

21. *Peace and War*, 611.

22. *Personal Letters, 1928–1945*, 1143.

23. *Personal Letters, 1928–1945*, 1148-1150.

24. *Public Papers, 1941*, 187-190.

25. *Peace and War*, 718-719.

26. *Public Papers, 1941*, 390.

27. *Personal Letters, 1928–1945*, 1159.

28. *Personal Letters, 1928–1945*, 1194-1195.

29. Joseph C. Grew, *Ten Years in Japan* (Simon and Schuster, 1944), 360.

30. Grew, *Turbulent Era*, II, 1233.

31. *Personal Letters, 1928–1945*, 1189.

32. *Personal Letters, 1928–1945*, 1246.

33. Walter Millis, *This Is Pearl! The United States and Japan—1941* (William Morrow and Company, 1947), 354-355, 357, 359-364.

chapter **12** AMERICA AT WAR

The President who stood in the House Chamber to address a stunned and sober Congress, was firm, confident—a symbol of courage. The words were brief. He had written them himself:

Yesterday, December 7, 1941—a date which will live in infamy—the United States of America was suddenly and deliberately attacked by naval and air forces of the Empire of Japan. . . .

No matter how long it may take us to overcome this premeditated invasion, the American people in their righteous might will win through to absolute victory.

I believe I interpret the will of the Congress and of the people when I assert that we will not only defend ourselves to the uttermost but will make very certain that this form of treachery shall never again endanger us.

Hostilities exist. There is no blinking at the fact that our people, our territory and our interests are in grave danger.

With confidence in our armed forces—with the unbounded determination of our people—we will gain the inevitable triumph—so help us God.

I ask that the Congress declare that since the unprovoked and dastardly attack by Japan on Sunday, December seventh, a state of war has existed between the United States and the Japanese Empire.[1]

The Congress was all but unanimous. Senator Arthur

H. Vandenberg's diary explained the feeling of the isolationist bloc:

> Congress declared war on Japan today—with but one dissenting vote. . . . There was no other recourse—in answer to what was probably the most treacherous attack in all history. . . .

We have little or no information regarding the peace negotiations. . . . It has all been secret—secret even from the Senate Foreign Relations Committee. Perhaps this was necessary. But I hope that some day the whole record will be laid bare. I should like to know what the price of peace in the Far East would have been. I have the feeling that it would have been necessary for us to yield but relatively little—and nothing in the nature of "appeasement." . . . Without condoning for an instant the way in which Japan precipitated hostilities, I still think we may have driven her needlessly into hostilities through our dogmatic diplomatic attitudes. . . .

But we have asked for this—and other—wars. Now we are in it. Nothing matters except victory. The "arguments" must be postponed.[2]

Every man soon marshaled his own memories of that fateful December 7. Secretary Hull had been trembling almost beyond control as he had told the Japanese ambassadors: *"In all my fifty years of public service I have never seen a document that was more crowded with infamous falsehoods and distortions—infamous falsehoods and distortions on a scale so huge that I never imagined until today that any Government on this planet was capable of uttering them."*[3]

The President himself was calm and decisive from the first moment of disaster. Frances Perkins remembered of that night:

> The President nodded as we came in, but

there was none of the usual cordial, personal greeting. . . . He was concentrated; all of his mind and all of his faculties were on the one task of trying to find out what had really happened. His voice, as he told Naval aides what to reply to dispatches was low. He wasn't wasting any energy. . . .

He began in a low voice, "You all know what's happened. The attack began at one o'clock [our time]. We don't know very much yet. . . ."

A great change had come over the President since we had seen him on Friday. Then he had been tense, worried, trying to be optimistic as usual, but it was evident that he was carrying an awful burden of decision. The Navy on Friday had thought it likely it would be Singapore and the English ports if the Japanese fleet really meant business. What should the United States do in that case? I don't know whether he had decided in his own mind; he never told us; he didn't need to. But one was conscious that night of December 7, 1941, that in spite of the terrible blow to his pride, to his faith in the Navy and its ships, and to his confidence in the American Intelligence Service, and in spite of the horror that war had actually been brought to us, he had, nevertheless, a much calmer air. His terrible moral problem had been resolved by the event.[4]

As the harried Army and Navy sorted out the fragments of information, rumor and recrimination grew. Eventually four distinct investigations would comb the evidence in a sad crusade to fix the blame. In fact, it was everyone's fault—and no one's. Each partisan detective would find what his prejudgments had led him to seek. The range would run from the inconceivable and unprovable indictment that Roosevelt had planned to trick his country into war, to the hapless search for scapegoats among the duty officers that morning at Pearl.

The facts which filtered in from the Pacific were unbelievably grim. Japan had created terms for the war which would eventually destroy her. But for the moment she rolled inexorably south, with only the shattered fragments of allied fleets, doomed and determined scatterings of troops and occasional beat-up, obsolete aircraft to challenge her. For months the southwest Pacific seemed an unblocked highway to Australia.

Ten hours after Pearl Harbor, American air power in the Philippines had been all but smashed on the ground. The British ships, Repulse and Prince of Wales, were sunk off the Malayan coast. The American naval base at Cavite in the Philippines was pulverized by steady bombing from carrier-based planes. The enemy poured ashore, and General Douglas MacArthur's American and Philippine troops were carefully withdrawn to Bataan Peninsula. He was outnumbered by the Lingayen Gulf landing force; and there were others. Bataan proved a death trap for the pitifully inadequate force, with no supplies, no food, no reinforcements, no air or naval support except from submarines and torpedo boats, little medicine—and, after a while, no hope. Later that year one of the torpedo boat officers explained to American newsmen what happened to American tanks on Bataan:

Four tankloads of them had been sent in to head off a Jap landing near Batangas—they were to go ahead of four columns of infantry and pave the way for retaking a little fishing village held by a small Jap force.

The boys said their major had assured them the Japs had nothing bigger than 50-caliber machine guns—of course their armor would stop that. So they started on in, when all of a sudden— Bam! The Japs had waited until they got within good range, and then opened up with an anti-tank gun which knocked the doors off the lead tank, and then, because the road was too narrow for the rest to turn around on, they knocked the treads off all the others except one.

"Well, then what did you do?" I asked the kids.

"Fired about two hundred rounds of 50-caliber and four rounds of 37-millimeter cannon."

"Which way were you shooting?"

"Every which way. You see, it all happened so fast we couldn't tell where the Jap fire was coming from. At the end of five minutes, three of those tanks ended up in the rice paddy—they were fourteen-ton light tanks—two of them with the doors blown off, and in one of these, the Jap machine-gun fire had cut the legs off the lieutenant in command. The others were riddled with holes. Our tank was the only one that wasn't hurt."

"So what did you do?"

"Tried to turn it around and get the hell out of there. But the road was too narrow, and then the tank got stuck in reverse, and ended up on its side in the rice paddy."

"What did the infantry do?"

"Ran like rabbits."

"Didn't they have any guns?"

"Only rifles—not a machine gun in the crowd. . . . So there they were, being cut to ribbons by concealed machine-gun fire, and nothing else to do but get for cover." . . .

"We were lying on our side in that paddy, and the Japs would come over and look at us. We played possum in there all day. They tried to open our door with bayonets, but we had it locked. In the afternoon a Jap officer looked at us through the slots—all of us lying still, holding our breath, and then he said, in English, 'They're all dead.'

"But we figured it was a trick—kept right on playing possum and, sure enough, in about an hour they came back for another look. But we were lying in exactly the same positions. This time they gave a few disgusted grunts and walked off. About an hour after dark we listened carefully, and then unlocked our door. Sure enough, they'd gone, so we beat it for the road." [5]

Bataan was epic tragedy. America watched, helpless except to bring out by crawling torpedo boat General MacArthur and a handful of special experts. On April 8 the peninsula fell; on May 6 General Jonathan Wainwright surrendered the maimed, hungry, hopeless remnants in the rock-fortress of Corregidor.

Meanwhile the combined American-British-Dutch fleet fragments were cut to pieces in a brave but impossible defense of the Dutch Islands. Java had fallen the first week in March; Guam, Hong Kong, Wake Island had been gobbled up in December. In February, the great British bastion at Singapore had gone the way of the Maginot Line—its defense prepared for the sea, the attack had come from the jungles in the rear. By early March the Japanese were marching across the south Pacific to stake their advance line in the Solomons. By the end of the month, New Guinea seemed in danger—and then Australia itself!

The peril was imminent; but the prospects for reply were weak. The battle of production had still to be fought out at home before American carriers could roam the Pacific armed with Hellcats and Corsairs, before American Marines could go ashore with decent equipment and adequate supplies, before the United States Army could return to the Dutch and Philippine Islands with forces to match the swarming Nipponese. The very pilots and marines and jungle troops had yet to be trained in many cases. And there were other wars to be won. For while the Japanese scourge was flowing inexorably across the Pacific, American ships were being torpedoed as they lay silhouetted against the bright skies of New York and Miami Beach; China's lifeline, the Burma Road, had been cut; Rommel was racing across North Africa toward the Suez Canal; Hitler's troops were deep in Russia forcing the mammoth but undergunned Soviet nation to its knees.

Worse yet for the Pacific, agreement had long since been reached by the British and American staffs that top priority must be given to Europe. Hitler was thought to present the most massive danger to American security; only in Great Britain did it seem possible to conduct the long, slow build-up of troops and supplies required by a major effort.

Throughout 1942 the massive war machine which was to crush Hitler, Tojo and Mussolini ground with confusion and friction. At one point, Harry Hopkins complained:

> Estimates can be made and agreed to by all the top experts and then decisions to go ahead are made by the President and the P.M. and all the generals and admirals and air marshals—and then, a few months later, somebody asks, "Where are all those landing craft?" or "Whatever became of those medium bombers we promised to China?" and then you start investigating and it takes you weeks to find out that the orders have been deliberately stalled on the desk of some lieutenant commander or lieutenant colonel down on Constitution Avenue.[6]

As production stepped up drastically, the demands increased beyond all conceivable limits. In the first eleven months of 1942, German submarines sank 8,000,000 tons of shipping, nearly cutting off the supply lines to Europe; only in the early fall of 1943 did the sinkings begin to be matched by new construction. In May, 1942, Soviet Foreign Minister Molotov came secretly to Washington to beg for an immediate second front to take the pressure off his beleagered nation, and there was an incessant clamor for more and more Lend-Lease for Moscow.

One example will illustrate the complexity of the production problems. Donald Nelson has described the difficulty of conversion in the automobile industry which had appeared even before Pearl Harbor:

> ... there could be no such thing as partial conversion in the automobile industry. Charles E. Wilson, president of General Motors, told me, as other motor magnates were to tell me later, that you do not "partly convert" a production line. You do it all the way or not at all. ...

Consequently, converting the automobile industry was, in a sense, destroying it—and its owners did not quite see fit to demolish this industrial colossus without knowing what would take its place. ...

Most auto firms date their transformation to a wartime industry back to a memorable meeting which took place in Detroit on October 25, 1940. ...

To the meeting ... Bill Knudsen, working on his idea about putting the motor industry back of airplane production, called together everyone who had anything to do with automobile manufacture: the primary producers, the parts and appliance makers, the tool and die makers. ...

Knudsen had brought to the meeting bits and parts of airframes and, I believe, some engine parts. Major Jimmy Doolittle ... asked the manufacturers what they could do about reproducing the specimens which were on exhibit. They were asked to study them and deliver a verdict.

They handled, measured, inspected the specimens, and decided that probably they could do much about reproducing them in their own plants. There was one dissenter—Charles E. Sorenson of the Ford Co. The company, he stated, would not make parts; it would make the whole plane—engines, frameparts and all—or nothing. He declared that Ford would not consider manufacturing odds and ends of parts to be shipped to a plane builder, only to have him, an alien personality, grouse that the parts didn't fit, that this or that had not been done correctly.

As a result of this most informal meeting—held together by Bill Knudsen's prestige in the industry—De Soto, Chrysler, Hudson, and the Goodyear Rubber Co. were soon building a long line of parts for Martin. The Murray Corporation was accomplishing the same thing for Boeing's Flying Fortress, and the Fisher Body Division of General Motors and Briggs were making parts for North American. . . .

At this meeting, too, the American bomber program really came into being. . . .

Shortly after the October 25, 1940, conference, the great Sorenson visited an aircraft plant where B-24s were being assembled. Men were crawling over fuselages, getting in each other's way, making scores of useless gestures, and occasionally hammering one another over the head. The whole procedure was a negation of mass production as Sorenson understood it, and few men alive understood it better.

While gaping at these strange antics, Sorenson is reported to have made a hurried drawing for the biggest aircraft plant in the world—Willow Run.

Later, Sorenson and his associates elaborated on the sketches, and from these grew a veritable Gargantua of aircraft production—larger than the combined pre-war plants of Boeing, Douglas, and Consolidated. It was a mile long and a quarter of a mile wide. Into this enormous cavern went 1,600 machine tools, 7,500 jigs and fixtures (some of which, I heard, were seventy-five feet long), an overhead conveyor system, and other gadgets which made possible the mass production of planes on a scale never thought possible before. This cradle of destruction seemed to spring from the ground

almost as soon as the Ford Co. reached its decision.
Eleven months after ground was broken at Willow
Run the first four-engine Ford-made Consolidated
bombers were assembled—the B-24s, which swept over
the battlefields of Europe and the Pacific at a speed of
more than 300 miles per hour, with a four-ton bomb
load potential, and a range of 3,000 miles. . . .[7]

The nation was fortunate indeed that mobilization
had begun long before Pearl Harbor. But there were
constantly new challenges. Aircraft were hardly in
production before they were obsolete. The crude B-17s,
for example, had been found in the Philippines to be
fatally undergunned. Gradually the Air Corps added
nose and tail, belly and top turrets, power driven and
armed with two machine guns each. Mechanical im-
provements were constantly being made. The B-24
bomber went through multiple modifications until, by
1944, the models were being labeled H, and J, and K,
and then L. The slow P-40s which fought sadly against
the Zeros in China and the Philippines gradually gave
way to the sprightly Mustangs, the twin-boomed Light-
nings and the heavy Thunderbolts. Often the demands
of war outpaced communications; modifications currently built into planes were sometimes modified again
as soon as they reached their overseas bases. The race
was never-ending. And, known only to a handful of
people, scientific and construction crews worked round
the clock in Tennessee and Washington to perfect the
atomic bomb.

Often sacrifices in pace had to be made to practicality
in production. By 1944 American airmen in Europe
would be desperately concentrating upon Germany's
oil refineries to keep down the Nazi jets which were
sitting in numbers on the German fields. The only
American jets were unarmed exhibition models flown
about the theater for demonstration.

There were errors, some tragic, some merely annoying:

shipments misplaced, production held up for the lack of crucial tools or of one small part; aviation cadets enlisted in large numbers and then left to walk the streets for months for lack of training facilities. But the eventual record was astounding. By the end of the war the United States had produced more than:

> 5,000 cargo ships and transports
> 6,000 naval vessels
> 64,000 landing craft
> 86,000 tanks
> 296,000 aircraft
> 2,500,000 machine guns

There were grievous administrative problems at home. And there were problems of public morale, especially during the first hectic year when disaster seemed everywhere. Lacking victories in those first months, Roosevelt had to try to buck up the will to win by dramatizing stories of individual heroism. The press followed suit. Colin Kelly, John Buckley, and others became symbols of a determination that could bring real results only one or two years away.

Roosevelt sought to strike a balance between democracy and security. An Office of Censorship was set up shortly after Pearl Harbor, but security within the nation depended heavily upon the voluntary code of self-discipline which newsmen phenomenally respected. Sometimes security problems overrode all sense of legal procedure and of justice. The mass movement of Japanese from California to "Relocation Camps" was the worst by far. Citizens and aliens alike were herded by force from the coastal areas, leaving their business and homes behind. Deep-rooted prejudice and economic envy all too obviously reinforced the wartime hysteria. Inflation was even more difficult to fight. In January, 1942, the President outlined the basic economic program he was to follow throughout the war.

Its essential aspects were four. Taxes and heavy government borrowing tended to sop up excessive funds. The Federal Reserve System used its control of credit to stop excessive private borrowing. The Office of Price Administration set maximum prices on a vast variety of goods and then supplemented this with direct rationing as shortages developed or military necessity dictated. Americans became familiar with sugar, coffee and gasoline rationing in 1942, with the doling out of shoes, meat, fats and cheese in 1943. Finally the problem of holding wage lines was managed in extreme cases by governmental seizure of plants to break off strikes and dictate terms. Thus Montgomery Ward's facilities were taken over on more than one occasion when it refused to accept War Labor Board rulings; once its crusty Chairman, Sewell Avery, was carried bodily from his office by Army troops. Thus the coal mines and the railways were taken over when strikes were called. Typical of the complaints against the program was John L. Lewis's blast on behalf of his coal miners in April, 1943:

Twenty-three million on the farms and 52,-000,000 employed in gainful occupation cannot be restrained in their attempts to maintain a participation on an effective and cooperative basis in our national economy while the government pours $6,250,000,000 of profit in nine months into the laps of the coupon clippers of America.

A farmer or a miner is more important to the war effort and the future destinies of this republic than a fat investor in corporation securities. . . .

If sacrifices are called for, we'll make them, but let industry and finance make equal sacrifices.[8]

As chief administrator of the war machinery the President was reduced to merely managing the worst

288 FRANKLIN D. ROOSEVELT

disputes among his chief subordinates. Frances Perkins
has said:

> . . . he was the catalytic agent through whose
> efforts chaotic forces were brought to a point where they
> could be harnessed creatively. He was a creative and
> energizing agent rather than a careful, direct-line ad-
> ministrator. He trusted people to whom he gave a job to
> do it. If they couldn't or wouldn't or didn't, he ap-
> pointed someone else or gave part of it to someone
> else. If he had taken the time and the energy to
> straighten out major and minor administrative diffi-
> culties, if he had heard judicially the complaints and
> arguments of all the men who thought their duties were
> in conflict, he would have done little else, and he would
> not have been able to get on with the war.°

There were three roles the President could not ab-
dicate to others. He remained the chief spokesman and
propagandist; his was the final decision on military
strategy; and his the decision on shaping the peace.

Early in 1942 he confided to an old acquaintance
some of the problems he faced in trying to keep up the
public morale:

> Sometimes I wish I could carry out your
> thought of more frequent talking on the air on my part
> but one thing I dread is that my talks should be so fre-
> quent as to lose their effectiveness. . . .

There is apathy, though frankly I think it is lessen-
ing. . . .

The best comment I have heard was by Elmer Davis
after I spoke at the end of February. He said: "Some
people want the United States to win so long as England
loses. Some people want the United States to win so
long as Russia loses. And some people want the United
States to win so long as Roosevelt loses."

I think we must avoid too much personal leadership—my good friend Winston Churchill has suffered a little from this. It must grow more slowly—remembering always that we have only been in the war for three months.[10]

Sometimes he could be biting in his impatient replies to criticism, as he was when he wrote in March, 1942:

You wax positively gruesome when you declare solemnly that had it not been for the thirty million man-days lost by strikes since the defense program began, the Philippines, the Dutch Indies and Singapore would all have been saved. You sound like Alice in Wonderland.

So let me tell you something more fantastic than that. If, since the defense program started, we in the United States had not lost sixty million man-days through that scourge of Satan, called the common cold, we could undoubtedly have had enough planes and guns and tanks to overrun Europe, Africa and the whole of Asia.

Take good care of yourself. Don't go on strike and for God's sake don't catch a common cold![11]

Roosevelt was proud of his education in military and naval affairs. He wrote an adviser in 1939, ". . . I do not have to have military and naval operations explained to me at length."[12] He insisted that the principle of civilian control of the military be maintained. Nevertheless, he respected the judgment of his professionals, once he had collected the team on which he thought he could rely. The war strategy was tailored essentially by General George C. Marshall for the Army, Admiral Ernest J. King for the Navy, General Henry H. Arnold for the Army Air Corps, and Admiral William E. Leahy, the President's personal military aide. Dwight D. Eisenhower, Marshall's Chief of Planning, played a crucial role, as did Admiral Chester Nimitz at Pearl Harbor, General Douglas MacArthur in the South Pacific, Admiral Harold L. Stark in London, and the civilian secretaries, particularly Henry L. Stimson. The President supported their hard-negotiated compromises, and strongly, in the conferences with the allies. His own views undoubtedly strengthened such crucial decisions as those to win in Europe first, to make the assault on Europe in France rather than in the Balkans. Only occasionally did he override them, as on the decision to strike in North Africa in 1942. More often than not, the military decisions for which the President was personally blamed were those in which his staff had fervently agreed.

He did insist on constant and detailed briefings. He could intervene, and sharply, when it seemed essential. Thus, he wrote to Knox and Stimson in March, 1942:

> I have only one objective in mind. The crux of the use of aerial torpedoes in the Southwest Pacific is from now for the next ninety days. I do not care who fires the torpedoes—Army fliers or Navy fliers. The point is that they must be fired at Japanese ships. This is the critical time for the use of these torpedoes. I do not give a continental about the use of these torpedoes after the next ninety days. . . .[18]

It was in the role of representing the United States with the leaders of Great Britain, Russia, France and China and a dozen other nations that Roosevelt had to act most directly and personally. There were at least fourteen such conferences with Churchill, Stalin, de Gaulle, and Chiang Kai-shek between December, 1941, and February, 1945. Churchill was almost a commuter

between Downing Street and the White House, and
he lived for long periods in the President's home at
Washington or Hyde Park. Other conferences took
Roosevelt himself to Casablanca in January, 1943; to
Quebec in August, 1943, and September, 1944; to Cairo
and Teheran in November and December, 1943; and to
the Russian Crimea in February, 1945. They were a
tremendous drain on both Roosevelt's time and energies. One of his secretaries complained in May, 1943:

> The difference between the President and
> the Prime Minister is this: the P.M. has nothing on his
> mind but the war. The President, besides planning war
> strategy with the P.M., must also conduct the Govern-
> ment of the United States and cope with the coal-mine
> strike, Ruml Plan tax bill, and the rest of it. In social
> habits F.D.R. is no match for W.C., who is the em-
> bodiment of the character Mr. Ingoldsby calls "a
> certain Count Herman,"

> "A highly respectable man as a German,
> "Who smoked like a chimney,
>   and drank like a merman." [14]

Despite his fatigue, F.D.R. thrived on these personal
contacts and insisted that they were essential. He explained privately the trip to Casablanca:

> "We were not getting anywhere in our plans
> for operations. . . . Our Joint Chiefs of Staff would meet
> and they could decide what in their opinion ought to
> be done and they'd report to London. The British
> joint staffs could agree among themselves, but they
> could not reach an accord with our joint staffs. They
> reported back and forth between London and Washing-
> ton but without results.
> "What to do?" he continued. "Always there was the

personal equation. The prima-donna temperament. If
I sent Stimson to London, Knox would have thought
he should go. It was the same between the Army and
Navy in London. Churchill and I were the only ones
who could get together and settle things." [15]

He was irritated with de Gaulle, mystified at Stalin.
But with Churchill, Roosevelt developed a warm and
intimate rapport, although there was always something
of the game of "oneupmanship" between them. As
John Gunther sees it:

> Many obvious points of similarity exist be-
tween the two, but Churchill was probably a better
gambler, and took chances more; also he was a better
bargainer. It is unlikely that FDR would ever have put
up such a bluff as, for instance, Churchill did in 1943,
when he tried to bludgeon the Turks into entering the
war by threatening to "give" the Dardanelles to Russia.
Churchill wrote more eloquent and brilliant prose. He
had a deeper apperception of historical realities. He
trusted his experts more, and avoided government-by-
crony. He was more accessible to controversy. It is
interesting that Henry Stimson records that he "could
cut loose at the Englishman as he never felt free to do
with his chief"; . . .

> . . . Between them something like 1,700 telegrams,
letters and other communications passed in five and a
half years, starting with Roosevelt's sympathetic initiative to the "Naval Person" when Churchill became
First Lord of the Admiralty in 1939. . . .

Churchill's letters to Roosevelt . . . constitute one of
the supreme feats of political argument of all time. He
"armed" FDR with patient lessons; he laid the framework for the destroyer transfer; he ceaselessly cajoled,
explored, exhorted; he wheedled him, encouraged him,
and called out sternly "Do It Now" . . . he analyzed

history for him as he made it, in documents of unprecedented insight, brilliance, variety, and vigor. But one must not think that Roosevelt was a dupe or that he played second fiddle. The Churchill salesmanship was masterly; but FDR did not need to be sold on the major premises. . . .

According to Churchill's own calculation they had 120 days of close personal contact in all. Nothing in the contemporary—or other—annals quite matches the dramatic intensity and importance of this series of monumental conferences; it is quite safe to say that never before has talk between two men so influenced the course of world history, both military and political. Roosevelt once telegraphed to Churchill, "It is fun to be in the same decade with you," which would appear to be one of the more massive understatements of the age.[16]

As the strategy evolved during the 1942 conferences Roosevelt described the terms of the situation to South Africa's Jan Smuts:

I am in accord with the thought that the objectives of 1942 differ from those of 1943. This situation arises from necessity.

In 1942, while our strategy because of circumstances must be essentially defensive, tactics may be offensive in one or more operations.

Both strategy and tactics in 1943 will, however, depend on several factors and, while we can and should plan to meet each and every one of the events of the next six months, the United Nations cannot adopt a hard and fast strategical policy at this time except that the United Nations must seek a little later on to gain the initiative in 1943.

The factors relate to certain main problems not yet clearly foreseeable. The main ones are:

(a) The outcome in Russia that runs from pushing the Germans back at one end to Russian collapse at the other end, including in between three or four different kinds of situations as of December 1, 1942.

(b) The results in the Middle East, Egypt, Syria, Iraq, Basra and the Caucasus line of communications.

(c) The control of lines of communications by the United Nations to Murmansk and Archangel, to Gibralter and the west coast of Africa, to Egypt and to the Persian Gulf, including mastery of the India Ocean.

At this time I do not bring warfare in the Pacific into the picture because I greatly hope that while the Japanese offensive may be pushed forward into the Bay of Bengal, into the New Guinea area and even to a greater distance into the Aleutians, it seems probable that most of India will be safe and that the United States can maintain the route to Australia and to Alaska.

American reserves and American planes and tank production are at least up to all reasonable schedules, but the controlling factor is to get these reserves and munitions to the scene of actual fighting.

I believe that the holding of the Middle East is of prime importance and that the so-called Second Front must be launched in 1942.

The United States is engaged in the twofold task of sending all possible help to the Middle East and, at the same time sending all possible troops and munitions toward the objective of a Second Front. What that Front will be must depend essentially on agreement between the British and American Staffs."

To Queen Wilhelmina of the Netherlands he more plaintively explained:

. . . It is difficult for us to do much that is practical in regard either to the Netherlands Indies or the Philippines at this time and all that is possible for us is to keep a stiff upper lip and vow that between us we will rescue the Islands from Japanese domination, even though it might take two or three years. . . .

In other words, we are forced to come to the conclusion that our major strategy must be the defeat of Germany this Summer in her Russian effort, for the very simple fact that if this can be accomplished the probability is that Germany cannot survive another year.[18]

But major commitment to the war in Europe did not mean that Japan was to be given a free hand. Long before the Japanese had driven into the Solomons, the Navy had begun a series of moves designed to harass the enemy, to reassure the home front, and to set limits to Nipponese expansion. The core of the strategy was the carrier force. Pearl Harbor had taught the Navy in one fateful day the dimensions of the new, mobile, air warfare. Happily Hornet, Saratoga, Lexington, Enterprise, Wasp and Yorktown were intact, as were a reasonable number of fast cruisers and destroyers.

In February, 1942, Admirals William F. Halsey and Frank Fletcher conducted lightning air and cruiser raids on the Marshalls, the Gilberts and Wake Island. On April 18 Tokyo itself was bombed by General Jimmy Doolittle's twin-engined B-25s, flown at great risk from the deck of the Hornet, 700 miles off the Japanese coast. This was the only trained B-25 squadron; every ship was lost. But most of the crews were saved, and the surprise raid boosted American morale, while raising profound doubts among the Japanese.

Despite the pitifully small American forces, the turning point came in May, 1942. Encouraged by successful carrier strikes on Japanese bases in New Guinea, the Yorktown and Lexington carrier groups challenged the enemy fleets headed for Port Moresby, the jumping-off point for any Australian invasion. The Japanese decision to break off, when their newest carrier, the Shoho, was sunk, marked high tide. This Battle of the Coral Sea was a brilliantly fought carrier action for the Americans; and it undoubtedly saved Australia. But the sinking of the Shoho was matched by damage to the Yorktown and the loss of the "Lady Lex." Samuel Eliot Morison has told the story:

The end of the battle found Lexington listing seven degrees, with three boiler rooms partially flooded, plane elevators inoperative and three fires burning; but before gun barrels grew cold, the flight deck was readied to launch and recover aircraft. While the planes settled on her deck, damage control and black gang brought her back to an even keel by shifting oil ballast. An hour passed, and the ship's company had reason to rejoice. The proud Lady was bloodied, yet showing a clean pair of heels and conducting nearly normal flight operations. Commander H. R. Healy, the damage control officer, in a telephone report to Captain Sherman, grew facetious: "We've got the torpedo damage temporarily shored up, the fires out and soon will have the ship back on an even keel. But I would suggest, sir, that if you have to take any more torpedoes, you take 'em on the starboard side."

No sooner were those words out of "Pop" Healy's mouth than, at 1247, a devastating internal explosion shook the carrier from stem to stern. Gasoline vapors, released by one of the torpedo hits, had been ignited below by a motor generator left running. More eruptions followed, each more violent than the last. Internal communications deteriorated rapidly. Central station, the nerve center of damage control, suffered major damage and casualties, Commander Healy among them. Smoke burst from the lower decks.

Even then the situation seemed hopeful to sailors on the bridge. Flight operations continued, planes of the morning attack group were recovered, the last plane being received on board at 1414. The ship still made 25 knots. Only as link after link in the communication system was severed did the officers come to the reluctant conclusion that the Lady was too hot to handle.

A second internal explosion at 1445, which wrecked the ventilation system of the fire and engine rooms, caused Captain Sherman to ask assistance from other vessels in fighting fires. Half an hour later flight operations were abandoned. . . .

With engine rooms untenable and communications reduced to one slim telephone line, the black gang was ordered to make its way topside after securing engines and boilers. Steam safety valves were lifted and the ship, drained of her life blood, wallowed to a stop at 1630. All hands prepared to abandon ship. . . .

The curtain for the last act began to descend at 1707 when Admiral Fitch called down from his bridge to the Captain, "Well, Ted, let's get the men off." . . . Abandonment was deliberate, methodical and exceedingly reluctant. . . . One group of men, awaiting their turn to go over the side, scooped up what ice cream remained in the ship's service store. Nobody who went overboard was drowned; even the Captain's dog was saved. . . .[19]

The lessons learned in the Coral Sea were quickly applied to block the enemy's advance in mid-Pacific. At Midway, June 3 to 6, the carrier groups stopped the strike which the Japanese had designed to smooth out their line of defense—from Attu and Kiska in Alaska (attacked in the same operation) to the Solomons in the south.

Midway was the first massive defeat for the Japanese Navy, and it cleared the way for the American island-hopping campaign that would lead eventually to Japan itself. On August 7 American marines went ashore on

298 FRANKLIN D. ROOSEVELT

the fetid, steaming islands in the Solomons, Guadalcanal and Tulagi.

These were pestiferous battlefields where heavy
American and Japanese forces fought for months in the
crowded jungle. The marines went to school here for
the lessons that would pay off later at Bougainville,
Tarawa and Iwo Jima. John Hersey, living among them,
caught the tangled motives and maneuvers of the jungle
fighters for the folks back home:

On the eighth day of October in the first
year of our war, I went down into a valley with Captain
Charles Rigaud of the United States Marines. A small
skirmish took place down there. . . .

Our column moved in absolute silence. It is impossible to describe the creepy sensation of walking
through that empty-looking but crowded-seeming
jungle.

What made it eerie was that the jungle was far from
silent. The birds whose cries had sounded so cheerful
from the heights were terrifying now. Parakeets and
macaws screeched from nowhere. There was one bird
with an altogether unmusical call which sounded exactly
like a man whistling shrilly through his fingers three
times—and then another, far off in Japanese territory,
would answer. The stream made a constant noise, and
an annoying one. It seemed terribly important to listen
for the enemy (as if the Japs would be so stupid as to
crackle through the underbrush), but the stream's
continuous chatter, maddeningly cheerful, made that
impossible in any case. Off and on we could hear the
noises of our own power—planes and artillery—far above
the jungle roof. These should have been encouraging
noises. . . . But down here the noises were merely weird
—the eccentric whirr of the strafing P-39's, sounding as
if some big cog in each engine were unlubricated; the
soft, fluttery sound of shells in flight, like the noise a

man would make if he were to blow through a key-hole. . . .

. . . During one halt I noticed a hollow in one huge tree trunk, and in the hollow what seemed to be the head and left shoulder of a man, and below that a small point which I imagined to be a muzzle. In trying to make sure, I showed myself and drew no fire. I'm still not sure, in the light of what happened later, that that shape was not a Japanese shape.

Now I comprehended for the first time why the marines had been taking so few prisoners. It was not just that the boys were trigger-happy, as one had boasted. It was not just brutality, not just vindictive remembrance of Pearl Harbor. Here in the jungle a marine killed because he must, or be killed. He stalked the enemy, and the enemy stalked him, as if each were a hunter tracking a bear cat. . . .

The signal was a single shot from a sniper.

It came from somewhere behind us, but probably not as far as the first shots we had heard. The high flat snap was easily recognizable as a Japanese sound, and immediately after it, overhead, went the sound of the bullet, like a supercharged bee.

After a couple of too quick seconds, snipers all around us opened up. There would be the snap, and the whine, and then the tuck when the bullet went into the ground. There was no way of knowing where the next was coming from. The only thing you could be certain of was that it would come soon enough to take your eye off the place where you thought you might spot the last one.

Then machine guns from across the river opened up.

But the terrible thing was that Jap mortars over there opened up, too.

The first thing a green man fixes upon in his mind is the noise of these weapons. This was the first time I had ever been surrounded this way by the tight-woven noise of war.

Its constant fabric was rifle fire; this sounded like Bucks County, Pennsylvania, on the first day of the pheasant season, only nearby and not an amusement. Like a knife tearing into the fabric, every once in a while, there would be the short bursts of machine gun fire. The noise of the mortars was awful, a thump which vibrated not just your eardrums, but your entrails as well. Forward we could still hear our aviation—dived bombs fumbling into the jungle, and the laughter of strafing P-39's. And every once in a while the soft, fluttery noise of our artillery shells making a trip. The noise alone was enough to scare a new man, to say nothing of the things which were done by the things which were making the noise.

The Japs had made their calculations perfectly. There were only three or four natural crossings of the river; this was one of them. And so they had set their trap.

They had machine guns all mounted, ready to pour stuff into the jungle bottleneck at the stream's junction with the river. They had snipers scattered on both sides of the river. And they had their mortars all set to lob deadly explosions into the same area. . . .

Had we been infantry, the trap might not have worked. . . . Heavy machine guns take some time to be assembled and mounted. In that narrow defile his men, as brave as any, never succeeded in getting more than two guns firing. . . .

That was what made being on the receiving end of mortar fire so terrible: the next thing that those little tubes gave off might land anywhere. We would almost have felt more comfortable if something which could aim was aiming right at us.

When the first bolts of this awful thunder began to fall among Rigaud's men, we hit the ground. We were like earthy insects with some great foot being set down in our midst, and we scurried for little crannies— cavities under the roots of huge trees, little gullies, dead logs. I found a good spot to the left of the trail. . . . I grew very affectionate toward the spot; I embraced it. . . .

What was happening to his men was something terrible. The mortar shells were exploding among them and bleaching some of the bravery out of them. The noise and seeing friends hurt were not things to be dismissed. . . .

And all the while snipers and machine gunners wrote in their nasty punctuation. Our own guns answered from time to time with good, deep, rich sound, but not enough. . . .

We could not see the enemy, either on our side of the river or the other. All this hatred was pouring out of jungle too thick to see more than twenty or thirty feet. . . . You might have thought that the jungle itself had grown malevolent, and hated us. The trees were hurling little pellets at us; the vines were slinging explosions.

But even if we had been able to see the enemy, we could not have done anything to him. We couldn't get our weapons to work. We were helpless. Our men were being killed and wounded. We were trapped, hopelessly trapped.

Individually the marines in that outfit were as brave as any fighters in any army in the world, I am positive; but when fear began to be epidemic in that closed-in place, no one was immune. No one could resist it.

The first sign of flight among those men was in their eyes. At first they watched what was going on calmly as an audience at some play. Then suddenly they were looking around for the nearest exit. . . .

The next sign of growing fear was the way the men started moving around. . . .

The marines had been deeply enough indoctrinated so that even flight did not wipe out the formulas, and soon the word came whispering back along the line:

"Withdraw."

"Withdraw."

"Withdraw. . . ."

Then they started moving back, slowly at first, then running wildly, scrambling from place of cover to momentary cover. . . .

It was at this moment that Charles Alfred Rigaud, the boy with tired circles under his eyes, showed himself to be a good officer and grown man.

Despite snipers all around us, despite the machine guns and mortar fire, he stood right up on his feet and shouted out: "Who in Christ's name gave that order?"

This was enough to freeze the men in their tracks. They threw themselves on the ground, in attitudes of defense; they took cover behind trees from both the enemy and the anger of their captain.

Next, by a combination of blistering sarcasm, orders and cajolery, he not only got the men back into position: he got them in a mood to fight again.

"Where do you guys think you're going?" he shouted. And: "Get back in there. . . . Take cover, you. . . . What do you guys do, just invent orders? . . . Listen, it's going to get dark and we got a job to do. . . . You guys make me ashamed. . . ."

But the most telling thing he said was: "Gosh, and they call you marines." . . .[20]

Before Japanese resistance on Guadalcanal finally ended in February, 1943, the main naval forces of both countries had become deeply involved. The enemy came out of the struggle with his morale broken, his South Pacific fleet shattered. The price to the allies had been heavy. In the naval battles of the Solomons the carriers Wasp and Hornet and numerous other ships had been lost. In one disaster off Savo Island, the cruisers Quincy, Astoria, Vincennes and Canberra had gone down in rapid order. In the whole South Pacific only Enterprise

was left for the time to fly off planes. But under the
cover of Guadalcanal, General MacArthur's command
had reinforced Port Moresby and by November, 1942,
his Australian and American troops were laying siege to
Buna and Gona, the great Japanese bases on the north
shore of New Guinea.

While the war was turning back upon Japan in the
Pacific, the major effort was being thrown into fighting
the German subs in the Atlantic and preparing a
massive assault on the Germans.

In the fall of 1942 came the landings in North Africa.
The argument over this assault had been long and
intense at the strategic level. As Stimson's biographer
has summed it up:

> The TORCH decision was the result of two
> absolutely definite and final rulings, one by the British,
> and the other by the President. Mr. Churchill and his
> advisers categorically refused to accept the notion of
> a cross-Channel invasion in 1942. Mr. Roosevelt cate-
> gorically insisted that there must be some operation in
> 1942. The only operation that satisfied both of these
> conditions was TORCH. Stimson . . . could under-
> stand that for many reasons it was important that
> American troops should come to grips with the German
> enemy somewhere, as soon as possible.
> But in July, 1942, neither of these considerations
> seemed to him as important as the fact that TORCH
> would obviously force an indefinite postponement of
> effective action in the only decisive theater outside
> Russia, and he pushed his disagreement with the Presi-
> dent to the limits prescribed by loyalty. . . . TORCH
> had what BOLERO [the cross-Channel invasion] had
> never had, the enthusiastic support of the highest
> authorities, and it was therefore possible to give it
> priorities and exclusive rights with the kind of ruthless-

ness that Stimson had so ardently and fruitlessly urged
for BOLERO. . . .

In October and November there occurred two great
and unforeseen events which still further reduced the
dangers of TORCH. One was the successful Russian
stand at Stalingrad. . . . At the same time, in the battle
of Alamein, the British Eighth Army achieved a definitive victory over the Afrika Korps. To these two major
areas Hitler was forced to give new attention, and the
prospect of a counterattack through Spain against
TORCH was diminished. . . ."

The command was given to Eisenhower. In October
1942, General Mark Clark was sent in by submarine for
a secret meeting with Admiral Darlan, the chief of
French government in North Africa. Before dawn on
November 8 British and American forces, convoyed
from England, moved onto the beaches at Oran and
Algiers, and American forces, direct from the States,
assaulted Casablanca and Port Lyautey in Morocco.
Surprise and French help smoothed the way for easy
landings in Algeria. At Oran and at Casablanca, where
a Vichy French fleet lay at anchor, there was sharp
resistance. The first successes soon gave way to a dogged
war of resistance. Germans swarmed over unoccupied
France on November 11, and they were soon reinforc-
ing Tunisia, the back door to Rommel's already hard-
pressed desert brigades.

Eisenhower had hoped for a quick parade to Tunis.
The Germans frustrated this by building up an army
there more quickly than reinforcements could be
brought from Britain and the United States through
the sub-packs and over the one-track railway. By the
end of November the allied columns were stalled before
German positions and mine fields just west of the
Tunisian border. The German lines held, but they
were unable to roll back the allies. The new rocket-

firing bazookas punctured their tanks; increasing allied
air power and effective artillery held them in place. This
was the baptism of fire for the American G.I. Ernie
Pyle has recorded what it was like for the foot soldier
in North Africa:

> . . . men lived in a way that is inconceivable
to anyone who hasn't experienced it. They walked and
fought all night without sleep. Next day they lay flat
in foxholes, or hid in fields of freshly green, knee-high
wheat. If they were in the fields they dared not even
move enough to dig foxholes, for that would have
brought the German artillery. They couldn't rise even
for nature's calls. The German felt for them continually
with his artillery. The slow drag of those motionless
daylight hours was nearly unendurable. . . .

The second evening after the attack began, C rations
and five-gallon cans of water were brought across
country in jeeps, after dark. One night a German shell
landed close and fragments punctured fifteen cans of
water. The men ate in the dark, and they couldn't see
the can from which they were eating. They just ate by
feel. They made cold coffee from cold water.

Each night enough canned rations for three meals
were brought up, but when men moved on after supper
most of them either lost or left behind the next day's
rations, because they were too heavy to carry. But they
said when they were in battle and excited they sort of
went on their nerve. They didn't think much about being hungry.

They fought at night and lay low by day, when the
artillery took over its blasting job. Weariness gradually
crept over them. What sleeping they did was in daytime.
But it was never very much, for at night it was too cold
and in daytime too hot. Also the fury of the artillery
made daytime sleeping next to impossible. So did the
heat of the sun. Some men passed out from heat prostra-

tion. Many of them got upset stomachs from the heat. But as the third and fourth days rolled on, weariness overcame all obstacles to sleep. Men who sat down for a moment's rest fell asleep in the grass. There were even men who said they could march while asleep. Lieutenant Colonel Charlie Stone actually went to sleep standing up talking on a field telephone—not when he was listening, but in the middle of a spoken sentence.

When sometimes they did lie down at night the men had only their raincoats to lie on. It was cold, and the dew made the grass as wet as rain. They didn't dare start a fire to heat their food, even in daytime, for the smoke would attract enemy fire. At night they couldn't even light cigarettes in the open, so after digging their foxholes they got down and made hoods over their heads with their raincoats, and lighted up under the coats. They had plenty of cigarettes. Those who ran out during battle were supplied by others. Every night new supplies of water and C rations were brought up in jeeps.

You can't conceive how hard it was to move and fight at night. The country was rugged, the ground rough. Everything was new and strange. The nights were pitch-black. The men groped with their feet. They stepped into holes, and fell sprawling in little gullies and creeks. They trudged over plowed ground and pushed through waist-high shrubs. They went as a man blindfolded, feeling unsure and off balance, but they kept going.

Through it all there was the fear of mines. The Germans had mined the country behind them beyond anything ever known before. Our troops simply couldn't take time to go over each inch of ground with mine detectors, so they had to discover the mine fields by stumbling into them or driving over them. Naturally there were casualties, but not as many as you might think—just a few men each day. The greatest damage was psychological—the intense watchfulness our troops had to maintain.[22]

War reduced life to its elemental emotions. One tank man in North Africa wrote home:

> Now something about the Germans, not Hitler but the German people themselves. They are really behind Hitler and want him, that is the majority. So you really can't blame him for all of this. They did the same things in the last war. You must destroy them or they will destroy you. They use all of the devilish, fiendish devices of war, things that we don't dare use. . . .
> It's a very, very horrible war, dirty, dishonest, not at all that glamor war that we read about in the home town paper we read. Someone has to remember that when the showdown comes. I know that as for myself and the other men here, we will show no mercy.[23]

By the end of January, 1943, Rommel had retreated carefully into Tunisia, and early in February he attempted to break through the allied lines to the west. He was stopped. Allied attempts in March failed to penetrate his line, but Rommel was outnumbered. The British Navy and the American Air Force had smothered his supply lines. Early in April Montgomery's desert troops joined hands with the forces in Tunisia. A new assault now pushed the Axis troops back to the sea, inexorably encircled by the British to the south, Americans at the center, and a French force along the coast to the north. The surrender was complete by May 9.

As Stimson had predicted, victory in Tunisia led to more Mediterranean adventures. At Casablanca in January, 1943, Roosevelt, Churchill and their staffs came to three fundamental decisions: the cross-chan-

nel invasion would be postponed until 1944 and the
immediate concentration would be upon Sicily and
Italy; the solid front with Russia and China would be
affirmed by public pronouncement and stepped-up
aid; and the conditions of peace would be established as
"unconditional surrender." Roosevelt announced the
decisions to the nation in terms which indicated how
much the bitterness of the tanker and the infantryman
had flowed back to Washington:

> In an attempt to ward off the inevitable
> disaster, the Axis propagandists are trying all of their
> old tricks, in order to divide the United Nations. They
> seek to create the idea that if we win this war, Russia,
> England, China, and the United States are going to get
> into a cat-and-dog fight.
>
> To these panicky attempts . . . to escape the conse-
> quences of their crimes, we say—all the United Nations
> say—that the only terms on which we shall deal with an
> Axis government, or any Axis factions, are the terms
> proclaimed at Casablanca: "Unconditional Surrender."
> . . . In our uncompromising policy we mean no harm to
> the common people of the Axis nations. But we do
> mean to impose punishment and retribution in full upon
> their guilty, barbaric leaders. . . ."

The Sicilian invasion was staged on the night of
July 9-10. There were heavy casualties, some caused by
gales which disorganized both the landing and the
parachute attacks, some by confusion. In the worst
mishap the 82nd Airborne Division was cut to pieces
in the sky by its own antiaircraft fire. As the Germans
pulled back behind Mount Etna, the allies approached
Italy for a surrender. On July 25 Mussolini was replaced
by Marshal Badoglio who promptly sued for peace.
Meanwhile Eisenhower was authorized to invade the
peninsula itself.

The German strategy had destroyed the hopes of quick victory and easily-won bases for a southern France invasion. The Nazis pulled back slowly, and in order. Their artillery turned Mark Clark's Salerno beachhead into a bloody slaughterhouse. Then there followed a stubborn retreat which bought time for Hitler and extricated most of the German force intact, while positions were prepared for defense in the mountains north of Naples. It was not until September 27 that Montgomery finally captured Foggia on the east coast and assured possession of the great valley from which bombers of the Fifteenth Air Force could pound south Germany and Austria, and harass the Nazis in Hungary and the Balkans. It was not until October 1 that the Americans entered Naples to deal with a monumentally sabotaged harbor and a sickeningly starved and diseased population. The bloody crossing of the Volturno River in October only brought the Americans, along with the British from Foggia, into the mountains where they lay in icy cold before nearly impregnable German positions, such as the great fortress which had been constructed in and around the mountain monastery of Cassino.

Both Clark and Montgomery had been slow; but the campaign had been starved by the build-up for the cross-channel strike. Italian aid did not materialize. German commanders, who did not have to win, bought time stubbornly for their colleagues in Russia.

In January, 1944, an attack on Cassino was stopped dead with heavy losses. A flanking expedition at Anzio to the north turned into a desperate attempt to hold the beachhead itself. A second assault was staged at Cassino in March after monumental bombings had torn up the monastery, the town and the countryside. The Germans still held. After two months of American reinforcement and bombing, the Cassino line finally broke and allied troops smashed through the ring around

Anzio. Rome fell on June 4. But the push could not be
continued. The cross-channel invasion was about to
require all possible effort, and the destruction of roads
and bridges which had led to the break-through now
slowed the allied advance itself. By the end of June
the struggle in Italy had settled down to the snail's pace
of mountain warfare.

NOTES, *chapter 12*

1. Samuel Rosenman, ed., *The Public Papers and Addresses of Franklin D. Roosevelt, 1941,* 514-515.

2. Arthur H. Vandenberg, Jr., *The Private Papers of
Senator Vandenberg* (Houghton, Mifflin, 1952), 16-18.

3. Cordell Hull, *The Memoirs of Cordell Hull,* 1096.

4. Frances Perkins, *The Roosevelt I Knew,* 379-380.

5. W. L. White, *They Were Expendable* (Harcourt,
Brace, 1942), 40-43.

6. Robert Sherwood, *Roosevelt and Hopkins* (Harper,
1948), 556.

7. Donald M. Nelson, *Arsenal of Democracy* (Harcourt,
Brace, 1946), 218-221.

8. *New York Times,* April 11, 1943.

9. Frances Perkins, *Roosevelt,* 384.

10. Elliott Roosevelt, ed., *F.D.R., His Personal Letters,
1928–1945,* 1298-1299.

11. *Personal Letters, 1928–1945,* 1294-1295.

12. *Personal Letters, 1928–1945,* 920.

13. *Personal Letters, 1928–1945,* 1297.

14. William D. Hassett, *Off the Record with F.D.R.,
1942–1945,* 171.

15. Hassett, *Off the Record,* 151-152.

16. John Gunther, *Roosevelt in Retrospect, A Profile in
History,* 14-16.

17. *Personal Letters, 1928–1945,* 1337-1338.

18. *Personal Letters, 1928–1945,* 1304-1305.

19. Samuel Eliot Morison, *Coral Sea, Midway and Sub-
marine Actions. May, 1942–August, 1942, A History of the
United States Naval Operations in World War II,* Vol. IV
(Little, Brown, 1950), 57-59.

20. John Hersey, *Into the Valley: A Skirmish of the Marines* (Knopf, 1945), 3, 5-7, 52-55, 77-80, 83-84, 86-91.

21. Henry L. Stimson and McGeorge Bundy, *Active Service in Peace and War* (Harper, 1947), 425-428.

22. Ernie Pyle, *Here Is Your War* (World, 1943), 123-124.

23. Mina Curtiss, ed., *Letters Home* (Little, Brown, 1944), 65.

24. *Public Papers, 1943,* 73-80.

chapter **13** VICTORY

While American and British armies fought out their grim holding operation in Italy, the allies concentrated on four mammoth fronts. In Russia Soviet troops began to roll the Germans relentlessly back after their drive had been stalled in the ruins of beleaguered Stalingrad. This campaign would develop two gigantic arms, one sweeping across the Ukraine toward the Danube, toward Roumania, Hungary and Austria. The second would build up outside the stubbornly-resisting Moscow to drive across the level plains of White Russia and Poland toward Berlin. Mounting supplies of American tanks, jeeps, trucks, guns and Bell Aircobras moved through the frozen ports at the north and along the thin rail line across Iran. These substantially supplemented the production of Russia's own factories, many of which had been moved heroically, piece by piece, beyond the protective barrier of the Ural Mountains.

The Atlantic represented a second major front to the United States. At its worst submarine warfare sank as much as eighty per cent of the freighters in one northern convoy to Russia. As American efforts were stepped up, the subs began to run in wolfpacks. Aerial attacks on their pens in France proved costly and ineffective. The answer finally appeared in hastily-built escort carriers—merchant ships with small flight decks placed on them—and in rapidly increasing destroyer construction. The height of the battle was passed by the end of 1943. But submarines continued to harass the supply lines of the Atlantic until V-E Day.

A third front was in the air over Europe. By 1944 the role and methods of American strategic bombing had become clear, but there had been over a year of experiment and readjustment. Accuracy had not proved as high as optimistic airmen had predicted. All bombers needed heavy fighter cover. The B-17s and the B-24s had to be separated because of their differences in effective speed and altitude. It proved impossible to knock out completely one industry at a time; the patterns had to be varied as the bombers sought out now railway yards, now oil refineries, now aircraft plants, now docking facilities. Casualties were heavy. Certain raids were monumentally significant, and sacrificial. One such was the roof-top attack on the crucial Ploesti oil refineries in Romania.

When the weather lifted in the late winter of 1943–1944, the Germans lived under the constant terror of the bomber. The British hit at night, burying massive industrial areas under patterns of blockbusters and fire. By day the American precision bombers flew from Britain and Italy. In bad weather single ships found their way through the fronts to keep the harried populace on edge with assorted cargoes of fragmentation, demolitions, and noise-makers. German flak and fighters took a heavy toll, but Hitler was losing planes and crews faster by far; and the stream of planes from the United States seemed endless by the spring of 1944.

By the close of the war, more than 27,000 bombers and fighters were operating with the American and British forces. More than 20,000 bombers had been lost, but over two and a half million tons of bombs had been dropped behind German lines, and about 57,000 Nazi planes had been destroyed.

The final, and crucial front, was the build-up for OVERLORD, the major punch across the channel. Eisenhower's official report catches the enormous scale of the operation:

... The German philosophy was: "Deny the Allies the use of ports and they will be unable to support their armies ashore." For this reason the chain of Atlantic and Channel ports from Bordeaux to Antwerp was under orders from Hitler himself to fight to the last man and the last round of ammunition. . . .

... They had no knowledge of our artificial harbors, a secret as closely guarded as the time and place of our assault. The impossible was accomplished and supplies came ashore, not afterwards to support a force beleaguered on the beachheads, but actually with the troops as they landed. The Germans were, by virtue of our initial supply, denied the opportunity of dislodging us and were subsequently, throughout the campaign, under sustained attack as the result of the feats of maintenance performed by our administrative organizations. . . .

June, 1944, saw the highest winds and roughest seas experienced in the English Channel in June for twenty years. . . .

On D-day the wind had, as forecast, moderated and the cloud was well broken, with a base generally above 4,000 feet. This afforded conditions which would permit of our airborne operations, and during the hour preceding the landings from the sea large areas of temporarily clear sky gave opportunities for the visual bombing of the shore defenses. The sea was still rough, and large numbers of our men were sick during the crossing. The waves also caused some of the major landing craft to lag astern, while other elements were forced to turn back.

As events proved, the decision to launch the assault at a time when the weather was so unsettled was largely responsible for the surprise which we achieved. The enemy had concluded that any cross-Channel expedition was impossible while the seas ran so high and, with his radar installations rendered ineffective as a result of our air attacks, his consequent unpreparedness for our arrival more than offset the difficulties which we experienced. . . .

The high seas added enormously to our difficulties in getting ashore. Awkward as these waters would have been at any time, navigation under such conditions as we experienced called for qualities of superlative seamanship. Landing craft were hurled on to the beaches by the waves, and many of the smaller ones were swamped before they could touch down. Others were flung upon and holed by the mined under-water obstacles. Numbers of the troops were swept off their feet while wading through the breakers and were drowned, and those who reached the dry land were often near exhaustion. It was, moreover, not possible on every beach to swim in the amphibious DD tanks upon which we relied to provide fire support for the infantry clearing the beach exits. These were launched at Sword, Utah, and Omaha beaches, and, although late, reached land at the two former; at Omaha, however, all but two or three foundered in the heavy seas. At the remaining beaches the tanks had to be unloaded direct to the shore by the LCT's, which were forced, at considerable risk, to dry out for the purpose. Fortunately, the beaches were sufficiently flat and firm to obviate damage to the craft. . . .

Apart from the factor of tactical surprise, the comparatively light casualties which we sustained on all the beaches except Omaha were in large measure due to the success of the novel mechanical contrivances which we employed and to the staggering moral and material effect of the mass armor landed in the leading waves of the assault. The use of large numbers of amphibious tanks to afford fire support in the initial stages of the operation had been an essential feature of our plans, and, despite the losses they suffered on account of the heavy seas, on the beaches where they were used they proved conspicuously effective. It is doubtful if the assault forces could have firmly established themselves without the assistance of these weapons. . . .

During the next five days our forces worked to join up the beachheads into one uninterrupted lodgement area and to introduce into this area the supplies of men and materials necessary to consolidate and expand our foothold. . . .

Meanwhile, on and off the beaches, the naval, mercantile marine, and land force supply services personnel were performing prodigies of achievement under conditions which could hardly have been worse. . . . Off shore, enemy aircraft, although absent by day, laid mines each night, requiring unceasing activity by our mine sweepers. By 11 June, despite these complications, the machinery of supply over the beaches was functioning satisfactorily. . . . During the first six days of the operations, 326,547 men, 54,186 vehicles, and 104,428 tons of stores were brought ashore over the beaches.[1]

While American and British troops were establishing this most crucial of all beachheads, the President led the nation in its D-Day prayer:

       Almighty God: Our sons, pride of our Nation, this day have set upon a mighty endeavor, a struggle to preserve our Republic, our religion, and our civilization, and to set free a suffering humanity.

Lead them straight and true; give strength to their arms, stoutness to their hearts, steadfastness in their faith.

They will need Thy blessings. Their road will be long and hard. For the enemy is strong. He may hurl back our forces. Success may not come with rushing speed, but we shall return again and again; and we know that by Thy grace, and by the righteousness of our cause, our sons will triumph.

They will be sore tried, by night and by day, without rest—until the victory is won. . . .

Some will never return. Embrace these, Father, and receive them, Thy heroic servants, into Thy Kingdom.

And for us at home—fathers, mothers, children, wives, sisters, and brothers of brave men overseas—whose thoughts and prayers are ever with them—help us, Almighty God, to rededicate ourselves in renewed faith in Thee in this hour of great sacrifice. . . .

Give us strength, too—strength in our daily tasks, to redouble the contributions we make in the physical and the material support of our armed forces. . . .

And, O Lord, give us Faith. Give us Faith in Thee; Faith in our sons; Faith in each other; Faith in our united crusade. . . .

With Thy blessing, we shall prevail over the unholy forces of our enemy. Help us to conquer the apostles of greed and racial arrogancies. Lead us into the saving of our country, and with our sister Nations into a world unity that will spell a sure peace—a peace invulnerable to the schemings of unworthy men. And a peace that will let all of men live in freedom, reaping the just rewards of their honest toil.

Thy will be done, Almighty God.

Amen.[2]

The summer of 1944 was crucial in every area of the war. A week after D-Day the Germans began to throw against Great Britain the pilotless buzz-bombs. In August V-2 rockets first hit England, and were to make life a constant terror until occupation of the Netherlands eliminated the launching areas. On June 15, and a half a world away, the first United States Superfortress raid hit the mainland of Japan. On July 20 Guam was recaptured at last. On the same day some of Hitler's own generals attempted to assassinate him. On the twenty-fifth General Bradley's troops punched out of the Normandy pocket between St. Lô and Lessay, while Montgomery's English and Canadians held the German down on the left.

By August 11 United States forces had crossed the Loire. The next day the Germans began a general retreat. On the fifteenth the United States Seventh Army landed in southern France. By the nineteenth, Patton had reached the Seine. Romania collapsed before the Russian advance on the twenty-third. Marseilles fell the same day. Two days later Paris was liberated, and by the end of August American troops were in Rheims. Early in September the troops in Italy broke through to Pisa; Brussels, Liége and Luxembourg were cleared of Germans. On August 11 Patton's armored columns joined with the troops from southern France and the German border was breached for the first time north of Triers.

In the late summer the allied drive slowed against the Siegfried Line and the rough country along the German border. Immense supply difficulties had developed and the flashing maneuvers of Patton's armored columns gave way to relentless pressure on key strong points like Metz and Aachen. Then, on December 16, the German unleashed a counterattack. As Walter Millis has described it:

The plan itself was, as usual, technically skillful. The Ardennes front was chosen because it was lightly held. After it had been broken in by artillery and infantry assault, the whole of the Fifth and Sixth SS Panzer Armies were to be launched like a thunderbolt. The Sixth SS Panzer Army was to strike westward and then northwestward to reach the Meuse on either side of the major Allied base at Liége; the Fifth Panzer Army was to drive westward to secure the river on either side of Namur, from Huy to Givet. The Germans did not repeat their Normandy error of underrating Allied air power; they planned to use the winter fogs and cloud as cover against it, and their meteorological calculations were so good that they were actually to secure nearly a week of substantial immunity from air interference. All sorts of stratagems were added to confuse the enemy—paratroop drops, infiltration by Germans wearing Allied uniforms, the use of captured Allied tanks and vehicles painted with the Allied insignia. . . . If the armor could reach Liége, there would be a good chance of disorganizing the whole northern Allied flank; if that could be done, the way would in turn be open for a drive to Antwerp in a lightning stroke on the 1940 pattern, once more splitting the Allied armies as had been done then and thus leaving the British and Americans paralyzed for many months to come. . . . Hitler was confident. In his headquarters near Bad Nauheim, a few days before the operation was to be launched, he told his officers that "Americans don't know how or why they fight," and that "once we get behind their backs, they will run like scared rabbits." . . .

Thus, in the fog and darkness of December 16, Germany's last reserves were committed recklessly to the attack.

The Americans met it with a maneuver which they liked to describe, in the language of the prize-ring, as "rolling with the punch." Their front lines had vanished in the first hours and could not now be restored. Elements of the 28th and 106th divisions which had survived the initial onslaught fell back into St. Vith; here they were joined by the 7th Armored Division, and these troops together formed a knot of determined resistance in the center of the German advance. But the two panzer armies simply flowed past, one on either side . . . within a few days the position had to be abandoned. Meanwhile, the vital necessity was to hold the two shoulders of the salient, in the areas, respectively, of Monschau and Echternach, while yielding elsewhere so as to contain and channel the drive. . . .

On the 18th the situation for the Allies was graver still. The 12th SS Panzer Division was battering at the Monschau shoulder, evidently intending to strike down along the Allied rear. The 1st SS Panzers were now perilously near to both the gasoline dump and the American First Army Headquarters at Spa. . . . Despite great efforts, the dump could not be . . . moved; even less was it possible to move the enormous stores which had been built up around the Liége base, the center of the whole supply system for the American First and Ninth Armies. . . . The air seemed filled with the lethal robot bombs; and as the day wore on the last of the Headquarters troops—humorously referred to as the "palace guard"—were mobilized and send forward from Spa against the German SS panzers. They included such units as a smoke-generator company, a motorized cavalry troop, and a rear-area security battalion. The newspaper correspondents who had not left by that time watched with mixed emotions as the officers who had been censoring their dispatches solemnly picked up rifles and marched out, under the command of their major and chief censor, to defend Spa against German SS tanks.

And curiously enough, these scratch troops sufficed. December 18 was the critical day. The 1st SS Panzers got to within five hundred yards of the gasoline dump, but they were already moving uncertainly and tentatively under numerous harassments, and they never actually reached it. . . . Bastogne was completely surrounded on December 21, and next day the Germans summoned the garrison to an honorable surrender as the only means of avoiding "annihilation." It was the 101st's second in command, Brigadier General A. McAuliffe, who replied with the single, scornful slang word: "Nuts." The defenders were not annihilated and Bastogne was never taken.

The defense of Bastogne slowed the southern arm of the German drive, but the spearheads were still reaching westward. So far the Allies had successfully funneled the German effort away from its most vital objective—Liége. . . . They had yet to stop the drive itself; but the Germans, who had staked the fate of the nation on a shoe-string, were already running short of fuel, while the narrow margin which the weather had given them was evaporating. On December 23, the allied tactical air forces came suddenly back into the battles, flying three thousand sorties; they were to fly many times that number on the following three days. The counterattack from the south was already beginning, for it was on December 22 that Patton's 4th Armored Division struck north, initiating the movement that was to end in the relief of Bastogne.[3]

General Bradley recalls Patton's colorful words: " 'Brad,' he exclaimed, 'this time the Kraut's stuck his head in a meatgrinder.' With a turn of his fist he added, 'And this time I've got hold of the handle.' "[4] Millis continues:

On Christmas morning, the German 2nd Panzer Division was in sight of Dinant and reaching the village of Celles, some three miles from the Meuse, the initial goal which was to have been reached in two days. But the thrust was already spent. They had driven over fifty miles deep into Allied-held territory, but they had failed to take a single decisive objective and their strength, like their fuel, was nearing its end. . . . The Ardennes offensive had reached its high-water mark, and from that time onward the tide began to recede. With it there receded Germany's last, futile hopes in the west.[5]

By February, 1945, Eisenhower was ready to launch the last great drive in the west. When the United States Ninth Army jumped off on the twenty-third to spearhead the final assault, the Germans faced a retreat without reserves, with dwindling supplies and with constant fear of the Russians driving in from the east. The allies controlled the air so completely that they could cover the advance with flocks of planes in relays and could throw an air assault within an hour whenever the Germans halted for a moment to resist. By March 7 the 9th Armored Division had punched through the German lines to grab the crucial Rhine bridge at Remagen, south of Bonn. The Remagen bridgehead was an hard-fought salient, but on March 25 the Americans broke out; the barrier of the Rhine had been breached far more easily than anyone had dared to hope. Meanwhile, Patton had feinted to throw the Germans off-balance and then knifed up the Rhine to Mainz, sealing off large German formations to the west. Patton skimmed on through weak resistance to isolate the western front from the German forces retreating stubbornly up the Danube from Budapest. And all along the front from Montgomery's British on the north to Patch's United States Seventh and French First on the south, the line moved forward through April, chewing Germany into pieces while the Russians fought for Berlin, block by block and house by house. On April ninth Mark Clark broke through the Po defenses in Italy and swept north toward the Alps. On the twenty-ninth the Germans in Italy surrendered.

As the troops poured across the Rhine they uncovered the full extent of the brutal Nazi mass murders. General Bradley recalls his first experience with the concentration camps:

Third Army had overrun Ohrdruf, the first of the Nazi death camps, only two days before and George insisted we view it.

"You'll never believe how bastardly these Krauts can be," he said, "until you've seen this pesthole yourself."

The smell of death overwhelmed us even before we passed through the stockade. More than 3,200 naked, emaciated bodies had been flung into shallow graves. Others lay in the streets where they had fallen. Lice crawled over the yellowed skin of their sharp, bony frames. A guard showed us how the blood had congealed in coarse black scabs where the starving prisoners had torn out the entrails of the dead for food. Eisenhower's face whitened into a mask. Patton walked over to a corner and sickened. I was too revolted to speak. For here death had been so fouled by degradation that it both stunned and numbed us. Within a week we were to overrun others and soon the depravity of Buchenwald, Erla, Belsen, and Dachau would shock a world that thought itself inured to the horrors of war.[6]

Despite the stubborn resistance by die-hards in the Ruhr especially, the armies in Germany outran their schedules. At the line of the Elbe where the meeting of Russians and Americans had been planned by the high commands, Bradley's troops awaited the slow-moving Russian columns for days. To the south Patton had to be restrained from the eager advance into Czechoslovakia for which he and his troops clamored. To the north Montgomery plunged across the Elbe to seal off Denmark from the Russians. On May 7, after Hitler's suicide in the smoking ruins of Berlin, German resistance finally ended. And the new dimensions of the World were suggested by the uneasy meeting of Russian and American on the Elbe. General Omar Bradley has described some of these contacts:

Collins met us at Leipzig and convoyed us through the corridor to Torgau. He had made the trip himself almost a week before and while enroute to the Soviet lines was asked if he would object to seeing a division commander.

"Of course not," he answered and the column turned off to where a Soviet division occupied a position facing us.

The division commander was apologetic. "May I ask you a question?" he started.

"Go ahead," Collins replied.

"Are your people digging in opposite us?"

"Digging in?" Collins looked startled. "Why of course not. After all, we're allies, you know."

The Red commander called for a staff officer. "Cancel that order to dig in," he said. "We'll stay right where we are." . . .

Konev was waiting with his staff outside the gloomy villa he had commandeered for a CP. A powerfully built man with a huge bald head, Konev took me first to his office for a moment of private conversation through our interpreters. I gave him a map I had prepared for the occasion, showing the disposition of every U.S. division across his group front. The marshal started in surprise but did not volunteer to show me his own dispositions. Had he wanted to, he would probably have had to ask permission from the Kremlin. American lieutenants were delegated greater authority on the Elbe than were Russian division commanders.

Pointing to Czechoslovakia on the map I had given him, Konev asked how far we intended to go. He frowned as the interpreter translated his query.

"Only to Pilsen," I told him, "see it's marked here with a line. We had to go in to protect our flank on the Danube."

Konev replied with the trace of a smile. He had hoped we would go no farther.

The banquet table had been banked lavishly with fresh caviar, veal, beef, cucumbers, black bread, and butter. A row of wine bottles filled the center. Vodka decanters were spread liberally about for the toasts which started as soon as we sat down. Konev arose and lifted his glass. "To Stalin, Churchill, and Roosevelt—" he said, not yet having learned of Truman's succession. . . .

After dinner Konev led us into the great hall of his

house. A chorus of Red Army soldiers broke into the
"Star Spangled Banner" and their resonant voices filled
the room. Konev explained that the chorus had mem-
orized the anthem without knowing a word of English.
Then to the accompaniment of a dozen balalaikas, a
ballet troupe danced into the room.

"Why that's splendid," I exclaimed.

Konev shrugged his shoulders. "Just a few girls," he
explained, "from the Red Army."

Two weeks later when Konev repaid our call with one
to our CP, he was enthralled with the violin virtuosity
of a thin khaki-clad man.

"Magnificent," the marshal cried in delight.

"Oh that," I said. "Nothing, nothing at all. Just one
of our American soldiers."

We had pirated the violinist from Special Services in
Paris for the day. His name was Jascha Heifetz.

Germany had lost her war when Hitler had squeezed
himself between Russian manpower and American
production. But for the United States the victory in
Europe was only half the problem. As the nation cele-
brated V-E Day, it poised for the mammoth invasion of
Japan which would finish the business. The United
States had been pushing the bloody island-hopping
campaign all through 1943 and 1944. In January, 1943,
MacArthur's troops had taken Buna in New Guinea.
Throughout the winter and spring attempts to reinforce
the enemy troops in the Aleutians were fended off and
Attu was finally cleared of Japanese early in May. At
both ends of the gargantuan theater the Japanese resisted with a suicidal intent to win or die. In New Guinea
they had to be blasted from their jungle pillboxes, one
after another. On Attu the remnants of a doomed garrison destroyed itself in a suicide attack which engulfed
the American hospital and brought death to scores of
wounded, nurses and doctors. But when Kiska was

finally assaulted, in August, the Japanese had already evacuated this last of their Aleutian footholds.

To the south the United States and Anzac advance would move along two highways: MacArthur's command would consolidate its positions around Buna and drive painstakingly along the jungle coast which led back to the Dutch East Indies and the Philippines. Before much progress could be made here it would be necessary to gain control of the air and the seas along the New Guinea coast, and particularly to reduce the great Japanese base at Rabaul on New Britain. The road to Japan itself was the broad sea. But the Navy must breach, one after the other, a formidable series of defenses based on the heavily garrisoned airstrips scattered throughout the islands. The first ring was hinged on the Marshall Islands with advance bases in the Gilberts. The second, to the west, was built about Truk, the fabled Japanese Pearl Harbor in the Carolines. The inner defenses were hung upon the Marianas which lay astride the route to Iwo Jima and Okinawa where bases for the B-29 assaults on the mainland might be gained. At first it seemed essential to take the islands one by one in bloody and tedious assaults. In March, 1943, however, a major Japanese transport fleet was utterly destroyed in the Bismarck Sea by General George C. Kenney's land-based planes using the new skip-bombing technique. It had become clear that control of the air was the key to the whole Pacific, and numerous enemy garrisons were bypassed to wait out the war in isolation as the mobile battle moved beyond them.

While the Sicilian invasion was going on, in early July, the marines began to punch their way up into the central Solomons toward Rabaul. Losses were heavy, but slowly the massive Navy program of air training and light carrier construction began to pay off. At points the attrition in planes worked as much as ten to one against the Japanese. On November 1 the marines hit Bougainville and slowly wrested from the enemy an airbase from which Rabaul could be neutralized. By February, 1944, MacArthur was ready to drive along the narrow coast toward western New Guinea, while his bombers were already hitting the enemy in the Dutch East Indies.

Meanwhile the Navy was striking northwest through the Gilberts. From November 20 to 24, 1943, a heavy force of large, light, and escort carriers and new, fast battleships covered the invasion of Makin and Tarawa. The marines on Tarawa hit one of the toughest situations they had ever faced. The island was taken, but only at the price of costly bunker by bunker operations with flame-throwers and explosives. Casualties claimed over a quarter of the marines in the hellish four-day operation.

The Marshalls would be an even tougher challenge. The Japanese must hold here, and they had had over twenty years to prepare the defenses. Throughout December and January long-range bombers pounded the numerous airstrips throughout the Marshalls to neutralize the enemy's major advantage of land-based fighters and bombers. On January 31 Admiral Raymond Spruance's fleet, the 4th Marines and the 7th Army hit Roi and Kwajalein on the far western reaches of the Marshalls. They had bypassed the bulk of the chain and engineered a complete surprise. On February 17 Eniwetok, the westernmost of the Marshall atolls, was taken. On the same day Spruance hit Truk itself with his carrier planes, only to find that the Japanese fleet had been evacuated. In the vicious fighter battles over Truk, the Japanese lost 127 planes to Spruance's eighteen. The whole ring of Japanese defense had been punctured. More important, the basic technique of island-hopping had been vindicated, as it appeared that the enemy could not concentrate enough air power to challenge the fleets of fifteen to twenty fast carriers upon which the American strikes were based. And American shipyards were turning out new light carriers at the phenomenal rate of three or four a month. American submarines were cutting into Japanese shipping greatly in excess of replacement possibilities; food and oil supplies were short at home and the naval construction plans were scrapped in a desperate attempt to meet the supply problem.

Meanwhile the war had been going badly in the almost forgotten theater of China and Burma. Chiang Kai-shek's forces were isolated except for the gigantic airlift developed by the Army's Air Transport Command. It ferried equipment and arms across the Himalayas and brought out Chinese troops for training under General Joseph W. (Vinegar Joe) Stilwell. Throughout 1943 Stilwell fought the Japanese in Burma with a mixed force of British, Indians, Chinese and a few Americans. He managed to push the enemy back far enough for engineers to construct the Ledo Road which began to supply Chiang from India late in 1944. American B-29s did mount attacks on Japan from Chinese fields in the summer of 1944, but they were soon driven out as the enemy overran the bases. It was clear that Japan must be approached from the sea, and that even aerial bombings to soften her up must be launched from hard-won island bases.

On April 22, 1944, MacArthur's forces staged a gigantic leap to the beachheads of Hollandia in north central New Guinea. But the focus of the war turned rapidly to the north as the Navy poised for its strike against the Marianas, leaving the bypassed Carolines in the rear. The targets were Saipan, Tinian and Guam. H. C. O'Neill has described the crucial battles:

> It was the second week of June that the fast carrier Task Force appeared in the Marianas and for several days raided the airfields, harbors and ground defences of Guam, Tinian and Saipan. The island of Saipan lies only about 1,500 miles south of Tokyo; and when Admiral Spruance's 5th Fleet on June 15th

opened its bombardment, considerable damage had already been done. The 2nd and 4th Marine divisions and the 27th infantry divisions were, therefore, able to make good their landing swiftly. On this same day, in order to distract the attention of the Japanese, the first super-fortress raid was made from China on the industrial centre of Yawatta, on Kyushu.

A Japanese attempt to strike back at the 5th Fleet and crush the invasion with hundreds of aircraft failed completely. Nearly four hundred Japanese aircraft were shot down and the attack developed into the battle of the Philippine Sea. The Task Force turned on the Japanese fleet which had launched the air attack, sank one carrier, damaged a battle ship, two cruisers, three carriers and a destroyer and shot down numbers of aircraft. In the bad weather and the darkness, a quarter of the American aircraft failed to return; but fleet interference with the invasion of the Marianas was not attempted again, and task forces on July 3rd raided Japanese destroyers and several cargo ships were sunk; Iwojima in the Volcano Islands and the Bonins. Three Japanese destroyers and several cargo ships were sunk; and a number of others were destroyed the following day.

But the reduction of the island went steadily ahead. Already the Aslito airfield had been captured; and in a few days bombers were operating from it as far north as Tokyo and as far south-east as Mindanao. The Japanese forces were cut in two and the fierce struggle continued until July 10th when organized resistance ceased, though a few snipers continued to give trouble until a month before the final surrender. The Japanese lost, it was estimated, 25,000 killed and the Americans had 2,359 killed in action, 11,481 wounded and 1,213 missing.

But meanwhile they had turned their attention to Guam and Tinian. The former was shelled by Allied cruisers on July 8th; bombarded once more by United

States warships on the 17th and invaded on the 20th. Guam had, of course, flown the United States flag before the Japanese forced America into the war; and when the 3rd Marine division and the 77th infantry division landed they were undertaking a work of redemption. As in Saipan the resistance was stubborn and, although the airfield and naval base had been captured early and the United States flag flown once more, it was three weeks before organized resistance was over. By that time the Japanese had lost 17,000 killed and 500 prisoners, while the assaulting troops had 1,214 killed, 5,704 wounded and 329 missing.

During this short but bloody campaign, after a heavy bombardment, the Americans landed on the island of Tinian, which is separated by only two and a half miles from Guam. The two Marine divisions which had conquered Saipan quickly overcame the resistance there. By August 2nd the occupation was complete. With the clearing of Guam the conquest of the Marianas had been achieved. As the new Secretary of the Navy, Forrestal, said they could "provide the key which will unlock the door to Japan, the Philippines and the coast of China." [8]

The next step must be the severing of Japan's communications with her oil, rubber and tin empire in the Indies. As summer came on, MacArthur's troops plunged up the New Guinea coast, isolating and chewing to pieces the dens of Japanese resistance as they went. Early in September, 1944, the essential bases in the Carolines were seized. Halsey's carriers roamed the western Pacific unhampered, destroying Japanese planes by the hundreds in the Philippines, the Ryukyus and Formosa, to clear the air for the invasion. MacArthur's troops landed on Leyte on October 20, while Eisenhower's forces were stalled at the German borders. The Japanese decided to make a stand with their Navy. As Halsey knew, they thought they had sunk eleven carriers of his fleet off Formosa. In fact, they had merely damaged one cruiser. The Japanese admiral brought in forces from Manila, Singapore, Formosa and South China, and he had at his disposal the first of the kamikazes, pilots trained to fly their bomb-laden planes directly into American ships. Halsey's brilliant maneuvering and superior force crushed the Japanese in the Battle of Leyte Gulf.

MacArthur's Philippine campaign was a masterpiece of sound strategy and adroit tactics. He took the Japanese by surprise everywhere, and after the first dogged resistance by the now hopeless enemy on Leyte, he overran them, outflanked them, and divided them before major battle plans could be made. The campaign settled into months of piecemeal reduction of isolated Japanese forces which holed up for resistance to the last man. On December 15, the day before the Battle of the Bulge, the Americans had landed on Mindoro. January 9 saw the first of them in Luzon. By February 4 they had started working on Manila. On March 10 as Cologne fell on the German front, the B-29s staged their first incendiary raid on Tokyo, and MacArthur's men assaulted Mindanao to the south.

The return to Manila, Bataan and Corregidor had been a great moral as well as a great military victory. But now, as Roosevelt, Churchill and Stalin met in Yalta, the focus of the war turned far to the North. On February 19, 1945, the navy opened its campaign to take Iwo Jima, from which fighter cover might fly for the long-range B-29 strikes against Japan. It was the roughest and the costliest of all the great marine engagements. The struggle for the tiny keypoint went on until March 16. The marines sustained 20,196 casualties, 5,324 dead. They left 20,000 Japanese dead, strewn among the pits and caves cut into the lava rock. Offshore, the fleet fought desperately against the kamikazes which hurled themselves in waves against the supporting ships.

The ring had closed more tightly around Japan than she realized even in her mounting fear. The incendiary raid of March 9 burned a third of Tokyo to the ground. A marine assault was staged on Okinawa, 370 miles from the homeground of Kyushu, on April 1. Spruance's fleet and a strong British squadron sought out the remnants of the Japanese fleet and destroyed much of it while they also attracted hundreds of the kamikazes. There were losses, but the bulk of the suicide craft were destroyed either in the air or on the ground. Okinawa turned into a new and larger Iwo, bloodily and craftily defended, with operations constantly harassed by the kamikazes and their new mates—suicide torpedo boats.

It was a hopeless cause for Japan. Far to the south MacArthur was sealing off her oil supplies. Although the Okinawan campaign would go on until June 21, the collapse of Hitler released unprecedented supplies of troops, aircraft, ships and matériel—American, British and Russian. Roosevelt had arranged at Yalta for a Russian invasion of Manchuria as soon as Hitler was liquidated. And on July 16, unknown to all but a few Americans, the first atomic bomb was successfully exploded at Alamogordo, New Mexico.

To most of the world the future seemed to hold only the senseless slaughter of hundreds of thousands of Americans and Japanese and Russians as the home islands of the Empire turned themselves into new and more hopeless versions of Iwo Jima and Okinawa. United States Army Intelligence estimated the Japanese Army at five million men, three million of them spread overseas from the Dutch Indies and Burma to Manchuria and the bypassed islands. If these scattered forces held out defiantly, the war might last through all of 1946; American casualties might be 300,000 or more.

The only alternative lay with a relatively obscure

American politician who, on April 12, 1945, had suddenly become President of the United States. He made the decision, alone. He would follow the recommendation of Stimson and Marshall and use the two atomic bombs which the United States had.

On August 6 a single B-29 destroyed the city of Hiroshima and killed approximately 80,000 people—most of them civilians. On August 8 the Russians struck at Manchuria and destroyed the Japanese Army's hope that it might hold out there even after the homeland was lost. On August 9 the second bomb leveled most of Nagasaki. On August 14 the Japanese gave up.

The price of peace had been high for the United States as well as for its allies. Eleven million Americans had served. There had been 1,200,000 casualties. Britain had fought the battle of western civilization for almost two and a half years, and virtually alone, before the United States had finally thrown its weight into the struggle. Russia had paid the stark price of seven million casualties.

But the heaviest price of peace was sketched in the boundaries of the world the war had made. The most hopeful of its three dimensions was suggested on June 24 when the San Francisco Conference met to adopt the Charter of the United Nations. The second dimension was more grimly hinted in the uneasy meeting of Bradley and Konev on the Elbe. The third dimension was starkly written in the boiling cloud above Hiroshima. Science had shortened the war; and it had taught man how to destroy himself absolutely, beyond recall.

NOTES, *chapter 13*

1. *Report by the Supreme Commander to the Combined Chiefs of Staff on the Operations in Europe of the Allied Expeditionary Force, 6 June, 1944 to 5 May, 1945* (Government Printing Office, 1945), 11-12, 19, 22, 24, 25.

2. Samuel Rosenman, ed., *The Public Papers and Addresses of Franklin D. Roosevelt, 1944–1945,* 152-153.

3. Walter Millis, *The Last Phase: The Allied Victory in Western Europe* (Houghton, Mifflin, 1946), 79-87.

4. Omar Bradley, *A Soldier's Story* (Holt, 1951), 472.

5. Millis, *Last Phase*, 87-88.

6. Bradley, *Story*, 539.

7. Bradley, *Story*, 550-553.

8. H. C. O'Neill, *A Short History of the Second World War* (Frederick A. Praeger, 1950), 241-242.

chapter **14** THE HAZY FUTURE

As the war raged across the world, from Moscow to Munda, from Kunming to Kharkov, Roosevelt and his staffs had to face simultaneously the challenges of the future. They dealt with five intimately related problems. The solution of each would make its mark on the disposition of the others: co-ordinating the allies' efforts to win the war; deciding what to do with the aggressors; arranging a machinery for maintaining postwar peace; establishing the grounds for postwar co-operation among the great powers; and laying plans for dealing with displaced persons, underdeveloped countries and colonial areas in the years of reconstruction.

For Roosevelt these were personal problems. He presumed that only the President could represent the United States adequately in these crucial negotiations, and he loved this high-level maneuvering. He displayed all the exuberance of a small boy at a baseball game, mixed with the grim and mature satisfaction of a master chess-player at work. More important, in personal conferences with other Chiefs of State Roosevelt could utilize to the full his particular skills. Here elaborate problems could be reduced to specific decisions and discussed in the folksy, anecdotal manner to which he had become so accustomed. And here he could bring to bear the full weight of his personal charm and his deep commitment to compromise and accommodation as the paths to solution.

Stalin was a challenge. Inscrutable and cold to the

outside world, the Russian dictator was the definitive test of Roosevelt's political techniques. Despite his austerity, despite the language, cultural and ideological barriers, F.D.R. thought Stalin was "gettable." After the Teheran Conference, he told Frances Perkins of one incident of which he was particularly proud:

"You know, the Russians are interesting people. For the first three days I made absolutely no progress. I couldn't get any personal connection with Stalin, although I had done everything he asked me to do. I had stayed at his Embassy, gone to his dinners, been introduced to his ministers and generals. He was correct, stiff, solemn, not smiling, nothing human to get hold of. I felt pretty discouraged. If it was all going to be official paper work, there was no sense in my having made this long journey which the Russians had wanted. . . .

"I thought it over all night and made up my mind I had to do something desperate. I couldn't stay in Teheran forever. I had to cut through this icy surface so that later I could talk by telephone or letter in a personal way. I had scarcely seen Churchill alone during the conference. I had a feeling that the Russians did not feel right about seeing us conferring together in a language which we understood and they didn't.

"On my way to the conference room that morning we caught up with Winston and I had just a moment to say to him, 'Winston, I hope you won't be sore at me for what I am going to do.'

"Winston just shifted his cigar and grunted. I must say he behaved very decently afterward.

"I began almost as soon as we got into the conference room. I talked privately with Stalin. I didn't say anything that I hadn't said before, but it appeared quite chummy and confidential, enough so that the other Russians joined us to listen. Still no smile.

"Then I said, lifting my hand up to cover a whisper (which of course had to be interpreted) 'Winston is cranky this morning, he got up on the wrong side of the bed.'

"A vague smile passed over Stalin's eyes, and I decided I was on the right track. As soon as I sat down at the conference table, I began to tease Churchill about his Britishness, about John Bull, about his cigars, about his habits. It began to register with Stalin, Winston got red and scowled, and the more he did so, the more Stalin smiled. Finally Stalin broke out into a deep, hearty guffaw, and for the first time in three days I saw light. I kept it up until Stalin was laughing with me, and it was then that I called him 'Uncle Joe.' He would have thought me fresh the day before, but that day he laughed and came over and shook my hand.

"From that time on our relations were personal, and Stalin himself indulged in an occasional witticism. The ice was broken and we talked like men and brothers. . . .

"He is a very interesting man. They say he is a peasant from one of the least progressive parts of Russia, but let me tell you he had an elegance of manner that none of the rest of us had." [1]

Fundamentally, Roosevelt believed that decisions must be made by the nations with real power; for those nations, he believed, the commitments must be made by the individuals with authority to carry them out. As early as 1937 he had written, half-jokingly, to one of his ambassadors:

The trouble about any world conference, as you know, is that it would bring fifty-five or sixty nations around a table, each nation with from five to ten delegates and each nation, in addition, with no authority to agree to anything without referring the matter home. From a practical point of view, this type

of conference is an impossibility unless . . . there are
one or two simple principles on which all will agree
beforehand. . . . If five or six heads of the important
governments could meet together for a week with
complete inaccessibility to press or cables or radio, a
definite, useful agreement might result or else one or
two of them would be murdered by the others! In any
case it would be worthwhile from the point of view of
civilization! [2]

Nevertheless, Roosevelt had no delusions about the
limits of leadership in a democracy. It would always
annoy him that he could not persuade Stalin to take
seriously his need to heed public opinion and the Constitution. He was inhibited more than he needed to be.
He estimated too heavily the continuing weight of
isolationist opinion. In fact, the war, his own salesmanship and the mass of propaganda at home had wrenched
American opinion from its traditional bases and provided
an extremely favorable foundation for an internationalist
approach to the peace. But there were significant mix-
tures of opinion to make the President's appraisal uneasy.
One poll in the spring of 1945 indicated that eighty per
cent of the people still believed that the President
should have been trying to keep the nation out of war
in the weeks before Pearl Harbor. At the same time,
sixty per cent favored a postwar military alliance with
Great Britain.

Whatever their uneasiness about specifics and has-
beens, most Americans had probably accepted in 1943
the new mood which Wendell Willkie expressed in his
popular book, One World. Willkie's personal goodwill
tour around the wartime world dramatized what he
meant when he said:

America must choose one of three courses
after this war: narrow nationalism, which inevitably

means the ultimate loss of our own liberty; international imperialism, which means the sacrifice of some other nation's liberty; or the creation of a world in which there shall be an equality of opportunity for every race and every nation. I am convinced the American people will choose, by overwhelming majority, the last of these courses. To make this choice effective, we must win not only the war, but also the peace, and we must start winning it now.

To win this peace three things seem to me necessary —first, we must plan now for peace on a world basis; second, the world must be free, politically and economically for nations and for men, that peace may exist in it; third, America must play an active, constructive part in freeing it and keeping its peace. . . . [8]

Roosevelt himself entered wartime diplomacy with certain strong assumptions. His lifelong concern for conservation and agriculture made him see many of the long-range problems in terms of economic reconstruction based on conservation and rehabilitation of natural resources. He opposed colonialism in all its forms. He was strongly Anglophile. He had deep-rooted suspicions of the German people, and he was inclined to dismiss British fears that Russia might represent the greater threat.

Above all he saw the United States as the mediator among the allies. Sometimes he carried this to the point where he seemed exasperatingly pious about American disinterest and nobility.

But wartime diplomacy involved much more than idealism. Roosevelt soon discovered this in the tangle of relationships with the French. The United States recognized the Vichy government; it provided a listening post, a point at which persuasion might be exercised, and it provided hopes in the fall of 1942 for unopposed access to North Africa. Britain had taken under her protective wing General Charles de Gaulle, the self-identified leader of the "Free French," who had refused to capitulate to Hitler. The situation became most difficult because of Marshal Pétain's insistence that the Vichy government resist the African landings, and because of de Gaulle's prima donna insistence on his personal dignity and on the treatment of prostrate France as an equal among the Great Powers. Roosevelt did not like de Gaulle. His distaste was increased when the General broke allied traces, and seized tiny St. Pierre and Miquelon off the Canadian coast from Vichy without authorization. Distaste became disgust as de Gaulle continued to demand an equal seat in the allied councils and made it as difficult as possible for Roosevelt to talk with him.

And there were other allies with whom relations were tense. The most difficult problems were with nations which, in their extremity, could not afford to accept the limits of American ability to help. The charming but exasperating Madame Chiang pressed relentlessly the claims of her husband. China had been longest in the war; her case was desperate; and yet geography fated her to a peripheral position until Hitler was beaten. Similarly, the Russians pushed throughout 1942 for an immediate and massive second front in Europe and for more and more Lend-Lease. They were hard-pressed; but their demands could not be met. Roosevelt was exasperated by their suspicion that he was not trying, that he was playing a double game with them.

In the mutual Russo-American suspicions lay the real challenges to both wartime co-operation and postwar peace. Not the least of the confusion between Russia and the western allies was the concept of democracy for which they presumably were fighting. Stalin would never have understood Roosevelt's deep appreciation of the New Yorker's humorous comment:

"We received a letter from the Writer's War Board the other day asking for a statement on 'The Meaning of Democracy.' It presumably is our duty to comply with such a request, and it is certainly our pleasure.

"Surely the Board knows what democracy is. It is the line that forms on the right. It is the don't in don't shove. It is the hole in the stuffed shirt through which the sawdust slowly trickles; it is the dent in the high hat. Democracy is recurrent suspicion that more than half of the people are right more than half of the time. It is the feeling of privacy in the voting booths, the feeling of communion in the libraries, the feeling of vitality everywhere. Democracy is a letter to the editor. Democracy is the score at the beginning of the ninth. It is an idea which hasn't been disproved yet, a song the words of which have not gone bad. It's the mustard on the hot dog and the cream in the rationed coffee. Democracy is a request from a War Board, in the middle of the morning in the middle of a war, wanting to know what democracy is." . . .[4]

When Roosevelt read this squib to his friends, he would say, "Them's my sentiments exactly." [4a]

Stalin and Vishinsky missed the point completely when they observed at separate times that the way to make Americans go along with Roosevelt's decisions was to immerse them in propaganda, and that the American people ought to learn to obey their leaders.

On one thing there was agreement among Roosevelt, Churchill and Stalin from the start: the complete defeat of Hitler's Reich. Roosevelt's impromptu announcement at Casablanca of the "unconditional surrender" policy in 1943 seemed to mark this unanimity. Roosevelt's use of the words may have been hasty, but they expressed his view precisely and he held to them

---

[4] E. B. White, *New Yorker* (July 3, 1943), p. 13. Reprinted by permission; Copr. © 1943 The New Yorker Magazine, Inc.

staunchly throughout the war. He resisted the temptation to soften the impact of the slogan with tedious and disputed definitions. To Queen Wilhelmina he confided: "I think that both here and in England there are two schools of thought—those who would be altruistic in regard to the Germans, hoping by loving kindness to make them Christians again—and those who would adopt a much 'tougher' attitude. Most decidedly I belong to the latter school, for though I am not bloodthirsty, I want the Germans to know that this time at least they have definitely lost the war." '

But there were sharp disputes among the allies on specifics. They might be unwilling to make "conditions" to Hitler; they must, however, shape those conditions in their own minds. Stalin wanted the reduction of Germany to a second-rate power—better yet, its dismemberment—and he wanted heavy reparations both in money and in kind to rebuild Russia's devastated industry. He objected sharply to his allies' vagueness and indecision. At Teheran in 1943, as an American memorandum indicated:

> In regard to Germany, Marshal Stalin appeared to regard all measures proposed by either the President or Churchill for the subjugation and for the control of Germany as inadequate. . . . He appeared to have no faith in the possibility of reform of the German people and spoke bitterly of the attitude of the German workers in the war against the Soviet Union . . . . He seemed to think that this mentality of discipline and obedience could not be changed.°

In 1944, at Quebec, Roosevelt and Churchill hastily initialed Henry Morgenthau's plan for a Carthaginian peace. This would have destroyed German industry completely and reduced the nation to several dependent, agrarian states. Churchill had been most reluctant, and even Roosevelt later backed sharply away from the Morgenthau Plan as he came to realize that such an ultimatum might lengthen the war and create horrendous economic confusion in Europe.

The discussion went on to Yalta, and beyond.

Stimson's biographer describes a related issue which came up at Quebec:

> One of the proposals in the Morgenthau memorandum of September 6 was that a list should be made of German arch-criminals . . . and that upon capture and identification these men should be shot at once. . . . Stimson wrote:
> ". . . The method of dealing with these and other criminals requires careful thought and a well-defined procedure. Such procedure must embody, in my judgment, at least the rudimentary aspects of the Bill of Rights, namely, notification to the accused of the charge, the right to be heard and, within reasonable limits, to call witnesses in his defense . . . the very punishment of these men in a dignified manner consistent with the advance of civilization, will have all the greater effect upon posterity. Furthermore, it will afford the most effective way of making a record of the Nazi system of terrorism and of the effort of the Allies to terminate the system and prevent its recurrence. . . . They should be charged with offenses against the laws of the Rules of War. . . ."

The question of trial as against shooting was not decided at Quebec, but Stimson heard . . . that the President had there expressed himself as definitely in favor of execution without trial. . . .

Meanwhile the War Department committee worked on, and in January its report was completed. In January, too, the President, shifting somewhat from his earlier view, appointed Judge Samuel Rosenman to study the question for him. Meeting with Rosenman,

Joseph P. Davies, Attorney General Biddle, and others on January 18, [Stimson wrote] "I was glad to find they were all in favor of legal action rather than political action against the head Nazis, and secondly, that in their study of the proper kind of legal action they were coming to the view which I have held from the first that we had better stage up a big trial in which we can prove the whole Nazi conspiracy to wage a totalitarian war of aggression violating in its progress all of the regular rules which limit needless cruelty and destruction." [7]

Like most of the German issues, this one was postponed at Yalta, although Stimson's view eventually won out. As a recent scholar has concluded of the Yalta announcement on Germany:

This proclamation veiled the vast indecision of the great Allies in questions concerning Germany. They could not agree, and as long as Germany fought on they could not afford to disagree. But the prospects of Germany's early collapse had brought the western statesmen face to face at last with the greatest European dilemma of the twentieth century: how can the threat of German power be eliminated from Europe without leaving Soviet power dominant throughout the continent? . . .

Roosevelt . . . supported a principle . . . that it was not in the interest of the United States for any one state in Europe to dominate the whole. Churchill . . . consciously followed a balance-of-power policy. . . . Thus it came about that the discussions of German questions at Yalta revealed . . . the hard rock of Anglo-American solidarity and moderation toward Germany. The Russians failed to win full satisfaction on a single one of the demands they raised at Yalta concerning Germany's future.

The credits and debits of Yalta concerning the German problem read as follows: Stalin demanded a decision to dismember Germany; Churchill and Roosevelt postponed any specific plans, though they agreed in principle to the possibility of dismemberment. Stalin demanded a decision to deindustrialize Germany and rebuild the U.S.S.R. with German equipment; the President and the Prime Minister refused to agree to deindustrialization and postponed consideration of reparations. The Russians hoped that the western boundary of Poland might be drawn by Big Three agreement at the Western Neisse River and that the Ruhr and Saar would be separated from Germany; both Roosevelt and Churchill were opposed. The single set of demands concerning Germany which were met fully at Yalta were those which Roosevelt and Churchill advanced there: France was to have a zone of occupation and to participate in the integrated administration of Germany through the Control Council.[8]

The question of Poland was the most difficult of the many problems involving smaller nations. Czechoslovakia, Hungary and the Balkan states might presumably be reconstituted with their approximate prewar boundaries. Finland, as an ally of Hitler, would be left to deal with the Russians as best she might. Lithuania, Latvia and Estonia had hopelessly disappeared within the Soviet state. But Poland was to be both victim and gainer; and it was the major political football among the allies.

Stalin insisted that Russia would keep her pre-World War I Polish areas which she had regained in her deal with Hitler. He wanted to compensate Poland with German territories to the west. This would involve either the mass removal of German populations or the creation of a festering minority area of the kind which had bred so much trouble in prewar Europe. Worse yet, there were two Polish governments, one in exile in London, another on the scene at Lublin under Russian auspices. To Churchill it was a question of faith with the Polish government for whose integrity Britain had gone to war in 1939, and it was a question of the power balance on the continent. To Roosevelt it was a question of justice, permanent peace, and the Polish vote at home. The key to the situation was the Red Army. It was within one hundred miles of Berlin when the Yalta conference met, and it controlled Poland. It also controlled Romania, Bulgaria and Hungary and was moving into Czechoslovakia. There was nothing that Roosevelt and Churchill could, in fact, do except extract the maximum promises from Stalin and hope that he kept them.

The agreement at Yalta on the liberated nations was inevitably general. And it left them, inevitably, to the good faith of the occupying power. There was no hope of settling the incipient clashes between communist and noncommunist forces in the various nations. All that could be obtained was a formula for transitional coalition governments and for free elections. The agreement made the principle clear; but the dream of free elections in Eastern Europe was to prove a nightmare, as Soviet military power in the postwar world turned those countries inexorably to authoritarian control.

Nevertheless, there were other focuses of the wartime idealism in which Roosevelt had caught the "wave of the future." If he did not foresee the full dimension of Soviet imperialism, he did grasp the inevitable transformation of the older empires. Here his adversary was Churchill, not Stalin. The doughty conservative had balked at some of the implications of the Atlantic Charter. His government raised serious doubts whether India should be allowed to sign the Declaration of United Nations. He protested at Roosevelt's constant interest in independence for the colonies. F.D.R. was *frank, especially in his fight for the concept of United Nations Trusteeship. As early as January, 1944, he had explained to Hull:*

I saw Halifax last week and told him quite frankly that it was perfectly true that I had, for over a year, expressed the opinion that Indo-China should not go back to France but that it should be administered by an international trusteeship. France has had the country—thirty million inhabitants for nearly one hundred years, and the people are worse off than they were at the beginning.

. . . I see no reason to play in with the British Foreign Office in this matter. The only reason they seem to oppose it is that they fear the effect it would have on their own possessions and those of the Dutch. They have never liked the idea of trusteeship because it is, in some instances, aimed at future independence. This is true in the case of Indo-China.

Each case must, of course, stand on its own feet, but the case of Indo-China is perfectly clear. France has milked it for one hundred years. The people of Indo-China are entitled to something better than that.[9]

And a month later with regard to Morocco: "I am inclined to think that the Emperor and El Glaoui [the Pasha of Marra kech] the other leaders would like to have the French Protectorate changed into a Protectorate by three Trustees—a Frenchman, an Englishman and an American. They do not want to be exploited and, taking it by and large, they trust the Americans the most." [10]

Roosevelt won his battle with Churchill on trustee-ships, although when a reporter asked, "Do you re-member the speech the Prime Minister made about the fact that he was not made the Prime Minister of Great Britain to see the empire fall apart?" *the President an-*

swered ruefully, "Dear old Winston will never learn on that point. . . ." [11]

The crux of the colonial issue for Roosevelt was the economic rehabilitation which might provide a firm base for self-government in the future. He was particularly dismayed with what he saw in North Africa and the Middle East during his wartime trips. After Casablanca he wrote his old headmaster, Endicott Peabody: "I am glad to get away from the poverty and disease and barrenness of North Africa and Egypt and Palestine and Iran. But we can help those countries in the days to come—and with proper management get our money back—if only we do not revert to the ostrich policy of 1920." [12]

The help he envisaged was shaped by his lifelong interest in conservation. It was no accident that, while he was fighting hard at home in the winter of 1944–1945 for a Missouri Valley Authority, he was also thinking of what Harry Hopkins called a TVA for Europe, and similar conservation projects for the underdeveloped countries. On the way home from Yalta he told the newsmen some of his thoughts:

> Of course, the obvious thing for Persia to do is to improve its own country. Reforestation is the best hope, and the Nation then might sustain itself, its whole standard of civilization would be a great deal higher. They could make more things than it could sell, buy many things it could not make.

The same thing is true about Iraq, Arabia, Lebanon, Syria, Palestine and Turkey. They've got no purchasing power to do anything with. Their only purchasing instrument is oil. Their people are not educated, do not get enough to eat, cannot cope with health problems. We talked quite a lot about this at the conference.

Now, of course, all that is tied up more or less with peace. A country that isn't moving forward with civilization is always more of a potential war danger than a country that is making progress. . . .

Take the Arabian, for instance. If you want to start a farm, you might build a dam, or start a pond or lake, but it would all evaporate overnight, the air is so dry. But there is plenty of water lying fifty or sixty feet below the ground. Now, if you can keep it below the ground to prevent evaporation, and put in pumps run by oil, you can get it out of the ground and do your irrigating at a very low cost.

This is just an example of how to do the same thing from a different angle.

Question: Wouldn't that be a long-time proposition?

The President: Growing trees is a long-time proposition.

Q: Do you mean that the conference looked ahead over a great many years?

The President: Sure, we are looking at the human race, which we hope won't end in fifty years.[18]

Roosevelt's imaginative sparring with problems of colonies and conservation was both hopeful and harmless. The agreements on Europe were perhaps the best available, given the military situation. But the most immediate issue for the United States in the spring of 1945 was Russian participation in the war against Japan. It was the Yalta agreements to assure this that provided the greatest fuel for the postwar controversies.

The first significant step had been made at the Moscow Conference of Foreign Ministers in October, 1943. The aged Cordell Hull had flown there to hammer out an agreement stressing allied unity in the war and in the formation of an international organization to maintain the peace. The conference also sketched the plan under which democratic government, with freedom of speech, religion, press and assembly, was to be restored in Italy. Under relentless pressure from Hull, the Russians had

finally agreed to allow China to join Britain, Russia and
the United States in issuing the declaration. Roosevelt
wrote delightedly to Lord Mountbatten in India:

> I really feel that it is a triumph to have got
> the four hundred and twenty-five million Chinese in on
> the Allied side. This will be very useful twenty-five or
> fifty years hence, even though China cannot contribute
> much military or naval support for the moment.[14]

But Chiang remained an orphan. At Cairo in 1943
he persuaded Roosevelt to support significant assaults
in China and Burma. Yet within days F.D.R. ruefully
cabled him to cancel the commitment in the light of
the Teheran agreement to stress the cross-channel invasion of Europe. And at Yalta, when it was necessary
to deal directly with Stalin's objectives in the Far East,
Chiang's future was at least half-committed by Roosevelt without his consent.

The governing factors for Roosevelt were clear at
the time, although they have been much confused since
by Monday morning quarterbacking. Military advisers
were unanimous in their demands for Russian aid
against Japan. Russian aid could not be assumed, given
Stalin's past record, unless there were significant gains
in sight for the Soviet Union. Finally, Stalin was, in
fact, in a position to take what he wanted in Manchuria
and the northern Japanese Empire. George Lensen has
listed the balance sheet for the Far Eastern agreements
at Yalta in this way:

What Stalin asked for:	What Stalin got:
1. Status quo in Outer Mongolia.	1. Status quo in Outer Mongolia.
2. Southern Sakhalin and adjacent islands.	2. Southern Sakhalin and adjacent islands.
3. Lease of Dairen.	3. Internationalization of Dairen.
4. Lease of Port Arthur.	

5. Operation of Chinese-Eastern and South Manchurian railroads.
6. Kurile Islands.

4. Lease of Port Arthur.
5. Russo-Chinese operation of these railroads.
6. Kurile Islands.

What Roosevelt asked for:
1. Russian participation against Japan soon after end of war in Europe.
2. Conditioning of Outer Mongolia and railway agreements on Chiang Kai-shek's concurrence.
3. Promise of Russian support for Nationalist government.

What Roosevelt got:
1. Russian participation against Japan soon after end of war in Europe.
2. Conditioning of Outer Mongolia and railway agreements on Chiang Kai-shek's concurrence.
3. Promise of Russian support for Nationalist government.[15]

Russia did come into the Pacific war—in a hurry and in the wake of the atomic bomb. She made good on her demands and more. And her influence in China and Korea were to lead to two bloody wars and one of the hottest campaigns of political recrimination the United States has ever seen. Forrest C. Pogue, a careful student of the war, has attempted recently to cut through the arguments to the essential meaning, and has concluded:

. . . Actually, in 1945 the Generalissimo [Chiang] thought he had a good arrangement with Stalin and for a time after the war his armies seemed to be strongly situated in parts of northern China. Overextension of supply lines, failure to get firm possession of liberated territory, overconfidence, poor leadership, inflation, refusal to reform Kuomintang corruption, failure to satisfy the land hunger of the Chinese peasant, and, above all, the failure of Stalin to keep his promises to Chiang Kai-shek are the chief explanations for the Nationalist debacle of 1946-50. Strategically, the grant of the Kuriles and Southern Sakhalin to a potential enemy of the United States was unsound. In case of a future war between the United States and the U.S.S.R. the American position would be definitely weakened. But few Americans thought of such a war in 1945 . . . there is no real defense on moral grounds of the Far Eastern concessions to the Soviet Union. It is the one point at which Roosevelt openly went back to the type of arrangement which he and other western leaders had previously condemned. Morality and reality were in conflict; reality won. . . .

. . . the Far Eastern concessions at Yalta did not seem excessive in February, 1945. Even today it is difficult to avoid the conclusion that if Stalin had not received them from Roosevelt and Churchill he would have sought them—or even greater gains—from someone else or have taken them without Allied or Chinese consent. The terms of the Yalta agreements concerning the Far East were in the nature of a Roosevelt-Stalin contract and constituted not only concessions to Stalin but also restraining limitations. It was not Roosevelt's fault that Stalin later broke the contract.[16]

Whether Roosevelt could have obtained Russian participation for a lower price is a moot point now. But clearly the President's own presumption was that postwar peace depended less on the specific agreements at Teheran and Yalta than on a World Organization and continuing negotiations among the allies. His main goal was machinery to work out the future. He knew that this machinery must be in existence before the concrete problems of the peace had to be faced. Roosevelt had been preoccupied with this central issue throughout the whole war. As early as November, 1942, he had outlined some of his ideas to Clark Eichelberger:

The central idea involves a situation where there should be four policemen in the world—the

United States, Great Britain, Russia and China—charged with the responsibility of keeping peace. The rest of the world would have to disarm and until disarmament was effected there would be no peace gathering.

Inspection would be arranged by the four policemen in all the countries to see that they did not begin to arm secretly as Germany did after the last war. As soon as any of the other nations was caught arming they would be threatened first with a quarantine and if the quarantine did not work they would be bombed.[17]

In September, 1943, he told George Norris:

It took nearly ten years to sell the idea of peace and security among the American Republics. But today, there is substantial accord.

In a sense this great change which has come over the feelings of the people in this Hemisphere has been easy in comparison with the task before us in Europe and the Far East.

That is why I am inclined to believe that we should have a trial or transition period after the fighting stops—we might call it even a period of trial and error. . . .

Therefore, I have been visualizing a superimposed—or if you like it, superassumed—obligation by Russia, China, Britain and ourselves that we will act as sheriffs for the maintenance of order during the transition period. Such a period might last two or even three or four years. And, in the meantime, through the holding of many special conferences the broad ideals which you and I have in mind might be cleared up.[18]

By October, 1944, he was ready to tell the whole nation:

Peace, like war, can succeed only where there

is a will to enforce it, and where there is available power to enforce it.

The Council of the United Nations must have the power to act quickly and decisively to keep the peace by force, if necessary. A policeman would not be a very effective policeman if, when he saw a felon break into a house, he had to go to the Town Hall and call a town meeting to issue a warrant before the felon could be arrested.

So to my simple mind it is clear that, if the world organization is to have any reality at all, our American representative must be endowed in advance by the people themselves, by constitutional means through their representatives in Congress with authority to act.[19]

The road to the United Nations was easier at home than Roosevelt had ever dared to hope. Congress itself paved the way with nearly unanimous expressions of sentiment in 1943. The text of the Connally resolution indicated how far the Senate had come in the twenty-three years since it had refused to ratify the Versailles Treaty:

Resolved . . . That the United States, acting through its constitutional processes, join free and sovereign nations in the establishment and maintenance of international authority with power to prevent aggression and to preserve the peace of the world.

That the Senate recognize the necessity of there being established at the earliest practicable date a general international organization, based on the principle of the sovereign equality of all peace-loving states, and open to membership by all such states, large and small, for the maintenance of international peace and security. [20]

When Roosevelt went to Teheran later in 1943 he

raised the whole question with Stalin. The ensuing conversation, related by Hopkins's biographer, indicates the tone of the negotiations:

. . . Roosevelt gave Stalin an outline of his concept of an organization, based on the United Nations, for the preservation of world peace. It was to consist of three main bodies:

First—an Assembly composed of all members of the United Nations which would meet in various places at stated times for the discussion of world problems and the making of recommendations for their solution. Stalin asked if this Assembly was to be world wide in scope, or merely European, and Roosevelt said it should be world wide.

Second—an Executive Committee which would consist of the U.S.S.R., the U.S., the U.K., and China, together with representatives of two European nations, one South American, one Middle Eastern, one Far Eastern and one British Dominion. This Executive Committee would deal with all nonmilitary questions— such as economy, food, health, etc.

Stalin asked whether this committee would have the right to make decisions which would be binding on all the nations. Roosevelt was indecisive in his answer to that one. He did not believe that the Congress would permit the United States to be bound by the decision of such a body. He said that the Committee could make recommendations for settling disputes with the hope that the nations concerned would be guided thereby.

The third body, as set forth by Roosevelt, was what he termed "The Four Policemen"—the U.S.S.R., U.S., U.K. and China. This, as its name implied, would be the enforcing agency—with power to deal immediately with any threat to the peace or any sudden emergency. The President cited the Italian attack on Ethiopia in 1935 as an example of the failure of the League of Nations to deal promptly and forcibly with an act of aggression. He said that had the Four Policemen existed at that time it would have been possible to close the Suez Canal and thereby prevent Mussolini from attacking Ethiopia.

Stalin expressed the opinion that this proposal for the Four Policemen would not be favorably received by the small nations of Europe. For one thing he did not believe that China would be very powerful when the war ended—and, even if it were, European states would resent having China as an enforcement authority for themselves. He therefore suggested, as an alternative, that there be one committee for Europe and one for the Far East—the European Committee to consist of Britain, Russia, the United States and possibly one European nation. . . . Roosevelt doubted that the Congress would agree to American participation in a purely European committee which might be able to compel the involvement of American troops. He said that only a crisis such as the present one could compel the Congress to agree to such a step—that it would not have been possible to send American troops to Europe in the present war had it not been for the Japanese attack on Pearl Harbor.

Stalin said that if the President's suggestion for a world organization were carried out—particularly the Four Policemen part of it—this might require the sending of American troops overseas. Roosevelt said that he had only foreseen the sending of American naval and air forces to Europe and that any land armies needed in the event of a future threat would have to be provided by Britain and the Soviet Union.

He saw two possible kinds of threat—one minor, and one major—to world peace. . . .

The major threat would be provided by a gesture of aggression on the part of a large power; in this case the Four Policemen would send an ultimatum to the threatening nation and, if the demands were not immediately met, they would subject that nation to bombardment and, if necessary, invasion. . . .[n]

Meanwhile four significant planning conferences met in the United States. In May and June, 1943, plans were laid for the United Nations Food and Agriculture Organization. Later that year a temporary United Nations Relief and Rehabilitation Administration was set up to handle immediate problems in the war-torn nations. At Bretton Woods, New Hampshire, in July, 1944, the outlines of the two great financial institutions were sketched. The International Monetary Fund, with assets of nearly nine billion dollars, would seek to stabilize currencies and facilitate international exchange. The World Bank would use its nine-billion-dollar capital to make loans throughout the world for economic reconstruction and development. At Dumbarton Oaks, near Washington, the delegates of the United States conferred from August through early October with those of Russia, Britain and China on the outlines of a world security organization. Edward R. Stettinius has described these talks:

The American proposals on world organization were accepted by the other powers as the basic documents of the conversations. At this conference the representatives of the major powers drafted the document that was to be the basis of discussion at San Francisco the following spring. We agreed on a statement of principles and purposes, a General Assembly, a Security Council, a Secretariat, an International Court of Justice, and an Economic and Social Council. It was only the insistence of the United States that secured a provision for an Economic and Social Council. The Soviet Union, and to a lesser extent Churchill, did not seem to understand the American concern for an organization that was broader than just a security organization.

Although we had agreed at Dumbarton Oaks that Great Britain, the Soviet Union, China, the United States, and even France finally should be permanent members of the Security Council, we had come to no agreement as to the voting procedure. There was also complete disagreement with the Russians over their proposal that all sixteen Soviet Republics be admitted as members of the world organization. . . . There was no disagreement at Dumbarton Oaks regarding the desirability of having the Security Council function on the basis of a qualified majority vote, or of the necessity of having all procedural questions decided by a majority vote with no distinction made between the permanent and nonpermanent members of the Security Council. . . .

With the agreement that the permanent members of the Security Council had to be unanimous for any action involving sanctions, the unsettled question at Dumbarton Oaks was what the voting procedure should be on other substantive questions in case one of the permanent members was a party to a dispute. . . . The Soviet Union insisted that the right of veto should apply, and we disagreed with this position. We recommended instead that a special procedure be developed for dealing with these cases where one of the permanent members was a party to a dispute.

Throughout the discussions on the world organization at Dumbarton Oaks, Yalta, and San Francisco, it was constantly emphasized by the representatives of the three major nations that—regardless of the voting formula—unanimity of the major powers was in the final analysis vital for the functioning of the organization. It was obvious to all of us that the United Nations would collapse and peace would be endangered if any of the major powers failed to co-operate. . . .[22]

The agreements at Yalta on the United Nations were a substantial victory for American diplomacy. A contemporary historian points out:

. . . in the final analysis, Roosevelt's U.N. policy at Yalta must be praised or damned in terms of the desirability of obtaining British and Russian co-operation in the world organization. Without their support no U.N. could be founded or could work effectively; to get their support, compromise was essential. Therein lay the essential meaning of Yalta in the history of man's search for world order. Furthermore . . . Roosevelt's strong stand against sixteen votes for the Soviet Republics held the Russians to the minimum number they would settle for. While the concession was something Roosevelt did not care to defend, it was not a serious blow to the U.N. Charter and it gave the Russians no great increase in power in the Assembly, as events have fully shown. Moreover, Roosevelt at Yalta won approval of pre-April negotiations regarding the troublesome question of territorial trusteeships for the U.N. . . .

Most important of all, Roosevelt won from Churchill and Stalin an agreement to call the United Nations Conference on World Organization before the war's end.[28]

Roosevelt looked forward eagerly to opening the San Francisco Conference which would draft the United Nations Charter. And he was making plans: short-range ones for new economic reforms at home; long-range ones for retirement to his library at Hyde Park. But the hours were running out for him in the late winter of 1945. His friends noted how heavy a toll time, travel and tension were exacting. Still he was amazingly resilient. The same person might find him gay and dynamic at one moment, sadly old and shaky at another.

Nevertheless, there were unmistakable signs. Rosenman noticed that he had begun to "ad lib," sometimes irrelevantly and obscurely, from his prepared speeches. When he returned from Yalta he addressed the Con-

gress for the first time sitting down; he could no longer
bear the heavy braces, he told his audience frankly. He
was irritable and somewhat pathetic with subordinates
who brought him problems which had less than top
priority.

On March 1 he told the Congress of some of his
hopes and misgivings for the future, and he set the
challenge:

> This time we are not making the mistake of
> waiting until the end of the war to set up the machinery
> of peace. This time, as we fight together to win the war
> finally, we work together to keep it from happening
> again. . . .
>
> The structure of world peace cannot be the work of
> one man, or one party, or one Nation. It cannot be an
> American peace, or a British peace, or a Russian, a
> French or a Chinese peace. It cannot be a peace of
> large Nations—or of small Nations. It must be a peace
> which rests on the cooperative effort of the whole
> world.
>
> It cannot be a structure of complete perfection at
> first. But it can be a peace—and it will be a peace—
> based on the sound and just principles of the Atlantic
> Charter—on the concept of the dignity of the human
> being—on the guarantees of tolerance and freedom of
> religious worship. . . .
>
> There can be no middle ground here. We shall have
> to take the responsibility for world collaboration, or we
> shall have to bear the responsibility for another world
> conflict.[24]

He was already beginning to sense the immense
portent of the Soviet Union for the future. As Rosenman has noted:

> . . . During the two months he lived after

Yalta, the President began to get glimmerings of the dangerous new attitude of the Soviet Union. To several people he privately voiced his growing reservations and doubts about the good faith of the Soviet rulers and their willingness to live up to their agreements.

On March 27, he expressed to Churchill his "anxiety and concern" over "the development of the Soviet attitude." The Soviet Union was showing that she did not intend to respect either the spirit or the letter of her agreement regarding Poland. . . . Roosevelt on April 1, 1945, cabled Stalin that he was disappointed in "the lack of progress made in the carrying out, which the world expects, of the political decisions which we reached at Yalta, particularly those relating to the Polish question." He warned Stalin sharply against the plan merely to enlarge rather than to reorganize completely the existing Polish Provisional Government. The President also said that "any such solution which would result in a thinly disguised continuation of the present government would be entirely unacceptable, and would cause our people to regard the Yalta agreement as a failure." Marshal Stalin replied on April 7, admitting that the Polish issue had reached an impasse, but he evaded the question by charging that the impasse was due to the British and American Ambassadors. Before a reply could be prepared, Roosevelt was dead.

A few days before his death, the President received a request from Churchill asking what he might say to the House of Commons on the Polish question. From Warm Springs, Georgia, on April 12, 1945—the day the President died—he sent the following message to Churchill: "I would minimize the general Soviet problem as much as possible, because these problems, in one form or another, seem to arise every day, and most of them straighten out as in the case of the Berne meeting. We must be firm, however, and our course thus far has been correct." [25]

As Forrest Pogue has recently concluded:

Several courses were open to the western leaders at Yalta in dealing with the new set of power relationships. It was possible to make minimum concessions to Stalin and hope for Russian co-operation and goodwill; it was possible to break off discussions at the first sign of demands which would ratify the new power relationships or create a greater imbalance in world politics than already existed; and it was possible to state certain moral positions in indignant and ringing Wilsonian phrases. Roosevelt and Churchill selected the first course, believing and hoping that it would bring victory and at the same time save the peace. They gained something by forcing the Russians to put their promises on record; but they could not make Stalin keep his word.[26]

The President had to leave to others the guidance that would give meaning or mockery to Yalta. On April 12 he died, suddenly, without warning, in the midst of his work. In the words of one of his secretaries who was with him:

Today the great and final change. In the quiet beauty of the Georgia spring, like a thief in the night, came the day of the Lord. The immortal spirit no longer supported the failing flesh, and at 3:35 P.M. the President gave up the ghost. . . .

Of course I had seen it coming for all too long, but little thought the end so near. At 1:15—as near as I could learn—he suffered a seizure; at 3:55 it was all over. A massive cerebral hemorrhage had done its work.

It was late when I saw him for the first time today. He was in good spirits, but did not look well. Color bad; countenance registered great weariness. . . . Was shocked at the President's appearance. He was up and fully dressed, at the card table near the fireplace, seated in the stout leather chair which he favored—back to the windows that overlooked the pine trees. . . . Presently Mme. Shoumatoff, an artist . . . came in, set up her easel, and began sketching. . . . Through it all the President looked so fatigued and weary. . . .

Despite the handicap of the artist's continued interference, he went on with his work. As I went over the papers later with the newspapermen, I found that the last enrolled bill, which he signed, was a measure to continue the Commodity Credit Corporation and increase its borrowing power.

When he reached that bill, he said to Laura Delano, "Here's where I make a law." Then he wrote the word "Approved" along with his name and the date. I had seen him do it a thousand times—little thought this would be the last. Many, many times have I thought of the importance of that final stroke of the pen which gives effect to the sovereign will of the people as expressed in an act of Congress. . . .

But at last it was over. It must have been close to 1 o'clock when I left him. . . . A little later, Mike Reilly phoned me to come up. I was there within five minutes —about 1:30 P.M. The heavy breathing which I heard as soon as I entered the cottage told the story. I knew that the President was mortally stricken. Laura Delano and Margaret Suckley were in the living room where I had left them with F.D.R. so short a time before.

We sat in silence. Presently I went into the President's bedroom. Dr. Bruenn and George Fox were with him. His eyes were closed—mouth open—the awful breathing. . . . But the Greek nose and the noble forehead were grand as ever. . . . Presently, Dr. Bruenn came from the bedroom and said there was no telling how long the present situation would continue. . . . At 3:35, as I sat in the living room with Grace Tully, Laura Delano, and Margaret Suckley, the silencing of the dreadful breathing was a signal that the end had come. . . .

April 15, Sunday. Hyde Park. F. D. R. came home to-day—the long journey from Warm Springs over. The train, brought up via New York Central on the east bank of the Hudson, was stopped behind the home place, as occasionally in times past. I left the train early —morning brisk and cool but sunny . . . went up the woods road through the virgin forest which the Boss loved and of which he often spoke. Arrived at the home, went through the opening in the hemlock hedge and there was the open grave right in the spot where he had told me so casually that he wished to be buried.

The faithful Mr. Plog, in charge of the place for almost fifty years, had supervised the job of digging the grave. He was making the final inspection when I shook his trembling hand. Neither of us spoke. Like all the rest of us, he loved the Boss. . . .

. . . We waited in silence for the Chief's arrival.

The muted notes of the West Point band told that the horse-drawn caisson bearing the Commander in Chief was on the way up the hillside through the woods. I have no ear for music, unfortunately. Never before, however, was Chopin's "Funeral March" so grand. One by one, evenly spaced, came the staccato shots of the President's salute—twenty-one guns, fired from some-where outside the garden. They echoed and re-echoed across the Hudson Valley and faded into silence. F.D.R. was near home now. The band and escort of West Point cadets came into the garden from the east side. For the last time for F.D.R. came the familiar measures of "Hail to the Chief"—triumphant and majestic—one more token of man's mortality.

In silence broken only by the solemn notes of the funeral dirge, we waited for the Chief. Nearer and nearer came the doleful music. Then, through an opening in the hedge toward the house, came the little procession headed by the venerable Dr. Anthony, rector of St. James in Hyde Park. He was preceded by a youthful crucifer. Going on eighty, with faltering step, it seemed almost as though the aged clergyman had not sufficient strength to complete the way to the head of the grave. The lusty noncoms came next, the heavy burden of the great bronze coffin all they could carry. Immediately behind the coffin walked Mrs. Roosevelt, and Elliott, Anna and John Boettiger, Mrs. Elliott Roosevelt, and the wives of Jimmy Roosevelt, Franklin, Jr., and John Roosevelt. . . .

. . . Dr. Anthony, surplice and cassock fluttering in the crisp April breeze, was a magnificent figure—frail of stature; an ascetic countenance; goatee, this latter unusual among Episcopalian clergy; and a black velvet skull cap. He looked for all the world like the famous triple portrait of Cardinal Richelieu in the National Gallery of London.

In a deep and vibrant and cultivated voice, he read the committal words from the Book of Common Prayer. Never was Cranmer's matchless prose better spoken. In conclusion, he quoted the hymn with the familiar refrain, "Father, in Thy gracious keeping leave we now Thy servant sleeping." While Dr. Anthony was reading his lines, I noticed that just above the Hudson River side of the hedge a lilac bush was unfolding its blossoms —a reminder of Walt Whitman's tribute to Lincoln with its famous first line, "When lilacs last in the dooryard bloomed." F.D.R.'s burial was on the anniversary of Lincoln's death in 1865. And, like Lincoln, his work is done. God grant that those who follow will not make the mess of things that followed Lincoln's death."

NOTES, *chapter 14*

1. Frances Perkins, *The Roosevelt I Knew*, 83-85.

2. Elliott Roosevelt, ed., *F.D.R., His Personal Letters, 1928–1945*, 649.

3. Wendell Willkie, *One World* (Simon and Schuster, 1943), 202-204.

4a. E. B. White, in *New Yorker*, XIX (July 3, 1943), 13, quoted in Robert Sherwood, *Roosevelt and Hopkins*, 734-735.

5. *Personal Letters, 1928–1945*, 1535.

6. Sherwood, *Roosevelt and Hopkins*, 782.

7. Henry L. Stimson and McGeorge Bundy, *Active Service in Peace and War*, 584-587.

8. John L. Snell, "What to Do with Germany?" in John L. Snell, Forrest C. Pogue, Charles F. Dellzell and George A. Lensen, *The Meaning of Yalta: Big Three Diplomacy and the New Balance of Power* (Louisiana State University, 1956), 70-72.

9. *Personal Letters, 1928–1945*, 1489.

10. *Personal Letters, 1928–1945*, 1493.

11. *Public Papers, 1944–1945*, 564.

12. *Personal Letters, 1928–1945*, 1471.

13. Edgar Nixon, ed., *Franklin D. Roosevelt and Conservation*, 632-633.

14. *Personal Letters, 1928–1945*, 1468.

15. George A. Lensen, "Yalta and the Far East," *Meaning of Yalta*, 152.

16. *Meaning of Yalta*, 196-198.

17. *Personal Letters, 1928–1945*, 1366-1367.

18. *Personal Letters, 1928–1945*, 1446-1447.

19. *Public Papers, 1944–1945*, 350.

20. Senate Document #123, 81st. Cong., 1st. Session, 14.

21. Sherwood, *Roosevelt and Hopkins*, 785-786.

22. Edward R. Stettinius, Jr., *Roosevelt and the Russians, the Yalta Conference* (Doubleday, 1949), 16, 17, 19, 23.

23. Forrest C. Pogue, "The Big Three and the United Nations," *Meaning of Yalta*, 186-187.

24. *Public Papers, 1944–1945*, 578-579, 585.

25. Samuel Rosenman, *Working with Roosevelt*, 537-538.

26. *Meaning of Yalta*, 206-207.

27. William D. Hassett, *Off the Record with F.D.R., 1942–1945*, 333-337, 343-345.

Few men have been so much revered by so many of their own generation. Perhaps only Jefferson, Jackson and Lincoln have been so deeply hated.

Grace Tully, who took dictation from him for seventeen years, wrote of Roosevelt, "I long ago knew that it was my good fortune to work for a man of straightforward simplicity, courage, passion and honesty—one of the great souls of history." [1] John Gunther, the journalist, estimated him in glowing terms: "He created the pattern of the modern democratic state, and made it function . . . he made government a much abler process, on the whole, than it has ever been before." [2] John T. Flynn, a wholly hostile newsman, said of him: "Little by little a nature, not greatly unlike many well-considered public men of his type, disintegrated, until power corrupted him. In the end it corrupted him utterly." [3]

Fifteen years after Roosevelt's death, the picture of the man and his age remains confused. We are still too close. One cannot touch the world without feeling the beat of his pulse. There is broad agreement about the results of the Age of Action. But the sharp disputes over Roosevelt are largely in the realm of values and morals. Essentially, the conflicts arise over the difficult problems: Was it necessary? Was it well done? Was it good? But by whose standards?

Roosevelt's critics are unanimous that he brought a revolution to America. For them the expansion of federal government and presidential power, the proliferation of economic regulation, the catapulting of the

United States into world leadership were major trage-
dies. A yearning for mass security had endangered individual initiative and independence. The Constitution
of rights had been replaced by a Constitution of powers.
The nation had been committed to responsibilities
beyond its means and interests in world affairs.

Others tested the Age by its results and found them impressive. They saw the New Deal as a mere extension
of the progressive tradition, a generally successful attempt to solve certain urgent social problems without
destroying the foundations of democratic society. Indeed, it seemed, "The great achievement of the New
Deal was to introduce the United States to the twentieth century. Roosevelt redressed the defects of the
Jeffersonian tradition by equipping the liberal party
with a philosophy of government intervention—a belief,
as he put it, that 'the government has the definite duty
to use all its power and resources to meet new social
problems with new social controls.' . . . The New Deal
took a broken and despairing land and gave it new confidence in itself." [4] Changes had rescued democracy,
made it viable; holding blindly to traditions would have
destroyed it. In the realm of world affairs the Roosevelt
leadership had been positive; perhaps the major criticism
is that he moved more slowly than he might have
toward leadership in international affairs.

The differences arise from two basically divergent
judgments. If one feels that Roosevelt could have solved
the nation's problems without serious institutional
change, and if one believes that the United States could
have been defended from the western hemisphere, the
Age of Action must appear as an age of tragic failure. On
the other hand, if one presumes that the dimensions of
American society and world affairs had changed sufficiently to demand the new approaches, then Roosevelt
must seem a far-sighted and inspired statesman.

But in the face of these arguments, what can be

said of the Roosevelt that will linger as a dynamic factor in American society?

First, it is certain that F.D.R. will remain a great legend. It is not so much what, precisely, he did, as what people think he stood for in the great crises of modern life. In an age of slogans and images Roosevelt has become, like Jefferson and Jackson, a symbol of the humanitarian impulse in government, of democratic change. The legend of Roosevelt the democrat, the humanitarian, the world citizen, will remain one of the major bench marks from which we shall continue to run the lines of our social understanding. And for some, the many-sided man Roosevelt will remain a symbol of the demagogue who sold out our traditions for an easy popularity. Yet James Burns notes: "To examine closely single aspects of Roosevelt's character— as thinker, as organizer, as manipulator, as strategist— is to see failings and deficiencies closely interwoven with huge capacities. But to stand back and look at the man as a whole, against the backdrop of his people and his times, is to see the lineaments of greatness—courage, joyousness, responsiveness, vitality, faith, and above all, concern for his fellow men." [5]

Married to the legend of F.D.R. are specific results of the Age of Action which have irretrievably shaped the boundaries of the future. The largest of them are beyond dispute. The nation moved beyond 1945 with an unprecedented commitment to international leadership and to identification of its security with that of the entire world. At home, the American people emerged with a commitment to a new politico-economic arrangement in three parts. First, the nation had a mixed economy, neither the completely unregulated capitalism of the social Darwinist's dream, nor yet the socialist or collectivist economy which had been so much feared. A regulated capitalism, with some small segments of socialism, it met the demands of neither the planners nor the economic anarchists. But it had grown peculiarly from American experience and need; it was vital, and it had a future.

Secondly, it was a society of bigness, and democracy must learn to live with it. Nor was giganticism only a governmental problem. Bureaucracy, organization, procedures, red tape, the mechanization of human relationships had become the lifeblood of a society which kept score on electronic computers, reduced the individual to holes punched in file cards, and taught its sons and daughters to adjust to life rather than to aspire for greatness.

Finally, the nation was committed to government as the guarantor of economic security. Whatever else might be opaque, it was abundantly clear that Americans would never again suffer major depression without turning to government for aid.

The Age of Action left problems: some seemed all but insoluble. Commitment to world security was warped in the shape of the Russo-American conflict of ideals, interests and power. At home the monumental national debt was matched by a Gross National Product which was phenomenal by prewar standards. But the high fixed costs of government added a new dimension to the total pattern of society. There was a challenge to protect the dignity of the individual and basic freedom in a democracy from the cancerous degeneration which institutionalized life might bring.

And the radioactive shadow of the Bomb mushroomed over the entire landscape of human affairs.

These are among the most frightening problems in the nation's history. The stakes were never so high; the way out never so uncertain. But Roosevelt and his age left the nation in a condition to handle its problems. The economy was vital and strong; democracy was real both in procedure and spirit.

To blame it all on Roosevelt is easy—and ridiculous. Roosevelt or not, much of the postwar world would have been shaped as it is. No man, not even "that man," could have held back the intellectual, social and economic forces which set the dimensions of the new era. Roosevelt's own "last words" to the nation provided neither formula nor program but a call to faith. In the speech which he was never able to deliver, he wrote: "The only limit to our realization of tomorrow will be our doubts of today. Let us move forward with strong and active faith." [6]

NOTES, *chapter 15*

1. Grace Tully, *F.D.R., My Boss* (Scribner's 1949), 1-2.
2. John Gunther, *Roosevelt in Retrospect, A Profile in History,* 378-379.
3. John T. Flynn, *The Roosevelt Myth* (Devin-Adair, 1948), 286.
4. Arthur Schlesinger, Jr., in Seymour Harris, ed., *Saving American Capitalism,* 80.
5. James M. Burns, *Roosevelt, the Lion and the Fox,* 477.
6. Samuel Rosenman, ed., *The Public Papers and Addresses of Franklin D. Roosevelt, 1944–1945,* 616.

INDEX